Buena Vista

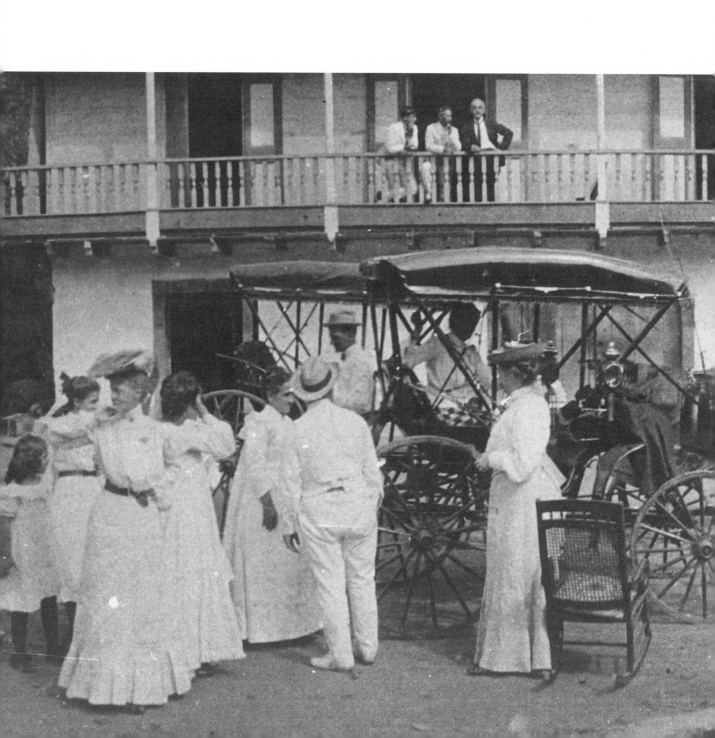

Buena Vista

Life and Work on
a Puerto Rican
Hacienda, 1833–1904

GUILLERMO A. BARALT

Translated by Andrew Hurley

The
University
of North
Carolina Press
Chapel Hill
& London

Originally published as *La Buena Vista, 1833–1904: Estancia de frutos menores, fábrica de harinas y hacienda cafetalera* by the Fideicomiso de Conservación de Puerto Rico © 1988 Fideicomiso de Conservación de Puerto Rico

English translation
© 1999 The University
of North Carolina Press

The translation and publication of this book were made possible through a generous grant from The Andrew W. Mellon Foundation to the Association of Caribbean Historians and The Johns Hopkins University.

Set in Minion and Meta
by B. Williams & Associates
Manufactured in the United States
of America

The paper in this book meets the guidelines for permanence and durability of the Committee on Production Guidelines for Book Longevity of the Council on Library Resources.

03 02 01 00 99   5 4 3 2 1

Library of Congress Cataloging-in-Publication Data

Baralt, Guillermo A., 1948–   [Buena Vista. English]   Buena Vista: life and work on a Puerto Rican hacienda, 1833–1904 / Guillermo A. Baralt; translated from the Spanish by Andrew Hurley.

p. cm.   Includes bibliographical references and index.

ISBN 0-8078-2474-7 (cloth: alk. paper).—ISBN 0-8078-4801-8 (pbk.: alk. paper)

1. Buena Vista Hacienda (P.R.)—History.   2. Haciendas—Puerto Rico—Ponce—History—19th century.   3. Grain trade—Puerto Rico—Ponce—History—19th century.   4. Coffee industry—Puerto Rico—Ponce—History—19th century.   I. Title.

HD1471.P92P66313 1999   972.95'7—dc21   98-37128   CIP

CONTENTS

hen *La Buena Vista* was first published in 1988, it received high praise from experts in many fields for both its broad scope and its attention to detail. Guillermo Baralt had ventured into the areas of architecture, technology, international economics, business management, labor practices, political behavior, working-class standards of living, elite lifestyles, and others, traditionally pursued by more specialized historians. The wealth of the materials at his disposition allowed him to provide readers with specific examples of the workings of the social and economic world he set out to describe. The result of his efforts received due recognition in 1992, when the Association of Caribbean Historians awarded the book the Elsa Goveia Prize, named after the prominent Guyanese scholar at the University of the West Indies who influenced an entire generation of historians in the English-speaking islands and the rest of the Caribbean before her death in 1980 and to this day. That *Buena Vista* is now available in English affirms the book's value to area specialists and points insistently to the importance of disseminating the results of local research.

Baralt's monograph is a major contribution to Puerto Rican historiography in two respects. First, it proves that raising minor crops for local consumption could be as profitable as producing sugar (or coffee, at century's end) for export. Buena Vista, first an estancia (a nonmanufacturing agricultural unit) and then a hacienda (where the processing of corn and coffee required industrial equipment), cultivated plantains, cotton, beans, and local fruits and root vegetables. Grown by slaves to feed the slaves of neighboring sugar plantations, these crops provided Buena Vista with a steady and sometimes considerable income. Second, this case study forces the reader to reevaluate accepted notions of Puerto Rican hacendados. Carlos Vives, the son of Buena Vista's founder, bought slaves as an investment, obtained loans from European bankers, placed his money on overseas ventures, subscribed to industrial magazines, and regularly used European and U.S. technicians as consultants. Both Buena Vista and Vives are welcome historiographical and historical anomalies.

More important, *Buena Vista* made advancements in Puerto Rican historiography that have since been furthered, with rewarding results, by a number of scholars. One of these corresponds to the history of science. In tracing the expansion of the technological capacity of the estancia-turned-hacienda as it strove to increase production to augment profits, Baralt points to the curious combination of European machinery, U.S. manufacturers, immigrant consultants, and Puerto Rican skilled craftsmen that characterized industrialization on the island. Carlos Vives, who managed the estate from 1845 to 1872, purchased from the West Point Foundry in

Cold Spring, New York, the hydraulic turbine that marked the turning point in the estate's trajectory. The design developed by Robert Bennet, the English engineer hired by Vives to work out the details of construction and installation, and by the foundry's manager and superintendent, resembled the one patented by the Scotsmen James Whitelaw and James Stirrat in 1841. Members of the team of experts hired by the Conservancy Trust to restore the hacienda in the late 1970s recognized the turbine as "remarkably sophisticated." As later works have continued to show, archaeological excavations of industrial sites uncover a wealth of information regarding Puerto Rico's sources of machinery and its adaptations to local conditions.[1]

Buena Vista was also a forerunner in business history. Baralt skillfully outlines the Vives's rational calculations upon entering the cornmeal market and while investing profits from the mill's operations as international conditions varied throughout the century and the political situation changed irreversibly in 1898. Buena Vista's founder, Salvador de Vives, figured that abundant corn and low production costs gave the cornmeal processed at the hacienda an advantage over expensive wheat flour imported from Spain. The captive market made up of slaves on surrounding estates assured him a successful business venture. His son, Carlos, proceeded to invest in European firms, which provided the family with credit and contacts in the old country. Taking advantage of the rising price of coffee, the third Vives began in the 1870s to cultivate coffee, a crop that was swiftly replaced by oranges when the tariff structure favored the latter after the U.S. invasion. Throughout these fluctuations, Baralt is careful to note, the internal operation of Buena Vista and the management of its (slave and hired) workforce remained relatively stable. It is noteworthy that others have followed the important step taken by the author to contextualize Puerto Rico's economic and political fortunes with international developments and with local considerations, as well as with the more evident U.S. and Spanish presence.[2]

Finally, Baralt's reference to the physical state of slaves and especially to the cholera epidemic of 1855–56 is an early effort to introduce the history of medicine into Puerto Rican historiography. His description of the spread of disease throughout the island and of the developing state-of-siege mentality of the estate's population as cases were reported in nearby areas adds a human element to an otherwise methodical treatment of the relationship between masters and workers. The author documents Carlos Vives's efforts to curtail the effects of the epidemic by medical supervision of the already afflicted and by quarantine precautions. The figures for losses incurred as a result of the ravages of cholera, much more than being simply statistical data, denote the fragility of life in the nineteenth century. Subsequently, the history of the Puerto Rican population's health alternatives has received the attention of other historians, a welcome development in Puerto Rican historiography.[3]

The excellent translation by Andrew Hurley deserves separate recognition, as it constitutes virtually another book. Hurley's product is faithful to the original, making Baralt transparent. In addition, it also has a number of explanatory notes that provide further context even to the most seasoned historian. Hurley has gone to the trouble of questioning the Spanish terms we have customarily picked up indiscriminately from the documentation in our quotations, tracing their etymology and providing several alternative interpretations, all equally satisfactory.

The publication of *Buena Vista* in English translation is a benchmark for Caribbean history. The efforts of the Association of Caribbean Historians, especially its president Bridget Brereton and its past president Woodville K. Marshall, of the Latin American Studies Program at Johns Hopkins University and most notably its former director Franklin W. Knight, and of the University of North Carolina Press, particularly its editor David Perry, and the financial support of the Mellon Foundation will undoubtedly be recognized for many years to come.

Teresita Martínez Vergne
Macalester College

his study was carried out with the support of the Conservation Trust of Puerto Rico and its director, Francisco Javier Blanco, to whom I am indebted for both the working and personal conditions that made the research and writing of this book possible.

It began in the summer of 1984, when Blanco asked me to look into the private papers of the Vives family of Ponce, whose coffee plantation, Hacienda Buena Vista, the Conservation Trust was about to restore, in order to establish on the grounds Puerto Rico's first living museum of science and art. The documents gathered through five generations of the Vives family proved to be of invaluable assistance in restoring the hacienda, as of course they were to me in the writing of this book.

Puerto Rico as a whole is indebted to Silvia, Carmen, Alicia, and Guillermo Vives, who donated to the Conservation Trust this treasure trove of documents that they, their father, Guillermo Vives Azcoaga, and his predecessors have saved over the years. I am grateful not only for their generosity but also for their enthusiasm and friendship. I will never forget those meetings in Ponce when we sat down together to pull back, with patience and astonished delight, the mantle of history that had fallen over Buena Vista.

I wish also to express my gratitude to Robert L. Johnson, scholar of water power and restorer of the hacienda, who shared with me more than ten years of his research into these subjects. To him I owe a great part of the material included here on the history of the hydraulic turbine. I am grateful for the help given me by Rafael Torres Colondres, who read the sections of the manuscript describing the functioning of the waterwheel and the turbine.

It would be unforgivable of me not to express my thanks to historians Humberto García, Fernando Picó, Gervasio García, and Luis de la Rosa, to the anthropologist Carlos Buitrago, and to the economist José Luis Barreto, all of whom carefully read the manuscript and offered valuable criticism and suggestions. Ernesto Ruiz de la Mata also made a number of useful suggestions and proofread the first draft of the book. And my thanks go as well to Mercedes López Baralt, who was of such great help to me throughout the entire process of the writing of the final draft. Special thanks to Sra. Luz M. Graziani, who provided me with extraordinary aid in the form of corrections, suggestions, and cooperation.

I am grateful to all those who have gone to Buena Vista with me: the Spanish engineer Manuel Díaz Malta, the writer José Luis González, the engineer Carlos Garret, the contractor Marcelo Colón, and many others with whom I have shared my findings. I have learned a great deal from these people's insights, knowledge, and experience.

I must mention many Ponceños who helped in various ways with my research: Rafael Pou Vives, who provided me with wonderful photographs; Pedro J. Vidal; Gladys Tormes, the director of the Ponce Municipal Archives; Néstor Murray, the president of the Ponce Folklore Society; Miguel and Delia Echevarría, the historians of Corral Viejo; Luis Becerra; Rafael P. Valls; and all those who worked on the restoration of Hacienda Buena Vista during all these years.

The editorial production of the original, Spanish edition of this book—concept, design, and layout—was in the clearly able hands of Aníbal Sepúlveda, Jorge Carbonell, and Néstor Barreto.

Guillermo A. Baralt

BVA   Buena Vista Archives, Conservation Trust of Puerto Rico

CHR   Center for Historical Research
(Centro de Investigaciones Históricas, University of Puerto Rico)

CTPR   Conservation Trust of Puerto Rico

FGE   Fondo de Gobernadores Españoles

GAPR   General Archives, Puerto Rico

HAER   Historic American Engineering Record, Library of Congress

NHA   National Historical Archives (Archivo Histórico Nacional),
Madrid

PMA   Ponce Municipal Archives

RAIC   *Revista de Agricultura, Industria y Comercio*

1 kilo = 1,000 grams = 2.2 pounds

1 *quintal* = 100 pounds

1 *arroba* = ¼ *quintal* = 25 pounds

1 ton = 20 *quintales* = 80 *arrobas* = 2,000 pounds

1 *almud* = 100 ears of corn ≈ 33 pounds

1 *fanega* of corn = 5 *almudes* = 500 ears

1 sack of cornmeal = 100 pounds = 1 *quintal*

1 barrel of cornmeal = 196 pounds

1 *almud* of coffee = 8 ⅓ pounds

1 *fanega* of coffee = 100 pounds = 1 *quintal* = 12 *almudes*

1 *vara* = 835.9 millimeters = 33 inches

1 *cuerda* = 0.97 acre = 3,930.39 square meters

1 *cuerda* of coffee = 100 coffee trees

1 *cuerda* of corn = 3 *fanegas* = 1,500 ears

1 *caballería* = 200 *cuerdas*

1 liter = 1,000 cubic centimeters = 61.02 cubic inches (dry)
    or 1 quart (liquid)

1 *real* = 12 ½ *centavos*

1 *peso* = 8 *reales*

1 silver peso = U.S.$1.00 (until 1898) or U.S. $0.60
    (after the currency exchange of 1899)

Buena Vista

hen, in the summer of 1984, I entered the residence of the descendants of Don Salvador de Vives (1784–1845), in the city of Ponce, for the first time, I found what I consider one of the greatest treasures in the social and economic history of Puerto Rico and the Caribbean. In that big old house, designed in 1859 by the famous architect Juan Bértoly, we opened dusty armoires, desk drawers, boxes, strongboxes, and safes to find documents, hidden away sometimes for more than a century, that revealed the entire history and development of Hacienda Buena Vista—farm, cornmeal mill, and coffee plantation— from 1833 to 1940.

The prompt organization and cataloging of these invaluable documents made the restoration of the buildings and machinery of the old estate much easier for the Conservation Trust of Puerto Rico. Today, the grounds of the estate are the site of Puerto Rico's first museum of the history of technology and agriculture. It is a living museum that encompasses both buildings and grounds, and it is invaluable as a door to the agricultural processes of the past. But that same labor of cataloging and evaluating the documents also led to this book, in which I discuss, among other topics, the history of nutrition in Puerto Rico during the nineteenth century. For this is the history of what began as a "truck farm," growing fruits and vegetables destined not for tables in Europe or America, as happened in the case of sugar, coffee, and tobacco, but rather for the tables of working Puerto Ricans—whether day laborers, salaried workers, or slaves—in and around the municipality of Ponce. The plantain, "the Puerto Rican's daily bread," was Buena Vista's principal crop for many years, and it was the origin of the Vives family fortune. With the income from this humble fruit, and over the course of three generations, the Vives family established first a milling operation, with two cornmeal mills from which sizable profits derived, and then a prosperous coffee plantation, while never abandoning what had been the source of the enterprise: fruits and vegetables. Diversity of production, in fact, was the key to Hacienda Buena Vista's continuing success.

The present work begins with a summary of the history of Ponce during the first half of the nineteenth century, when Don Salvador de Vives, the founder of the estate and future mayor, arrived in Ponce. These were the years in which the village of Ponce was on its way to becoming the island's foremost grower of sugarcane and producer of sugar. The port of Ponce, with its large warehouses and offices of the representatives of European and American trading concerns, became not only the island's main export point for sugar but also, by the end of the century, the port that handled the highest volume of the island's principal export product: coffee. It was this traffic that made Ponce, officially declared a "city" by royal decree

Above: Plantain tree, *Musa para-disiaca.* (Heck, *The Iconographic Encyclopaedia of Science, Literature, and Art*)

Right: Port of Ponce, the largest trading and shipping center in Puerto Rico at the end of the nineteenth century. (*Views of Puerto Rico*)

in 1877, the most dynamic, progressive, and cosmopolitan city on the Island.

The second chapter relates the story of the founding of Buena Vista on little-used or virgin land in Barrio Magüeyes. At that time, Hacienda Buena Vista was no more than a truck farm providing food to the slaves on the plantations along the coast and to the residents of the coast's largest town.

Following that, I tell a little of the history of the technology of water power in Puerto Rico during the nineteenth century, because in 1847 Carlos Vives, Don Salvador's son, wishing to convert the farm to a cornmeal mill, installed a waterwheel on the estate and then later, in another building, an ingenious reaction turbine. Both these installations were powered by water from the Canas River, which ran through the property. Because of drought and lowered river levels, waterwheels were being replaced by ox-turned wheels along the coast, and there was even talk of piping in water from the north coast, but at Buena Vista water was always the main source of energy for the mills. The hydraulic turbine installed at Buena Vista had been invented in 1841 by the Scotsman James Whitelaw and was manufactured, twelve years later, at the West Point Foundry in Cold Spring, New York.

We should not wonder at the presence of U.S. technology on the island, even in remote and impoverished Barrio Magüeyes, for long before the Spanish-American War in 1898 most of the ships that stopped at island ports, most of the buyers of sugar, and most of the providers of iron parts and machinery (not to mention other goods) were American. The presence of the United States permeated Puerto Rican trade even when Puerto Rico was a colony of Spain.

Above: Logo of the West Point Foundery [*sic*], Cold Spring, New York. (BVA)

Left: The streets of Ponce, with their sidewalks, were wider than those of San Juan and other cities, allowing both pedestrians and carts loaded with coffee on its way to the main trading houses of the city to comfortably share the thoroughfares. (*Views of Puerto Rico*)

Buena Vista cornmeals prospered, in fact, in the shadow of the Spanish flour monopoly. When Spain attempted to raise a wall of tariffs to protect Spanish flour from foreign (and especially U.S.) incursion into the market, a flour shortage and devastating rise in prices resulted, which in turn deprived most Puerto Ricans of bread. So it was that Carlos Vives asserted in 1847, in his request to take up water from the Canas River to drive his mill, that his cornmeal "would offer the municipality, and often the remainder of the district, an interesting resource or provision at lower cost than the foreign product."[1]

Demand for his cornmeal was instantaneous. On a workday, Buena Vista would look like a train station near some great market. Oxcarts full of corn would arrive from the coast, while others would depart the farm loaded down with cornmeal on its way to Ponce's main sugar plantations.

And yet the Vives family's admiration for foreign technology (an admiration shared by the owners of sugar plantations all across the island) and their installation of such technology at Buena Vista contrast strikingly with the presence of fifty slaves on the farm. Slaves were always Buena Vista's predominant labor force, as they were also a source of liquid capital. The Vives family bought and sold slaves for great profits. The old order of slavery and the new order of technological advances existed side by side at Buena Vista.

Curiously, the Buena Vista slaves worked to feed their fellow slaves throughout the sugar-producing coastal region around Ponce; they were farmworkers, carpenters, and masons, not cane-cutters. The moist and gloomy mountain forest and upland field were their home, not the dry, hot land of the coast.

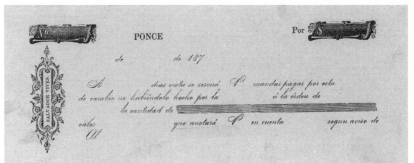

Top: Receipt for donation made by Carlos Vives to construction of the highway between San Juan and Ponce, 1853. (BVA)

Middle: The gas company was founded by Julio Steinacher in 1864. (BVA)

Bottom: Receipt to Salvador de Vives from the Agriculture Society of the Department (district) of Ponce, 1883. The Agriculture Society was formed on May 30, 1875, as a way of cutting government red tape and "destroying [those] practices in government and individual haciendas that stand in the way of the prosperity of the island." (BVA)

Right: Printed check, Salvador Vives, from the 1870s (note the three digits printed for the year). (BVA)

Slaves and day laborers, carpenters, masons, and cart drivers all contributed to the functioning of the operation—for the history of Buena Vista is not simply a history of its owners but also the history of its slaves and hired laborers. The Vives family serves as one link in that history, to which we must add the further links forged by the artisans and foreign engineers who immigrated to Ponce and made the technological progress of Buena Vista possible.

To make this microhistory more understandable, we should take into account a number of international factors, such as the tariff war between the United States and Spain, in which the victory of the sugar producer meant the miller's ruin, and the development of coffee at Buena Vista as a crop during the "bonanza years" at the end of the nineteenth century and the bust years of the early twentieth. Fluctuations in the price of coffee on the international market largely explain the rise and decline of coffee at Buena Vista. The hacienda's profits, invested with European investment houses, and the deals it carried out through letters of exchange are another example of the connections that existed between Buena Vista and off-island elements, this time in the world of international finance. So far from the capital of Puerto Rico, yet so near the investment houses of Murrieta and Company in London and Palmieri in Paris!

Last, I discuss the way the economic consequences of the Spanish-American War that reached Puerto Rico on July 25, 1898, the ravages caused by Hurricane San Ciriaco on August 8, 1899, and the bust in the coffee market changed the future of Buena Vista. In addition to these events is the fact that when U.S. flour became readily available on the island, Buena Vista cornmeal lost its captive market, and the hacienda was obliged to reorder its priorities. It turned back to its "truck farm" roots, to the production of oranges, which were packed, still green, for shipment to New York and beyond.

The great store of documents of Buena Vista itself has been complemented by the documents of the Ponce Municipal Archives, which allowed

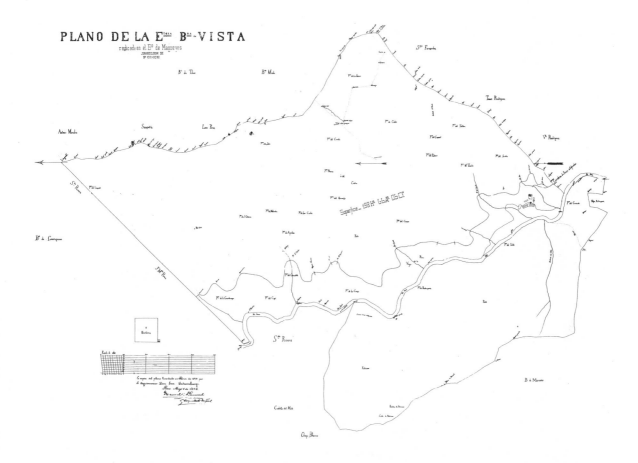

Manuscript survey plat of "Estancia Buena Vista" drawn by surveyor Guillermo Schomburg. Copy belonging to Manuel Domenech, Ponce municipal architect, 1896. (BVA)

me, among so many things, to compare Buena Vista's labor force and financial situation over the years with that of other farms, sugar and coffee haciendas, and cornmeal mills in the area. These documents also enabled me to see Hacienda Buena Vista in perspective vis-à-vis the history of Barrio Corral Viejo, Barrio Magüeyes, the town of Ponce, and the island of Puerto Rico as a whole; to corroborate or confirm the information that appears in the estate's private documentation; to delve into the history of the food of the slaves, day laborers, and small landowners of the municipality; and to study the role of the hacienda's founder, Salvador de Vives, not simply as landowner but also as mayor of Ponce; the public role of his son, the city councilman Carlos Vives; and the business acumen of his grandson Salvador Vives.

hen Salvador de Vives,[1] founder of the farm known as Buena Vista, his Venezuelan wife, Isabel Díaz, and their only son, Carlos, left Venezuela and came to the municipality of Ponce in 1821,[2] they found a rural village that was growing fast. Not so long ago the flatlands around Ponce had been a landscape of palm groves, the sometimes communal, sometimes private lots on which a few pigs and cows were raised, and impenetrable forests, dotted here and there with the homes of cattle ranchers and the cowhands that worked for them, farmers, campesinos, and smugglers, all living in humble thatched houses with walls of palm husks and banana leaves, known by their Taíno Indian name of *bohíos*. Now the landscape was beginning to be transformed into the site of a large and important city.[3] In 1850, while San Juan Bautista, capital of Puerto Rico and seat of the highest civil and ecclesiastical authorities on the island (the Capitanía General and the Intendencia), was a sober, walled, colonial fortress-city, Ponce was more open, more "energetic," and less constrained. Because it had no encircling walls it could spread out endlessly and thus was on its way to becoming the most cosmopolitan, dynamic, and progressive city in nineteenth-century Puerto Rico.[4] As the distinguished Puerto Rican educator Eugenio María de Hostos put it on the occasion of the 1882 Exposition held in Ponce, "Ponce is a city of initiative, understanding, and heart."[5]

Not since its founding had the city experienced such rapid economic and social development as that which occurred in the first quarter of the nineteenth century.[6] The boom was the result of the phenomenal growth of the region's sugar industry, which benefited from the increase in the price of sugar (the greatest in the history of the sugar market) that resulted from an unexpected shortage of sugar on the world market in those years.[7] For example, in Philadelphia, which was the principal market for Puerto Rican sugar in the United States, the price per hundredweight of sugar rose from $12.72 in the years 1800–1810 to $17.31 in 1810–20.[8] This increase was the incentive that made "entire regions" in the Ponce area "abandon their cultivation of many major crops such as corn, plantains, bananas, and sweet potatoes, and turn exclusively to sugar, some growers even going so far as to destroy their beautiful coffee plantations to plant their fields with sugar cane."[9]

By 1827 there were already forty-nine sugar plantations and many more smaller farms in the lowlands around Ponce, producing some three thousand tons of muscovado sugar,[10] twenty times more than the entire production of Puerto Rico in 1776.[11] Several factors favored Ponce: its fertile alluvial soils, which were among the best in the world for the cultivation of sugarcane; its port, which had been fitted out and open to trade since 1812;

CHAPTER ONE

Ponce in the First Half of the Nineteenth Century

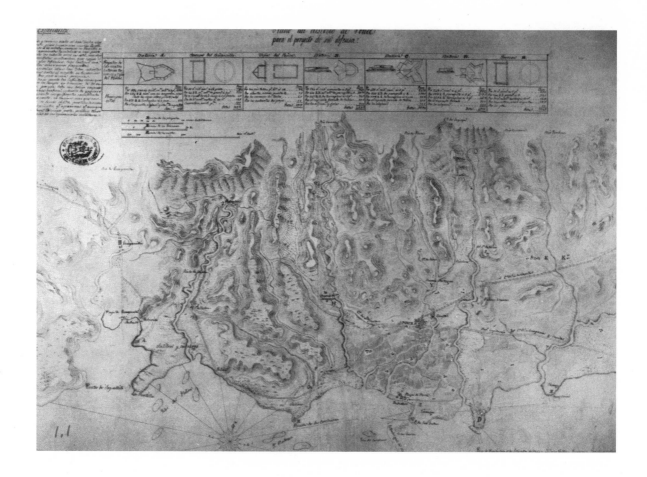

Map of the District of Ponce, made in pursuance of a defense plan for the city by Nicolás Valdés. Copy belonging to José Buenaventura de Vega, 1844. (Servicio Histórico Militar, Madrid, published in *Perfiles de Ponce*)

its mercantile contacts with the free port of St. Thomas; the availability of construction materials; the immigration of foreigners, some of whom brought capital for investment; and the presence of almost five thousand slaves. Because of these conditions, Ponce was expected to produce one-eighth of the island's entire wealth in 1828.[12]

An Irishman, Colonel George Flinter, who served as an officer of the British Army in the West Indies for twenty-one years and visited the island during the period from 1829 to 1832,[13] noted that this southern region of the island was known throughout the world for its extraordinary fertility in the growing of sugarcane.[14] It was wet during the early growth of the stalks and dry during the rest of the year. The dry conditions of the soil helped preserve the sucrose in the cane, leading to one of Puerto Rico's highest yields per acre.[15] This phenomenon had also been noted by Governor Miguel de la Torre's secretary of state, Pedro Tomás de Córdova, who observed that the lowlands that he owned were so fertile that they remained productive even after an entire year of drought. The moisture from dew and a single month of rain, he claimed, were enough to allow his lands to yield sizable harvests.[16] The terrible drought of 1821 and those that occurred between 1839 and 1842 only temporarily slowed the burgeoning development of the Ponce sugar industry.[17]

In 1828, more than 1,634 *cuerdas* (1,585 acres; 1 *cuerda* = 0.97 acre) were planted in sugarcane, and during the following decade the number doubled. The increase was so rapid that Secretary of State Córdova, wishing to dramatize it, indulged in the exaggeration that "in 1832 there were those still alive in Ponce who had seen the first stalk of sugar cane" introduced into the territory.[18]

The sparsely populated settlements and outlying regions along the coast had good access to the city. There were roads built by subscription of all those whose lands they bordered or crossed, private roads on the sugar plantations toward the east, and public cart roads.

In his report, George Flinter had ventured the opinion that "the low price of West India produce [on the market, leading to low profits on exported goods] has compelled the inhabitants of the south coast to think seriously of raising provisions for their negroes, and not to depend entirely on the imports from foreign countries." To move toward this important goal, he noted, roads had been cut up into the mountainous interior, "where various kinds of grain and roots are raised in abundance" on small farms called *estancias de frutos menores*. Flinter observed that one of these roads was so impressive as to strike one as a "carriage road"; this was the *camino real* that went from Ponce to the mountain village of Adjuntas, five leagues inland. Thus, even in times of drought and shortage of provisions, the coast could always be plentifully supplied with foodstuffs.[19]

In addition, the cart road that led out of the center of Ponce through a thick palm grove to the port village was as firm and substantial as that of the prosperous settlement of Mayagüez, and in excellent condition. Flinter describes these roads as "made in a most substantial manner, and their convex form . . . well adapted to preserve them from the destruction caused by the heavy rains of the climate." He says that these roads could not "be surpassed by any in Europe."[20]

The port, in Barrio Puerto Real just two miles from the village of Ponce, had been fitted out since 1812, and a naval customs office had been in service there since 1813. Located in a sheltered bay on the Caribbean side of the island, the port made it possible for ships of all types and nationalities and en route from all the major cities of the West to drop anchor in Ponce.

During the year 1828, some 256 ships anchored in the port of Ponce, of which 165 were Spanish and 91 under foreign flags.[21] Some years later, Spanish ships no longer stopped in Ponce, but they were replaced by ships under the U.S. flag.[22] These ships purchased much more than half the unrefined muscovado sugar exported through the port and in turn supplied the mu-

Manuscript map of Ponce, 1818, by Alejandro Ordoñez. (PMA)

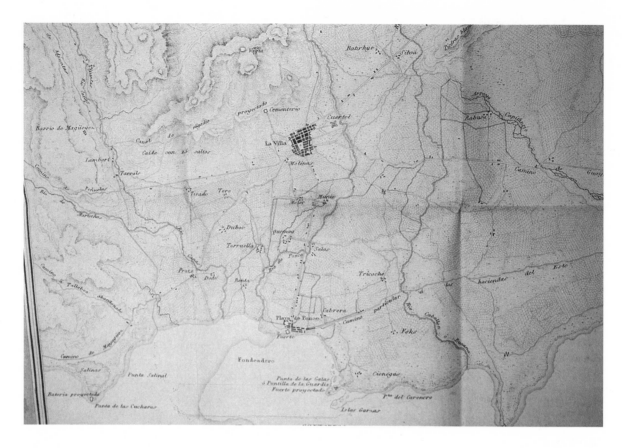

The town of Ponce encircled by sugar plantations; two miles south, the Playa de Ponce, which was the harbor area and a portside settlement. ("Contornos de Ponce" [Ponce and its surroundings], in Coello, *Atlas de España y sus posesiones de ultramar*)

nicipality with much of the provisions, lumber, equipment and machinery, and iron parts that it required. In fact, in 1858 the United States provided most of the machinery imported by Puerto Rico.[23]

In addition, the port area was the home of trading houses and mercantile corporations that were in direct touch with the foreign exporters that were the source for (among other goods) the machinery used in sugar processing. Here could also be found those who dealt in the slave trade, which continued to exist, though it had been abolished officially in 1817.[24] Thus, another settlement grew up around the port of Ponce, and soon a large population made its home in this village.

The port of Ponce had no rivals as the busiest port on the island for the movement of citrus, tuberous, and other agricultural products and for the export of coffee and sugar. An English-born resident of Ponce, Albert E. Lee, recalled that his childhood was filled with the "mixed smell of sugar, molasses, pine lumber, coffee, tar, and oakum" from the port of Ponce.[25]

Furthermore, the proximity of Ponce to the Danish island of St. Thomas, an important trading and financial center at the time as well as a free port, gave the haciendas and farms of Ponce access to loan funding and contact with foreign traders interested in buying their agricultural products.[26]

Top: The Caribbean, including the Antilles, Central America, and northern Colombia, 1835. (BVA)

Bottom: Road map of the island of Puerto Rico, 1860. (GAPR)

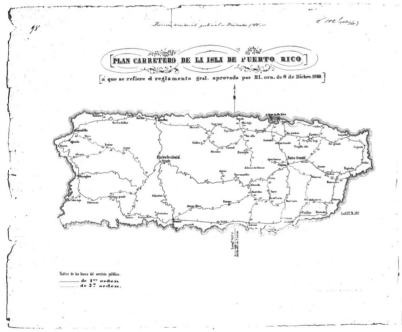

Without credit from St. Thomas and the commercial relationships that were established there with such firms as Grunner and Company, Santos Bartolomé Lange, Simmonds and Company, and the C. F. Overmann Company, many of the haciendas and large business establishments of Ponce would have had little success or failed altogether.[27]

Another factor that contributed to the rapid growth of the Ponce sugar

Above: Plaza de las Delicias (Plaza of Earthly Delights), Ponce's central square. The trees were planted at the order of Salvador de Vives, mayor. (Hill, *Cuba and Porto Rico with the Other Islands of the West Indies*)

Right: Front elevation of the Customs House in Ponce, constructed of cement in 1841. (GAPR, published in *Perfiles de Ponce*)

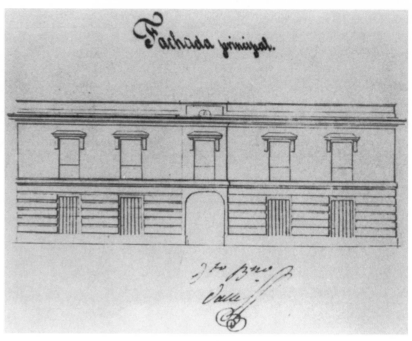

industry (which had already become the island's most important) was the ready availability of a wealth of raw materials for the construction of the agricultural, industrial, and mercantile buildings of the area. In the forests of the mountainous inland area of the municipality, in Barrios Guaraguao, Marueños, Tibes, and Mayagüeyes, there were many types of trees: the *tachuelo* (or fustic); the *capá prieto* (the salmwood or bohum); the *capá blanco* (or fiddlewood); the *ausubo* (or bulletwood tree); the *guayabacón* (perhaps the *guayabota*, a tree native to and found only in Puerto Rico); the *higuerillo* (or white fiddlewood); the *tortugo* (mastic or false-mastic); the *carne doncella* (which may have been the *maricao* or "barka-locust" tree, the *negra lora* or *Matayba domingensis*, or, less likely, the *palo de vaca* or "pigeonberry" [or pigeonwood] tree); the *caimitillo* (probably the tree known variously through the Caribbean as the caimite, *feuille dorée*, or wild star-apple tree); the *guayacán* (or lignum vitae); the *cedro* (Spanish cedar or West Indies cedar); the *nogal* (supposedly the "walnut," though the walnut tree never existed in Puerto Rico); the *aguilón* (though perhaps one of a number of varieties of locust); and the *paja de vaca* (perhaps the *palo de vaca*, as above).[28] These trees produced lumber for the construction of houses (which were quickly replacing the thatch *bohíos* of the past), buildings, and machinery of all kinds. The town, and later city, of Ponce, like all the great cities of Europe, was initially built of wood.

Unfortunately, many of these lumber trees were used not only for building the residences and other buildings of the town but also as fuel for the twenty-one installations of steam-driven cane-crushing equipment on the sugar plantations of the municipality (1866). Soon, deforestation brought on terrible droughts. As early as 1844, when there were only five steam-driven cane crushers, the mayor of Ponce, Salvador de Vives, who had recently ordered that trees be planted in the town plaza (the Plaza de las Delicias, or Plaza of Delights), tried to remedy the growing deforestation by making it illegal to clear trees on the slopes and summits of mountains or on the banks of creeks and rivers. In addition, landowners near the headwaters of rivers and creeks and along any banks that had been cleared were required to plant trees chosen from among a list of those that grew fastest in the island's soil and climate.[29] In the long run, however, the edict had little effect.[30]

In the nineteenth century, builders in Ponce began to use wood in combination with other construction materials such as stone, bricks, and mortar. Nearby, on the lower slopes of the peak known as El Vigia (The Watchtower), which lies above the town on the left bank of the Bucaná River in Barrio Sabanetas, there was a quarry belonging to Valentín Tricoche that yielded a white limestone that made excellent raw material for lime and bricks. Stones, cement made with that lime, and bricks were used in constructing canals, small fortresses, chimneys, larger buildings, houses, churches, and factories both on the haciendas and in town. There were many lime and brick kilns in Ponce. The number of lime kilns increased from two in 1828 to twenty-two in 1845, while in that same period, the number of brick kilns increased from six to thirteen. In Barrio Puerto Real, Salvador Arenas built the largest and most productive lime and brick kilns in Ponce.

With these facilities and supplies, the number of artisans in the construction trades—plasterers, masons, carpenters, ironworkers, and so on—living in Ponce increased substantially; there were more of these types of craftsmen in Ponce than in any other sugar-producing region of the island.[31] In later years, these artisans formed several guildlike organizations, such as the Círculo Ponceño de Artesanos (1873) and the Taller Benéfico de Ponce (1886).[32]

Another factor that helps to explain the expansion of the sugar industry in Ponce is the immigration of foreigners who saw a chance to profit from the high price of sugar, the wide market for it, and the land and trade privileges granted by the Cédula Real of August 1, 1815. This decree promised, among other things, free land: 680 hectares if the immigrant were white, plus 65 additional hectares for each slave he brought.[33] A number of foreigners from various European countries or their New World possessions arrived in Ponce with capital, excellent commercial contacts, and experi-

Rolling hogsheads of sugar through the streets of the port of Ponce to the docks. The largest year of production was 1871, with 35,274 hogsheads of muscovado sugar, 4,175 barrels of refined sugar, and 15,140 casks of honey. (Olivares, *Our Islands and Their People*)

ence in the Antillean sugar industry.[34] With the purchase of good land and the installation of modern processing equipment, in less than twenty years these immigrants had displaced several of the old Spanish landowners in Ponce.

In 1845, the Englishman Jaime Gilbee, the American/St. Thomian Estevan Julio Dubocq, the German Guillermo Oppenheimer, the Frenchman Julio René Mirailh,[35] and the two Irish brothers Josiah W. and Robert Archebald were proprietors of what were some of the largest and most important sugar plantations in Ponce. It was in 1823, at the Archebald brothers' Hacienda La Citrona, the most productive estate in Ponce, that the first steam *trapiche*, or cane-crushing mill, was installed in Puerto Rico.[36] In addition to its steam-driven equipment, La Citrona had a waterwheel, located on the Inabón River, which turned the gristmill where various grains were ground and powered a sawmill.

The Ponce sugar industry also provided opportunities to other foreigners who, though they did not own haciendas, worked in satellite enterprises: the trading houses, factories, artisans' shops, and hardware-supply houses that also served the coffee, cotton, and cornmeal producers, among

TABLE 1.1. Population of Ponce, 1846

Color/Status	Men	Women	Total
Free whites	3,814	3,516	7,330
Free mulattoes	4,864	4,232	9,096
Free black	119	284	403
Slaves	2,728	2,242	4,970
Total	11,525	10,274	21,799

SOURCE: Legajo 578, expediente 366: "Población del partido de Ponce," 1846, PMA.

Simón Bolívar (1783–1830), the Liberator of South America.

others, and lent Ponce its considerable store of technical expertise. In time, some of the members of these mercantile and artisan classes became owners of haciendas. The Englishman Gilbee, for example, arrived from the British Virgin Islands as a specialist in the construction of windmills; soon he became one of the largest holders of sugar-producing land. Another case is that of the mulatto blacksmith Mateo Rabainne, who came to Puerto Rico from the Dutch colony of Curaçao in early 1830 to work on machinery for the sugar and other industries. In time, he not only had a large shop but also was the owner of a sugarcane plantation.[37]

Some of the immigrants who owned sugarcane plantations were also the largest owners of slaves in Ponce. Other immigrants, such as the Americans James Atkinson and Arthur Roger or the Germans Juan David Wedstein and Fernando Overmann, were slave traders.[38] Because of the constant rise in the price of slaves, the slave trade was a very lucrative business in this sugar-growing region that depended so heavily on the cruel institution.

In 1821 Ponce had 1,480 slaves. During the next two decades, with the arrival of hundreds of African-born slaves (who were called *bozales*, or "people that have a hard time expressing themselves in good Spanish"), the slave population increased to a total of 4,970 in 1846. In Ponce, more than any other region of the island, sugar and slavery were synonymous, especially on the large haciendas that belonged to foreign landholders.

In 1846, slaves constituted 11 percent of the population of the island as a whole; in Ponce, they totaled 23 percent. Nonetheless, the largest group of "nonwhites" in Ponce consisted of those called the free "dark-skinned" or mulattoes. For that same year, there were 9,096 mulattoes, or 40 percent of the entire population. In the nineteenth century, this group (made up of small landowners, agricultural workers, and artisans) showed the highest rate of increase in the municipality.[39]

To this mixture of off-island and island-born whites, blacks, and mulat-

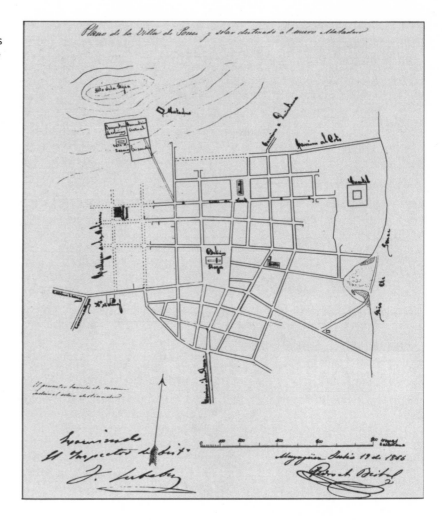

Map of the town of Ponce, with the lot north of the laid-out streets intended for Pedro A. Bisbal's new slaughterhouse (in bold as *Matadero*), approved by Timoteo Lubelza, 1866. (GAPR, published in *Perfiles de Ponce*)

toes were added others: immigrants from Spain (especially Catalonians from Barcelona and Gerona) who settled in the municipality of Ponce and devoted themselves to all types of agriculture and trade and to such financing ventures as factor's liens to the sugar producers.

Finally, during and after the Spanish-American Wars of Independence (1810–23), many ships departing South America brought Spanish and Venezuelan soldiers, army officers, and civilian employees of the colonial government to the shores of Puerto Rico.[40] Among these were the merchant Francisco González de Linares, first civilian governor of Puerto Rico (1822–23), and Miguel de la Torre, who bore the military title *mariscal* ("marshal") and who was made governor of the island from 1823 to 1837.[41] One of the largest waves of immigration occurred beginning on October 15, 1821, after the surrender of Cumaná, when an entire garrison, composed of four generals, 666 soldiers, and 599 "other persons," arrived in Ponce.[42]

Top: West facade of the Ponce market, the Plaza del Mercado Isabel II, with stalls along the pavement in front. This market was built in 1863, replacing the old town market located on the main square. Ramón Marín, a journalist of the time, noted that "outside the building, in portable stalls with canvas awnings, one might see several most humble restaurants set up at night, where the working class would go to eat" (*El Vapor* [newspaper], Ponce, 1877). (Olivares, *Our Islands and Their People*)

Bottom: South facade of the market. Inside the building vendors sold meat, local produce, and staples. (*Views of Puerto Rico*)

Most of these newcomers remained in Ponce and settled there; thus, as the nineteenth-century historian Salvador Brau pointed out in his book on the founding of Ponce, the municipality received a large influx of educated settlers from Venezuela.[43] Many of these immigrants contributed in no small way to the public and social life of the town. Because legally they were also able to use their Venezuelan currency (the *macuquina*), their impact was soon felt in every sphere of Ponce life.[44]

Old and new seals of Ponce. The new seal introduced a lion in place of the traditional lamb. The change was suggested by Salvador de Vives while mayor of Ponce; the governor of Puerto Rico, the Conde de Mirasol, approved the change on September 5, 1844.

TABLE 1.2. Institutional and Administrative History of the Municipality of Ponce, 1800–1877

1812	Dredging, construction, and so forth for the opening of the port of Ponce
1812	Establishment of first constitutional city government (*ayuntamiento*) in Ponce
1813	Establishment of naval customs office in Ponce
1814	Construction of first cemetery
1816	Declaration of Ponce as seat of the Southern District government
1819	First public scrivener appointed in Ponce
1820	Foundation of a boys' school
1820	Declaration of Ponce as one of the island's seven judicial districts
1820	Appointment of the first sanitation board
1821	Declaration of Ponce as headquarters, Southern Military District
1827	Construction of wooden slaughterhouse in Ponce, managed by one of the city's *regidores*, or city councilmen
1836	Inauguration of the Ayuntamiento General in Ponce
1839	Transfer of the Court of First Instance from Coamo to Ponce
1840	Establishment of the Income Tax Administration
1846	Royal decree organizing the municipal government of Ponce
1848	Royal decree making Ponce officially a "town"
1877	Royal decree making Ponce officially a "city"

To take one example, Gregorio Medina, a native of the Canary Islands who had been living in Venezuela, came to Ponce and in time became one of the largest merchants and wealthiest hacienda owners in the area.[45] One note, however: Medina had been able to leave Venezuela in 1816, before the war was over, with enough capital and other resources to allow him to "get ahead" quickly. So while Medina was establishing Hacienda Vayas on the coast in 1820, it took Salvador de Vives, who had lost everything in the war, twelve years to establish a farm on which to grow fruit and vegetable crops in Magüeyes, one of the poorest barrios in Ponce.

With the increase in the number of farms and haciendas that cultivated sugarcane in the rural areas, the urban center of Ponce experienced a notable expansion. In spite of the terrible fire that swept the town on February 27, 1820, and left it virtually in ashes, during the next few decades Ponce grew quickly. In the area around the main plaza with its traditional church and government offices, people began establishing not only their homes but also offices for doctors, attorneys, and engineers, shops for blacksmiths and other artisans, consulates, the offices and stores of mercantile agents, butcher shops, such businesses as general stores, dry-good stores, drugstores and the like (the forerunners of department stores), military offices, and the many government agencies needed by the prosperous city government of Ponce (see Table 1.1). In addition, hundreds of wage laborers and the dispossessed, mostly blacks and mulattoes, congregated in the working-class slums of Barrio Canas and La Cantera and along the bank of the Portugués River to the east of town.[46] These slums of thatched *bohíos* and shanties built with the wood of shipping crates occupied a quarter or more of the total area of the city, and at the end of the nineteenth century, a full quarter of the city's population lived in them.

In the heart of the city, on Marina Street, was located the town's first marketplace, the Plaza Real. Farmers and campesinos would bring in the produce they grew on their land, and for two hours each morning fruits and vegetables were sold wholesale at the market. From ten o'clock on, peddlers and shop owners would buy the produce that had not yet been sold in order to resell it at stalls around the plaza, in pushcarts, or in their stores.[47]

Thus the small town of Ponce gradually became the largest and most important commercial, military, and government center on the south coast of Puerto Rico. In 1816, Ponce was made the seat of the district government. Five years later, when Governor Gonzalo Aróstegui divided the island into four military commands, Ponce was made Southern Command headquarters. One year later the Central Postal Administration for the region was established in Ponce, and in 1840 the Tax Administration and the Court of First Instance were established there. Eight years later, on July 19, 1848, having reached such a degree of population size and economic development, Ponce was declared a *villa*, that is, a "town" in the legal definition of the term then in force, and on August 16, 1877, was promoted to the status of city.

CHAPTER TWO

The Founding of Buena Vista

From Farm to Cornmeal Factory

n 1873, leaving the town of Ponce and heading inland, toward the north and the municipality of Adjuntas, one came to the flat plains of Barrio Magüeyes, where several farms and sugar haciendas were located, among them those of the Bernardino and Chardón families and that belonging to the heirs of the Catalonian immigrant Ramón Tarrats, an estate named Hacienda Feliz. Continuing northward along the old *camino real* that crossed and then ran directly alongside the Canas River,[1] one came first to the hacienda of Catalina Sabater and, farther along, to that belonging to Robert Bennet, an English engineer, as well as to other sugarcane fields and some twenty *estancias de frutos menores* that grew the fruits and vegetables, mainly tubers and plantains, that made up most of the diet of the Puerto Ricans of the time.[2]

Up to the place along the road that people called Corral Viejo, Magüeyes was essentially a sugarcane-growing barrio. From Corral Viejo on, however, the land began to rise, and sugarcane gave way to rich stands of timber. At the end of the carriage road there was a good highway, which finally climbed to an elevation of about five hundred feet above sea level.[3] One had reached the steep region known as Barrio Guaraguao and toward the left could admire one of the waterfalls along the Canas River[4] (from which there was a *buena vista*, a "lovely view"), known at that time as the Vives waterfall.[5]

It was here, on the land bordering this waterfall, that Salvador de Vives, a Spaniard born in Vilobi, in Catalonia, in the diocese of Gerona,[6] after having lived for a time in the town of Cura in the province of Caracas, Venezuela, came to live, and where he founded the estancia known as Buena Vista.

When he arrived in Ponce in early July 1821, at the age of thirty-seven, Vives had had twelve years of experience working for the Spanish colonial government. His first job after studying philosophy, Latin, and mathematics for four years (1804–8) at the Royal University of Toledo[7] had been as comptroller of hospitals in his native city of Gerona (1808), but when in 1808 the French invaded Spain for a second time, Vives was commissioned in the defense of the port of Santa Bárbara, at El Saladero in Madrid, where he was captured and sent to France.[8] A year later, he escaped and made his way to Cádiz, from which he sailed for Caracas.[9] On September 7, 1812, Vives was appointed comptroller of hospitals in Caracas, and two years later, on July 24, 1814, he was named administrator of the Treasury and Postal Service in the department of Villa de Cura and city of San Sebastián de los Reyes, Caracas. There he distinguished himself in his handling of the taxes and other matters with which he was charged.[10]

Salvador de Vives

But he was not to find any more peace in Venezuela than he had experienced in Spain, since the Wars of South American Independence had broken out toward the end of 1810. During the short-lived Spanish reconquest of the ravaged city of Caracas, he set up hospitals and organized all aspects of the economy, bringing it as well as he could back to the conditions it had been in before the city fell into the hands of the rebels.[11]

Five years later, in the midst of the renewed Wars of Independence that now were spread all across the country, Vives was also made administrator of supply warehouses for armies under several commands, in particular those of the deserts of Arauca. In addition, he served as commissary general, acting consul, and administrator of the postal service and range rights for Venezuela.[12] Finally, on June 27, 1821, three days before the decisive battle of Carabobo, he was given leave to migrate, through Puerto Cabello, to Puerto Rico.[13]

Once on the island, Salvador de Vives was appointed paymaster in the Registry and Clerk's Office for the Municipality of Ponce, and four years later he purchased the office of clerk of the Royal (that is, Spanish) Treasury and Registry for the municipality.[14]

The farm that Vives brought together between 1833 and 1838 was the result of the gradual purchase of nine parcels of contiguous land, totaling 482.5 _cuerdas_ (some 467.5 acres), predominantly impenetrable woods, fertile pastures, and clayey soils.[15] Though the lowland acreage was somewhat arid, by the highest point of the estate, almost 2,000 feet above sea level, the land turned moist and shady. At the time of its purchase, neither coffee nor any other citrus or food crop was planted on the land.

As I have indicated, the island's most important Caribbean port for the export of sugar was on the coast, about two miles south of Ponce, and it was also in that area, along the coastal plains, that one found the most prized land of the time, known around the world for its extraordinary fertility and virtually perfect suitability for the cultivation of sugarcane. On this coastal plain were found almost all the most modern and most prosperous haciendas in Ponce and in all of Puerto Rico. But lacking the large capital resources that other immigrants had brought with them, Salvador de Vives was unable to purchase that prized acreage. What he bought was cheap virgin land in impoverished Barrio Magüeyes;[16] the land was steep, sometimes mountainous, and not at all close to Ponce. Buena Vista, then,

Left: Certificate of studies granted Salvador de Vives by the University of Toledo in 1804. (BVA)

Right: The wagon road (formerly the *camino real*) from the town of Ponce to the municipality of Adjuntas. This road cut through Buena Vista. Map redrawn from the original manuscript, 1873. (PMA)

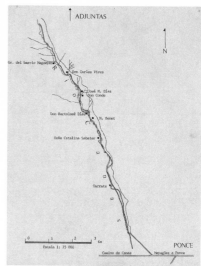

was not founded on land near the coast, the town, or the main agricultural establishments of the municipality, yet in the course of time the land purchased by Salvador de Vives in Barrio Magüeyes revealed itself to be an excellent buy.[17]

The First Years (1833–1845): The Estancia

During its first years of agricultural production, Buena Vista produced a wide variety of foodstuffs: plantains, bananas,[18] *yautía* (generally called taro or, when processed, manioc in English), and sweet potatoes. Of these, the plantain (*Musa paradisiaca*) was the estancia's principal crop. This plant, native to the East, adapted quickly and easily to the Antilles and the tropical regions of Central and South America. Rich in carbohydrates, from the earliest days of colonization the plantain proved a rich source of nourishment to the settlers.[19]

Dr. John Layfield, chaplain of the Count of Cumberland's expedition that seized the island for England in 1598, described the banana-like fruit in the following way:

Plantines [*sic*] are a fruit which grow on a shrub betwixt an hearb and a tree, but it is commonly called, a tree of the height of a man, the stem of it as bigge as a mans thigh, the fruit it selfe, of the bignesse and shape of a Goates horne, it groweth yellowish and mellow being ripe either upon the tree, or with keeping, and then eaten raw or roasted, it is a good meat, comming neere to the rellish of an Apple-John, or a Duson that hath beene kept till it is over-ripe, saving that me thought I still found some taste of a roote in it, the meat of it is lapped up in a thin skin,

The port (top) and town (bottom) of Ponce. Drawings by the French naturalist Auguste Plée (1821–23). (Alegría, *Los dibujos de Puerto Rico del naturalista francés Augusto Plée*)

which being scored the long way with a knife, easily delivereth what is within it.[20]

In 1644, Fray Damián López de Haro, bishop of Puerto Rico, observed that plantains, "of which there is a great abundance[,] . . . are the lifeblood of the Negro, and even of many poor whites, because the mature fruits

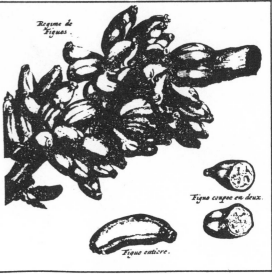

Top: The plantain, "the Puerto Rican's daily bread." (Labat, *Viajes a las Islas de la América*)

Bottom: Francisco Oller, *Plátanos amarillos* (yellow plantains), ca. 1892–93. (Ponce Museum of Art)

serve for bread, while the unripe fruits are roasted and baked as we bake potatoes or carrots; laborers roast them like chestnuts, and make many sorts of stew with them; it is a healthful food."[21] Two hundred years later, toward the end of the eighteenth century, both Fray Iñigo Abbad and the French naturalist André Pierre Ledrú, men who wandered the island from coast to coast, agreed that the green plantain, roasted, was the Puerto Rican campesino's "daily bread."[22] Fray Iñigo went so far as to describe the plantain as the handsomest and most useful plant grown on the island.[23] As the nineteenth century advanced, cultivation of the plantain increased enormously, and because the crop required little investment, it became the most important subsistence crop on the island.

By ten years after the founding of Buena Vista, there were already forty *cuerdas* on the property dedicated mainly to growing plantains. The "lots" planted in this crop were estimated in 1845 to have a value of six hundred pesos.[24] They were the farm's major source of income.

But quite the opposite was the case in the municipality of Ponce as a whole, since from 1828 to 1841 land dedicated to the raising of plantains had decreased by 398 *cuerdas*, from 1,597 to 1,199.[25] Sugarcane was crowding out food crops, and especially plantains, throughout the fertile coastal lowlands.

The terrible drought that began in 1839 was another factor that adversely affected the already reduced production of food crops, with resultant shortages of rations and even hunger among poor wageworkers and slaves. Slaves, whose diet consisted basically of plantains, went hungry, and as the mayor of the neighboring town of Guayama pointed out, "The man that

goes hungry is greatly to be feared."[26] Slave rebellions soon broke out in various places along the island's south coast. On December 18, 1841, the largest slave uprising in the history of Puerto Rico was uncovered in Ponce.[27]

Because Buena Vista was located inland, in the mountains, it was not so severely affected by droughts as were the lowlands. In fact, except for the drought year of 1856, Buena Vista's production of plantains steadily increased, from 329,200 in 1852 to 475,380 in 1860, and it was able to sell them both to the sugar haciendas on the coast, for feeding their slaves, and (to a lesser extent) to resellers and peddlers in the marketplace in town.[28] Week after week, oxcarts from the largest sugar plantations in Ponce—Guillermo Oppenheimer's La Isabel, Luis Lambert's La Perseverancia, the Widow Echevarría's La Bagatela, Julio René's Vayas, and Haciendas La Matilde, Quemado, and Canas, which though belonging to different owners were all under the administration of the Catalonian businessman Juan Pratts—were sent to be loaded up with Buena Vista plantains. Oppenheimer was the main purchaser; in 1850, to take but a single year, he purchased more than 129,000 plantains in fifty-four loads, one a week for the entire year.[29] Like all the big buyers, Oppenheimer paid an average of five *reales* per thousand plantains. The price to haciendas was less than to the stalls in the plaza.[30]

In addition to plantains, Vives diversified his crops to accord with market demands. (Table 2.1 lists the fruits, grains, beans, and tubers grown during this period at Buena Vista.) And so it was in response to a rise in the price of coffee that Vives cleared eleven *cuerdas* of his farm and planted the land in coffee.

TABLE 2.1. Commercial Crops, Buena Vista

Avocados	Genip	Plantains
Balsa wood	Gourds	Pomegranates
Bananas	Guavas	Prickly pears
Beans	Lemons	Rose apples
Cacao	Limes	Soursops
Choky apples	Mammee apples	Star apples
Coffee	Mangoes	Sweet potatoes
Corn	Manioc, cassava	"Sweetpeas" (a tamarind-like fruit)
Cotton	Oranges	Wild pineapples
Custard apples	Pineapples	*Yautía* (a root vegetable)
Figs		

SOURCE: "Frutas, 1840," BVA.

Near the main houses of the estate but on the other side of the waterfall, on the western bank of the river, lay the pasturelands that Vives devoted to cattle. Cattle had been the old, traditional source of wealth for the first settlers of the region, those "on the banks of the Portugués River," as the "Memoria topográfica de Ponce," a yearly report prepared by the town's mayor, José Ortiz de la Renta, put it. By 1846, that same document reported, cattle raising no longer held the importance it had in earlier years; no one raised cattle to the exclusion of other animals or crops.[31]

Unlike on the northern side of the island, where some of the harvested sugarcane was transported to mills by water, on the south coast, and especially around Ponce, cane was moved by oxcarts. The mill wheels, too, were turned by oxen, rather than horses, mules, or men. For that reason and because of the scarcity of the animals, there was a great demand for oxen on the south coast, and they brought high prices.[32]

In 1846 there were fifty bovine animals at Buena Vista, of which thirty-two were oxen.[33] Hundreds of oxcarts filled with foodstuffs (plantains, cornmeal, coffee, and fresh fruits) left the farm each year en route to Ponce. Hundreds more returned with the goods and supplies needed by Buena Vista for subsistence and development.

The profits earned in this first period of Buena Vista's existence, when it was little more than a farm raising fruits and vegetables, especially plantains, allowed Vives to accumulate a good deal of capital and thus begin to move the property toward its later industrial incarnation.

In view of the fact that many of the crops raised on the farm had little commercial future unless they were processed (the case, of course, with coffee, cotton, and corn), in 1837, only four years after Vives had purchased his first *cuerdas* of land and established Buena Vista, he took out a loan for

Francisco Oller, *La ceiba de Ponce* (Ponce's silk-cotton tree). The *ceiba*, or "silk-cotton," tree (or at least this species) is native to the New World and is one of the hemisphere's largest trees, with the trunk sometimes growing to between five and eight feet in diameter. With its broad, horizontal spread of branches, it is an excellent shade tree. The standard text for the trees of Puerto Rico and the Virgin Islands, *Arboles comunes de Puerto Rico y las Islas Vírgenes* (by Little, Wadsworth, and Marrero, illus. Horne), says that "in many towns, one finds a gigantic, wide-spreading ceiba tree in the center of the town square" (434). Its name in Spanish is said to be taken from the Carib Indian word meaning "boat," because its wood was easily hollowed out for canoes. The fibrous "silk-cotton" capsules of the tree are used for kapok. This particular tree was famed in Ponce for its size and cool shade.

two thousand silver pesos, free of interest, from his compatriots, the Catalonian businessmen and brothers Manich and Esteban Domenech,[34] and with the two thousand pesos he purchased a cotton gin, a rice mill, a machine to remove the pulp from the raw coffee beans, and a corn mill with its shellers. All this machinery was run manually or with horses. The corn mill cost less than the other equipment and in the long run turned out to be the best investment, certainly the most profitable equipment on the estate.

But Vives did not live to see the fruits of his ambitious plan; he died after a long illness on May 25, 1845, at the age of sixty-one. His only son, Carlos, who for several years had also served with "distinction and exactitude" as the clerk of the Municipal Customs-House, took up Don Salvador's work with great dedication and success.[35]

The Second Period: The Corn Mills

This first step toward Buena Vista's industrialization was unquestionably successful, because eight years later, in 1845, the estate was the scene of ambitious construction projects. In the southwest part of the property, on its lowest-lying land and nearest the market at Ponce, a machine shed was erected for mill equipment, and alongside the shed, a roasting shed was constructed with a well-ventilated furnace, chimney, and warehouse area. Nearby, a two-story house was built for the family to live in, with a large open space for the living and dining room, a pantry, a kitchen (with its own oven and chimney), and four bedrooms in the upper story and a warehouse below. This house, which on a small scale represented the prototypical colonial house of Venezuela, was built of wood, though its foundations, lower story, and northwest elevation were of concrete and brick.[36] Last, next

Top: Document showing number of cattle and other livestock, Buena Vista, 1846. (BVA)

Bottom: Mule-powered mill. (Detail of a drawing by José A. García-Diego; manuscript attributed to Juanelo Turriano, Biblioteca Nacional, Madrid)

TABLE 2.2. Inventory of Livestock, Buena Vista, 1846

CATTLE	COWS
1 ox—yellowish	1 red and white, with male calf
1 ox—black	1 dark male
1 " —mule-colored	1 heifer, terra-cotta
1 " —bright with white patches	1 heifer, terra-cotta
1 " —yellowish	1 black cow
1 " —dark	1 black-yellow cow
1 " —black	1 one-eared cow
1 " —bay	1 dark cow, with broken horn
1 " —yellowish black	1 dark black cow
1 " —dark, horns turned down	1 dark calf, male
1 " —terra-cotta	1 yellow cow
1 " —spotted terra-cotta	1 dark male calf
1 " —brown and white	1 male calf
1 " —dark brown and white	1 dark, brown and white
1 " —black and white	
1 " —white and red	BEASTS
	1 mule
8 yokes — 16	1 blind horse
	1 burro
1 ox—spotted black	2 female burros
1 young bull—spotted	60 [illegible]
1 young bull—brown and white	25 goats

SOURCE: Inventory, January 17, 1846, BVA.

to the main house in this compound area was a concrete warehouse building that also served as a storm house.

There were also two wooden buildings: one for the hired laborers and another, much larger, of two stories, for housing more than fifty slaves. This barracks was constructed only sixty-two feet from the owners' residence. Finally, for the horses and carriages, wagons, and so forth, there was a building to one side of the warehouse.

On April 8, 1847, Carlos Vives notified the Ayuntamiento of Ponce ("city hall," basically), where he had been one of the city councilmen, and later notified the governor, Rafael de Arístegui, count of Mirasol, that he planned to install a waterwheel on the Canas River. (This river, as I have noted, flowed through his property.) In the document he sent to the Ayuntamiento, Carlos requested that he be allowed to take up the water of the river, promising that he would return the water clean to the streambed, with no harm or damage done to any resident of the district; his intention, he said, was to irrigate some of his land and to produce various types of cornmeal. Vives added that cornmeal, when fresh and unadulterated, was a

most healthful food and that his would offer "the municipality, and often the remainder of the district, an interesting resource or provision at lower cost than the foreign product."[37] At this juncture, in spite of the fact that the Ayuntamiento was attempting to find solutions to local conflicts between hacienda owners who were disputing water rights along the coastline, it saw no obstacle to Vives's request, and on June 12 Governor Arístegui gave Vives permission to take water from the Canas River for the purpose of irrigating his land and installing a water-powered mill.[38]

The use of wooden waterwheels to power mills was nothing new. Waterwheels had been known since antiquity, and the vital role they played in the production of flour and meal in Byzantium, Greece, Egypt, and especially Rome is well documented. One of the earliest authorities on the design and application of the undershot wheel and bucket chain and the gear mechanism for regulating its speed was the Roman architect and engineer Marcus Vitruvius Pollio (ca. 25 B.C.), whose text *De Architectura* documents the technology of his time.[39]

During the Middle Ages and with the proliferation of dikes, dams, and irrigation canals, the waterwheel spread throughout Europe. In England, by the time of William the Conqueror's Domesday Book in 1086, Lewis Mumford tells us, "there were five thousand water-mills in England alone—about one to every four hundred people."[40] (Jean Gimpel gives the

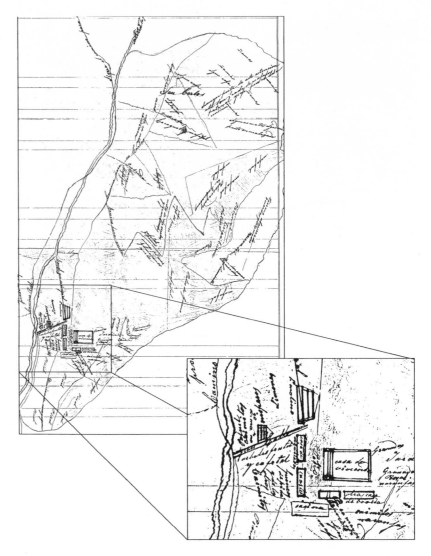

Map of Buena Vista, with crops, roads, buildings, plots of land, bordering property, etc., 1860. In the enlargement, the larger striped "building" is the mill; the straight line running north from it up to the river (see full map) is the canal that brings water to the mill; and the point where the canal meets the river is noted as "*toma de agua*," or "water intake." The main house is to the lower right of the mill, labeled "*casa de vivienda*," or "living quarters." (BVA)

number as 5,634.)[41] In the seventeenth century, Mumford says, "the most powerful prime mover in existence was the waterworks for Versailles: it developed a hundred horsepower and could raise a million gallons a day 502 feet" (117).

In his classic *Technics and Civilization*, Mumford describes the many uses of the waterwheel through history:

Grinding grain and pumping water were not the only operations for which the water-mill was used: it furnished power for pulping rags for paper . . . ; it ran the hammering and cutting machines of an ironworks . . . ; it sawed wood . . . ; it beat hides in the tannery, it furnished power for spinning silk, it was used in fulling-mills to work up the felts, and it

The main house at Buena Vista, constructed between 1845 and 1847. (Photograph, 1904, Grace Hartzell Collection, GAPR)

turned the grinding machines of the armorers. The wire-pulling machine invented by Rudolph of Nürnberg in 1400 was worked by waterpower. In the mining and metal working operations, . . . water-mills were used for crushing ore. The importance of water-power in relation to the iron industries cannot be over-estimated: for by utilizing this power it was possible to make more powerful bellows, attain higher heats, use larger furnaces, and therefore increase the production of iron. (114–15)

Indeed, it was water-powered machinery that permitted the growth and development of metalworking and the mechanization that resulted from it.[42] Likewise, the European textile industry achieved an unheard-of level of production thanks to the power of the waterwheel (Mumford, 118).

From the end of the eighteenth century to the middle of the nineteenth, with the many demands made by capitalist industrial growth, on the one hand, and the limited supplies of water, especially in England, on the other, the design and construction of the traditional vertical waterwheel was forced to change.[43] The traditional practice of building waterwheels intuitively, without a fixed plan, was abandoned, to be replaced by quantitative analysis and theory. The usual separation between the miller and the scientist had ended (Reynolds, 195, 196ff.). One of the main goals of the new "science" of waterwheels was the more efficient use of water, so that water entered the wheel without impact and left it with no velocity (258). To accomplish this, the design of the wheel's buckets (whether in the form of blades or float boards and riser boards) and bucket walls evolved, so that the buckets became curved; wheels began to be constructed of iron rather than wood, first in parts such as the axle and the shrouds and then in their

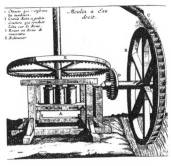

Top: Overshot waterwheel. This wheel has "buckets," rather than the curvilinear vanes that would characterize later evolutions of the waterwheel. (Singer, Holmyard, and Hall, eds., *A History of Technology*, vol. 4)

Bottom: Vertical waterwheel linked to the *trapiche*, or sugarcane crushing wheel mechanism. (Labat, *Viajes a las Islas de la América*)

entirety.[44] Iron made it easier to manufacture more durable, efficient, and powerful wheels. Another important development was the recognition that gravity-driven wheels (overshot and high-breast wheels) are more efficient than impulse-driven wheels (undershot and low-breast wheels) (258). And the most important technological change of the first half of the nineteenth century was the replacement of traditional overshot and undershot vertical wheels with what was called the "breast wheel," which received its water somewhere between the top and the bottom (278ff.). During the second half of the century, breast wheels became the best source of energy for America's and Europe's heavy industry.

In the New World, wooden waterwheels had been used to power sugarcane mills for extracting the juice from the cane for more than three hundred years, since the beginnings of the sugar industry in the sixteenth century. In Puerto Rico, Gregorio de Santaolalla first installed a horse-driven mill on his sugarcane plantation in the district of Bayamón in 1548, but a few months later he brought Puerto Rico's first water-driven mill to the district of Yabucoa. According to the bishop of San Juan, Rodrigo de Bastida, his plantation was called Nuestra Señora del Valle Hermoso, or Our Lady of the Lovely Valley.[45] Some years later, in 1555, Luis Pérez de Lugo, an accountant, installed another water-driven mill on the banks of the Canóvanas River. Others followed in Bayamón.[46] Alonso Pérez Martel was also to install a water-powered mill near the strong-running Toa River.[47]

The evolution of these waterwheels, like the technological progress of the Puerto Rican sugar industry as a whole during this period, is somewhat obscure. In spite of their having been the most powerful, efficient, and costly mills of the first three hundred years of sugarcane history in Puerto Rico, water-powered mills were replaced by what were called *trapiches de sangre*—"blood-driven mills," which was the general term for those powered by horses, mules, oxen, or slaves.[48] Even in the early nineteenth century, when the number of sugarcane plantations increased to 789, only a few waterwheels were installed, in the municipalities of Mayagüez, Arecibo, Vega Baja, Toa Baja, Ponce, and Fajardo. In his *Memoria acerca de la agricultura, el comercio y las rentas internas* (1847), Darío de Ormachea noted that there were very few waterwheels on the island.[49] During the first half of the nineteenth century, in the district of Ponce, where there were six considerable rivers, there were only four water-powered mills in operation—on the haciendas belonging to Torres and Torruellas and on the two haciendas belonging to the Mandrí, Rabasa y Mila company.[50] Shortly after the terrible droughts of 1838–42, which severely reduced the production of sugar on these plantations, even these few water-powered mills were converted to oxen.[51]

The falls on the property of the Vives family, Buena Vista Plantation. (Postcard, ca. 1890, BVA)

Nevertheless, precisely at this time of meteorological crisis and of struggle among landowners for control of the rivers' water, Carlos Vives constructed an aqueduct, or canal, to bring water to a waterwheel that would turn his cornmeal mill. We should recall that the droughts affected the coast more than the mountains and also that a strong current of water from

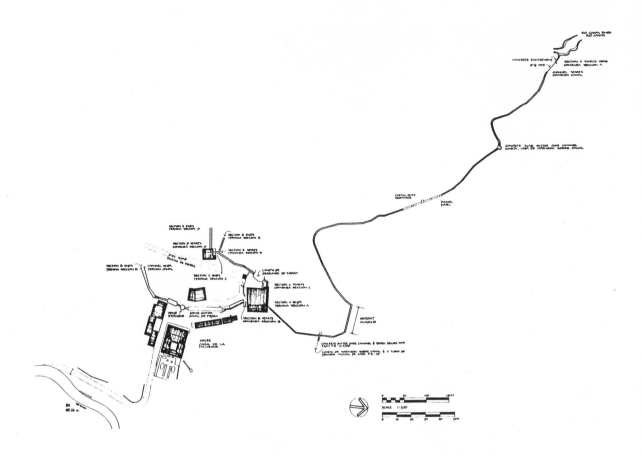

The canal, showing its course from the Canas River, above, through a tunnel to protect it from landslides, over a bridge or aqueduct, and to the millhouse. The canal is 360 meters (1,180 ft.) long, 44.45 centimeters (about 17.5 in.) wide, and 45.72 centimeters (about 18 in.) deep. (HAER, drawing by Reinhard A. Valle, 1977)

a powerful river was *not* necessary for moving a waterwheel; what was needed was a constant volume of water, and this could be obtained either by damming water, creating a holding tank, using a series of sluice gates, or, of course, employing gravity. The purpose, whatever the means, is to obtain a regular flow of water.

Vives took his water from a natural pool upstream at what in essence had become "his" falls on the Canas River. Once the water was contained, a sluice gate could be opened and the water would flow rapidly through a rectangular canal seventeen and half inches wide by eighteen inches deep and constructed of brick and cement. The dimensions of the canal keep the current slow enough so as not to destroy the aqueduct yet fast enough to prevent sedimentation. (I now use the present tense because the canal still functions.)

The canal runs for 360 meters (about 1,200 ft.) downhill (the water moving by gravity) through a wooded landscape of fruit trees and timber. It follows the twists and turns of the topography, bordering the hillside, and sometimes goes underground through a tunnel, to avoid the frequent landslides. It crosses a bridge (or aqueduct in the old Roman sense) that is one

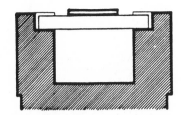

of Buena Vista's most impressive, elaborate, and costly features, and comes to a holding tank (the canal itself, deepened and widened), where the water is held to assure regularity of flow farther along the canal as the water flows into the mill. Because the water comes to a virtual halt in the holding tank, all the suspended soil, rocks, and leaves and foliage settles out or floats and can be skimmed off.

From this tank, clear water flows along a continuation of the canal that acts as the mill's headrace, leading finally into the millhouse, where one can clearly hear the rush of waters. There, the water passes through a switching channel with three sluice gates,[52] and at last to another sluice gate and the vertical wooden wheel, which stands 16.6 feet (5.06 m) in diameter and 2.6 feet (0.80 m) wide. The water falls "without losing a drop" into the wheel's fifty-six buckets.

As José M. Vallejo points out in his classic *Tratado sobre el movimiento y las aplicaciones de las aguas* (Treatise on the movement and applications of water, 1833), the bucket should be set on the wheel so that it holds only the amount of water that will escape at the bottom of the rotation; for maximum speed and efficiency of rotation, the water should never spill over into the next empty bucket.[53] The energy generated by the wheel was transmitted by a main gear (sometimes the waterwheel itself would have a toothed shroud) to a conical pinion mounted on an axle, and then to several further gears and eventually the millstone. It was the upper millstone, known as the *corredera*, or "runner stone," that turned, while the lower, called the *solera*, or "bed stone," remained fixed.

As work progressed on the canal and the millhouse in September 1847, Vives ordered a new corn mill from Hatch and Pritchard, a company with offices in Ponce, though it was the Columbian Foundry of New York that actually manufactured the pieces.[54] The new mill, with its greater grinding capacity than the old one, cost three times what the old one had: $334.51 in gold. But its design and the principles behind it were the same. It had two stone millstones, set one atop the other, with a small space separating them; the corn was fed into this space to be ground.

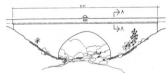

Top: Section of the canal. (HAER, drawing by Robert Fraga, Charles F. D. Egbert, and Reinhard A. Valle, 1977)

The Buena Vista aqueduct/bridge is 9.14 meters (30 ft.) long and 4.57 meters (15 ft.) high. The inscription at the center of the aqueduct, which can be seen in the photograph, reads "Buena Vista, Año de 1851." (HAER, drawing by Robert Fraga, Charles F. D. Egbert, and Reinhard A. Valle, 1977)

Whitelaw's Hydraulic Turbine

The first five years of cornmeal production at Buena Vista (1847–52) were characterized by good profits and a captive market. Soon, therefore, excavation was begun on a pit or shaft in which to install a hydraulic turbine, and construction started on a building above the shaft for a second corn mill. This was the single most important and costly investment ever made on Hacienda Buena Vista, as the estancia now began to be called.

The investment was well justified, however, because the upper, or "first,"

MUELAS HORIZONTALES.

MUELAS DE PIEDRA FRANCESA ESCOGIDA.

Above: Catalog from Blackstone and Company, Ltd., Stamford, England, ca. 1887. (BVA)

Right: Isometric projection of the Buena Vista waterwheel and its gear mechanism. (HAER, drawing by Richard A. Howard, 1977)

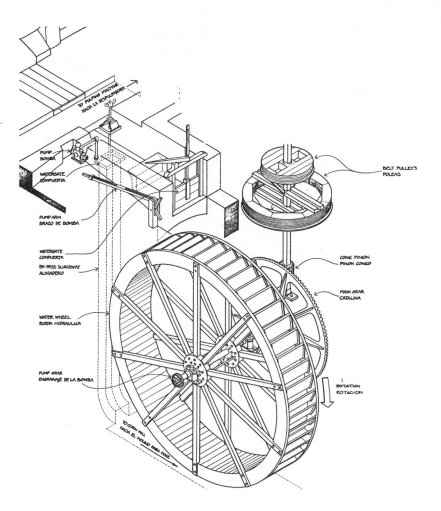

mill, as it was known, was not productive enough to keep pace with the demand from the market in Ponce and the surrounding vicinity. Nor was the waterwheel strong enough to turn two heavy mills at once; in addition, there was not enough space in the "first" millhouse to install the gears needed for two mills.

The second building, also known as the "downstream house," was constructed south of the first mill, where, as we have seen, the waterwheel, the roasting house, and the first millhouse were located. A canal, known technically as a water race, joined the first millhouse to the second; at the second, Vives had a reaction turbine instead of a waterwheel installed to turn the millstones. The water that came off the upper waterwheel was ingeniously reused: as it flowed out of the buckets of the upper wheel, it ran into the second canal and on into a forty-five-foot vertical feed pipe eleven inches in diameter, known as a penstock, installed in the shaft of the "downstream millhouse."

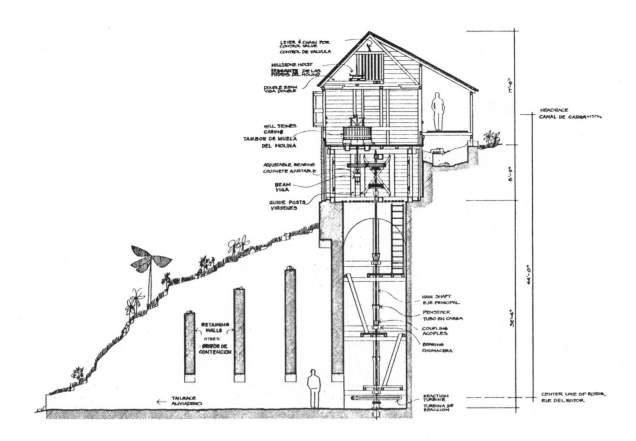

LEVER & CHAIN FOR CONTROL VALVE / CONTROL DE VALVULA

MILLSTONE HOIST / PESCANTE DE LAS PIEDRAS DEL MOLINO

DOUBLE BEAM / VIGA DOUBLE

MILL STONES CASING / TAMBOR DE MUELA DEL MOLINA

ADJUSTABLE BEARING / COJINETE AJUSTABLE

BEAM / VIGA

GUIDE POSTS / VIRGENES

RETAINING WALLS / MUROS DE CONTENCION

TAILRACE / ALIVIADERO

HEADRACE / CANAL DE CARGA

MAIN SHAFT / EJE PRINCIPAL

PENSTOCK / TUBO EN CARGA

COUPLING / ACOPLES

BEARING / CHUMACERA

REACTION TURBINE / TURBINA DE REACCION

CENTER LINE OF ROTOR / EJE DEL ROTOR

Carlos Vives hired Agustín Belmi and Florencio Serrano to construct the turbine shaft and housing. The contract, notarized on November 28, 1853, reads in part as follows:

> They [Belmi and Serrano] shall construct of cement a shaft forty-five English feet deep (of which, from eleven to twelve shall stand above ground level) and seven and eleven feet in diameter, with the arches and other construction features as shown in the plan and as needed, having been imposed with great care; the walls and bottom shall be two feet thick, as shall the drain [that is, the tailrace] from [*sic*] the river, which shall be of cement and following the terrain, this work being for the purpose of installing a machine like that of the Messrs. Tarrats Brothers, which [Belmi and Serrano] have seen.[55]

> They shall also construct the canal, which shall be made to join the drain [that is, tailrace] from the present [upper] mill in such a way as to direct its water into the new machine, which shall be inside the shaft; which canal joins the drain at ground level, and shall rise ten and twelve feet above ground level in order to be at the level of the water intake of the pipe [penstock] in the [new] machine.

The "downstream" millhouse, or second cornmeal mill, in which the Vives family installed the Whitelaw hydraulic turbine, 1853. (HAER, drawing by Charles F. D. Egbert, 1977)

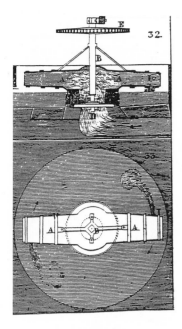

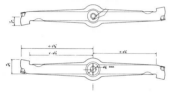

Top: Engraving of primitive wooden reaction turbine. (Vallejo, *Tratado sobre el movimiento y aplicaciones de las aguas*)

Bottom: Buena Vista turbine. Volume of water, 180 liters/sec.; hydrostatic load, 13,411 kg/m². (Drawing by Beatriz del Cueto Pantel and Juan Penabad, CTPR)

The thickness of this wall shall be three feet, in order that the canal that runs above may have an opening of twenty inches, [with] the work to begin upon the instructions of Vives, who shall pay for the cost of labor 300 pesos macuquinos, and supply all necessary laborers and materials. To all this, we voluntarily commit ourselves.

While construction on the shaft was proceeding, Vives ordered the hydraulic turbine that had been recommended (and was to be installed) by Robert Bennet, an English engineer who had arrived in Ponce during the 1840s. Like so many other foreigners, Bennet had immediately found work in the flourishing Ponce sugar industry. He ordered the turbine on Carlos Vives's behalf in August 1853 from the "classic factory," the West Point Foundry in Cold Spring, New York, through Maitland and Phelps Company, also of New York. The turbine was of the same design as that patented by James Whitelaw and James Stirrat of Paisley, County Renfew, Scotland, in 1841.[56] The Buena Vista turbine was not, however, strictly speaking the improved, or "Scotch," turbine with spiral- or S-shaped arms and an interior section that was not uniform throughout the length of the arm but decreasing outward from center to nozzle or jet;[57] it was a near predecessor of that machine. Nonetheless, both turbines operated on the same principle of reaction, and both received their water from below, through a buried feed pipe that lay under the center of the turbine runner (the part that turns, like the modern-day lawn sprinkler). It was the introduction of water from below that had been Mathon de LaCour's great contribution to the primitive "Barker's Mill"–type turbine at the end of the eighteenth century, and the feature that Whitelaw later improved on and patented.[58]

The order that Bennet sent to the West Point Foundry specified that a cast-iron turbine five feet in diameter was to be built; its fall, or head, of water was to be forty-five feet, and it was to rotate at 170 revolutions per minute.[59] Given West Point's experience with this sort of machinery (it had already produced several), the turbine's manufacture was expected to take little time.

Since its founding in 1817, one of the West Point Foundry's major clients had been the U.S. government, and the foundry was known for the excellence of its products: cannons for the army and navy, steam engines for ships such as the *Missouri* and the *Merrimac*, the Cornish pumping machinery at Belleville for the Jersey City aqueduct, a pump for the dry dock at the Brooklyn Naval Yard, the first two practical steam locomotives built in the United States, and steam engines and boilers for the sugar industry.[60] Many of these machines were manufactured for export.

By the middle of the nineteenth century the West Point Foundry was already famous in Cuba, not only for the number of sugar mills and other

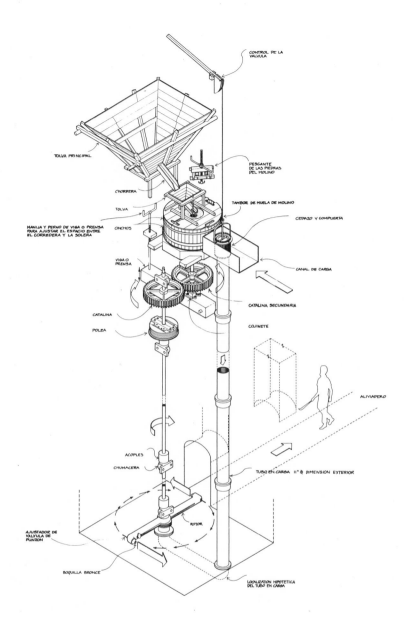

Isometric projection of Buena Vista's second cornmeal milling mechanism, including hopper and turbine. (HAER, drawing by Reinhard A. Valle, 1977, redrawn by Richard K. Anderson, 1978)

types of machinery that it manufactured for Cuba's main sugar plantations but also because it demanded "cash on the barrelhead." That stipulation meant that the foundry's clients had to be solvent; some of the Cuban clients, prominent landowners, thought they deserved a greater benefit of the economic doubt.[61]

Both the foundry manager, William Kemble, and the superintendent, Robert Parrott, played a role in the construction of the Buena Vista turbine.[62] When they received the order, they asked James Finlay, the representative of the Whitelaw and Stirrat patent in the United States, to install it,

Improvement to the hydraulic turbine, submitted to U.S. Patent Office (facing page, left) by James Whitelaw and James Stirrat, James Finlay, patent representative, 1843.

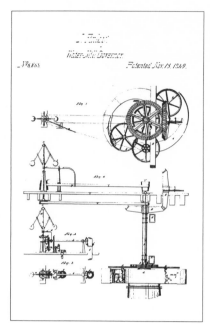

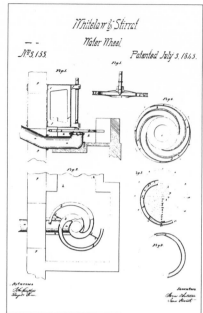

and he agreed, though he recommended several changes to Bennet's plan, innovations that Whitelaw himself had already begun to introduce in places where the turbine was to be used with long falls and ample supplies of water.[63] Finlay also recommended that to achieve the revolutions needed, the turbine should be eight feet in diameter rather than the five feet Bennet had originally proposed and that a governor and a spigot tube be incorporated, so that adjustments might be made to it.[64] Finlay believed that these modifications would produce an improved turbine.

Robert L. Johnson and Patricia O'Reilly, investigating the ruins of Hacienda Buena Vista in 1978, noted the following about the modernity of the installation:

> The construction of the turbine . . . is remarkably sophisticated. Well executed in cast iron, it is fitted with elements advanced for their time, such as cleanout ports covered by removable metal plates. Most remarkable of all, it has jet nozzles of brass fitted with pear-shaped nozzle valves. Nozzles and valves are threaded, permitting adjustment both to balance the thrust of the two arms and thereby reduce vibration, and to vary the quantity of water. These are ancestors of the needle-regulating nozzles invented and patented over a half-century later by Abner Doble as improvement to the Pelton impulse turbine.[65]

In December 1853, five months after the order was placed, the English brig *Velocity*, sailing out of New York, anchored in Ponce harbor with sev-

UNITED STATES PATENT OFFICE.

UNITED STATES PATENT OFFICE.

JAMES WHITELAW AND JAMES STIRRAT, OF PAISLEY, ENGLAND, ASSIGNORS TO JAMES FINLAY, OF NEW YORK, N. Y.

IMPROVEMENT IN WATER-WHEELS.

Specification forming part of Letters Patent No. 3,153, dated July 3, 1843.

To all whom it may concern:

Be it known that we, JAMES WHITELAW, engineer, and JAMES STIRRAT, manufacturer, both of Paisley, in the county of Renfrew, North Britain, have invented Improvements in Rotary Machines to be Worked by Water; and we do hereby declare that the following is a full and exact description of the same, reference being made to the accompanying drawings.

Figure 1 is an elevation, and Fig. 2 a plan, of the first of our improved rotary machines to be worked by water.

In these figures the same letters point out the same parts.

The main pipe *a a* conducts the water which drives the machine into its arms from a reservoir or head on a higher level than the arms.

b b b are the arms, which are hollow. The water passes into them at the center part *c*, and escapes at the jet-pipes *d d*. The motion of the arms is communicated to *e e*, the main or driving shaft of the machine, and by means of a wheel-pinion or pulley fixed on the shaft *e e* its rotary motion may be communicated to any machinery which the water-mill may be intended to work.

f f f f is a large bracket which is fixed to the wall or building *g g*. This bracket supports the shaft *e e*. The tail-race is marked *h h*. As the arms have a rotary motion, and the pipe *a a* is fixed to the building under the machine, there must be means provided to prevent the escape of water at the place where the main pipe meets the arms. A contrivance suitable for this purpose is shown at Fig. 1. It consists of a ring *i i* round the under side of *c*, the central opening or aperture leading into the arms, and of a part *k k*, turned cylindrical at the place where it fits into the bored part on the top of the pipe *a a*. The part *k k* has a groove or grooves turned round its outside near to its bottom end. The groove or grooves is or are to be wrapped full of soft twine or other like material to prevent the escape of water between the pipe and the cylindrical part of *k k*. There is a flange outside of the part *k k*, and rope-yarn is wrapped round in the space between this flange and the top of the pipe for the purpose of keeping the top of *k k* in contact with the bottom of the ring *i i*. The ring *i i* is not sectioned in Fig.

1, but the other parts of the water-tight joint and the main pipe are represented in section in this figure. It will be clear that if the ring *i i* and the part *k k* be accurately turned and ground upon each other at the place where they meet the rope-yarn in the space between the flange outside of *k k* and the top of the main pipe will press the part *k k* into contact with *i i*, and in this way keep the joining of these parts water-tight.

We will now explain the manner of forming the arms of the machine, as shown in Figs. 1 and 2.

In the diagram Fig. 3, let 1 4 9 be a circle of the same diameter as that described by the center of the jet-pipes, and let this circle be divided into, say, twelve equal parts in the points 1, 2, 3, 4, 5, 6, 7, 8, 9, 10, 11, and 12, and let the radius 1 *w* be also divided into twelve equal parts in the points *a, c, e, g, i, k, m, o, q, s,* and *w*. From each division on the circle draw a straight line to the center *w*, and from the division at *a* on the radius draw from the center *w* a portion of a circle till it cuts the radius 2 *w* in the point *b*. From the same center *w* draw a portion of a circle through the second point *c* till it cuts the radius 3 *w* in the point *d*. In this way continue to draw concentric arcs from the divisions on the radius 1 *w*, making each concentric arc to terminate in that radius immediately following the radius in which the arc formerly drawn was made to terminate. The points of intersection 1, *b, d, f, h, j, l, n, p, r, t, w*, and *w* thus obtained will be points in the middle of the breadth of the arms, and a curve line traced through these points will be the curve of the middle of the breadth of the arm. After the curve line 1 *d l r w* is formed any number of points in the curve lines which form the sides of the arms will be obtained in the following way: With *w* as a center, draw such a number of concentric circular arcs passing through the curve line 1 *d l r w* as may give a sufficient number of the required points. Then with a pair of compasses take a distance equal to four times the width of the outer end of the jet-pipe and set off that distance upon each such concentric arc twice, measuring once upon each side of the curve 1 *d l r w* from the point of intersection of the arc and that curve. The points so marked off on one

UNITED STATES PATENT OFFICE.

JAMES FINLAY, OF COLD SPRING, NEW YORK.

REGULATOR FOR WATER-WHEELS, &c.

Specification of Letters Patent No. 6,868, dated November 13, 1849.

To all whom it may concern:

Be it known that I, JAMES FINLAY, of Cold Spring, in the county of Putnam and State of New York, have invented a new and useful governor or regulator suitable in its application to Whitelow and Stirrat's patent water-mill (usually called "the Scotch motor") and to all other mills when the aperture, sail, or part to be acted upon is carried around by the rotary motion of such mill; and I do hereby declare that the following is a clear and exact description of the construction and operation of the same, reference being had to the accompanying drawings, making part of this specification.

Figure 1 is a plan, showing the application of this governor to Whitelow and Stirratt's patent water mill, and Fig. 2 an elevation, in both of which figures the same letters and numbers point out the same parts.

A is the water mill of which the jet apertures *a, a,* are to be acted on by the governor.

B, B, are cog wheels for transmitting the power of the water mill to any required distance.

R, R, are the main beams which support the water mill.

C, is a cog wheel accurately bored and fitted to the turned part of the water mill shaft D, on which it acts. It is not keyed, but left loose, so as to revolve freely around on its seat; either in the same direction as that in which the water mill revolves, or in the direction contrary to it; accordingly as it is acted upon.

E, E, are cog-wheels which gear into C. They are something less than one half the breadth of C.

F, F, are spindles on which these cog-wheels are keyed. These spindles are secured in bearings G, G, to the top and bottom plates of the water mill; having screws *k, k,* cut in the lower ends which pass through the nuts *i, i*. These nuts have two projecting cylindrical ears, opposite each other, which are held in the forked ends of the horizontal arms of the bell-cranks *h, h*.

The other, or vertical arms *o, o,* are connected to the movable plates *l, l,* (which form the inner sides of the jet apertures *a, a,*) by the links *m, m. n, n,* are standards having a center pin, on which the bell cranks *o, h, o, h,* turns.

It will now be obvious that if the cog wheel *c,* be made to revolve in either direction, the cog wheels E, E, and spindles F, F will also revolve; and by the action of the screws, the nuts *i, i,* will either ascend, or descend in accordance with the direction of the motion given to C; and will act on the movable plates *l, l,* through the bell cranks *o, h, o, h,* and links *m, m,* so as either to push those plates outward and diminish the width of the apertures, or draw them inward and increase that width.

P, is a shaft secured in bearing Q, Q, to the fixed beam R, and floor *t*.

S is a cog-wheel of the same breadth as E, E, which also gears into C, above E, E, so as to allow these cog-wheels, when carried around by the revolution of the water mill to pass clear under it. This cog-wheel is keyed on the lower end of the shaft P, and consequently revolves with it. On the upper end of this shaft is fixed a conical drum T with the smaller and downward which is connected by means of a belt U, with a similar conical drum T', having the smaller end upward. The last conical drum is fixed on the spindle V, of an ordinary governor W, (such as are usually applied to steam engines). The belt U passes through an eye formed in the end of the bent lever *x,* shown at *y*. The other end of this lever embraces a groove in the sliding collar *z,* by means of a fork 1, formed on the end of it in the usual manner. Q is a standard having a pin 3 through the top, on which *z* turns as a fulcrum. A pulley 4, fixed on the governor spindle is by means of a pair of bevel wheels with the shaft P, and the other shall communicate with any convenient shaft driven by the water mill. In this case the governor W, must also be driven separately, either from the water mill shaft, or from any shaft connected therewith.

Such is the general arrangement here shown which will serve to explain the principle of the invention. But it will be obvious that this construction may be varied to suit existing circumstances. For instance, the conical drums T, T', may be mounted on separate horizontal shafts, in place of the vertical shafts as drawn. One of which shall be connected by the means of a pair of bevel wheels with the shaft P, and the other shall communicate with any convenient shaft driven by the water mill. In this case the governor W, must also be driven separately, either from the water mill shaft, or from any shaft connected therewith.

---

eral cases addressed to Carlos Vives. The cases contained a corn sheller, a winnower, and other accessories for a new mill.[66]

Due to an overload of work at the foundry, however, it was not until January 4, 1854, that the turbine itself and the parts for a corn mill arrived on the *Alexander Mitchel*.[67] The total price of the turbine, the corn mill, and all the parts was $1,630, and with the insurance, Finlay's commission (of 2.5 percent), and customs and other taxes, the final cost was $1,870.11.[68]

When the shaft and housing were completed and the turbine set in place in April 1854 (the day that had been agreed on), Carlos Vives hired Ramón Rosaly to build the millhouse, which was to be twenty-four feet long by sixteen feet wide and to sit on top of the shaft. The building would include a storeroom for the corn (like the other millhouse) and a space for the mill wheels. On July 16, Rosaly and his assistants completed construction, and they were paid the amount they had contracted for.[69]

During the years that followed, Bennet himself watched over the functioning of the turbine. He frequently visited the installation to fine-tune machinery, adjust the mills' functioning, repair the wheels' axle bearings,

Above: "Regulator for Water-Wheels, etc.," Whitelaw and Stirrat. Specifications submitted to U.S. Patent Office by James Finlay, 1849.

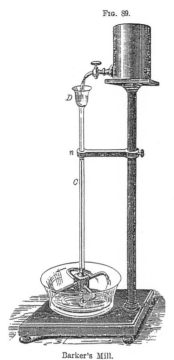

Fig. 89.

Barker's Mill.

WEST-POINT FOUNDERY
and
BORING MILL.

A LIST OF SPUR, BEVEL, AND MITRE WHEEL PATTERNS,
BELONGING TO THE WEST-POINT FOUNDRY ASSOCIATION.

IN ADDITION TO WHEEL PATTERNS, ARE ON HAND
PLUMMER BLOCKS, OF ALL SIZES; WINGED GUDGEONS; SHAFTS; ETC.

Above: "Barker's Mill," reaction turbine, eighteenth century.

Right: Logo of the West Point Foundery [*sic*], recognized in Puerto Rico in the nineteenth century as the United States's "factory par excellence." (BVA)

gudgeons, and drums, draw up plans for and install parts that were manufactured in his shop, and provide tools.[70]

As we have seen, Salvador de Vives, the estate's founder, was a man of letters, and even more a man of numbers. His son, Carlos, who had managed Buena Vista since 1845, was also a man of numbers. The Vives family brought inventiveness, experience, management skills, and business contacts to the industrial development of Buena Vista—though they were not always rewarded for it. For example, in the summer of 1862 Carlos went to Paris in search of a corn-pulverizing machine invented by Betz Penot, a Frenchman; Carlos tried to obtain an interview with Penot. In Carlos's note to Penot from his hotel in Paris, the Madrid et de la Michodière, he asked to see Penot's invention, but Penot never received Carlos, since a short while before, a prominent Havana plantation owner named Juan Poey had paid Penot a visit and bought his invention.[71] Poey was one of the most distinguished and respected men of the Cuban sugar industry. He owned one of the best and most modern corn mills in Cuba—Las Cañas, in Güines, and during the latter half of the nineteenth century, his was the most modern plantation in Cuba: a "model of its kind."[72]

For the engineering work on their estate (the plans and models, the research as to the best machinery, its purchase and maintenance, and improvements to the machinery and the project in general), the Vives family

sometimes went to off-island manufacturers, but they also employed carpenters, masons, blacksmiths, and engineers of great skill and experience who had workshops and offices in the town of Ponce. These were men who generally worked on or for the sugar plantations on the island's south coast. Some invented machinery and other artifacts that were patented during the second half of the nineteenth century.[73]

One of these inventors was Mateo Rabainne, a mulatto who had come to Puerto Rico from the Dutch colony of Curaçao. Rabainne founded a prosperous trading company and a carpentry and blacksmith shop in Ponce; he specialized in the construction and repair of sugar-industry machinery.[74] He was well known as an inventor, and one of his projects, a water pump, won a prize at the first Agricultural and Industrial Exposition in Ponce in 1853.[75]

Rabainne's workshop produced many of the parts that the Buena Vista mills and machinery needed. Documents show that the estate bought iron hammers for the millstones, iron ingots and pins, wheels, gudgeons, firebox doors, sluice gates, and so forth from Rabainne. He and his son Ricardo

View of north side of the plaza at Buena Vista. To the right, the coach house, and to the rear, the roasting shed (note the smokestack) with the millhouse beside it, ca. 1890. (Photograph donated by the Vives family to the CTPR)

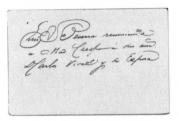

Top and middle: Business card from the Hôtel de Madrid and de la Michodière (printed in Spanish in spite of its Parisian location), with a recommendation on the back from Luis Becerra to the concierge Sra. Crespo. (BVA)

Bottom: Calling card sent by the inventor Betz Penot to Carlos Vives, 1862. (BVA)

also visited the various mills to cut millstones for them or adjust the gear teeth on the wheels.[76] In late 1850, they went into business with Robert Bennet, who designed the parts that the Rabainnes manufactured.[77]

Buena Vista's overseer, Domingo Roche, was another self-taught engineer. He not only was familiar with the process of grinding cornmeals but also knew from experience a good deal about the assembly and functioning of the wheels.[78] In 1856, when a new waterwheel arrived at the port of Ponce and was carted up to Buena Vista, the estate's administrator, Joaquín Mayoral, could find neither Bennet nor any other engineer to set it up, as they were all outside the municipality working on other machinery. So Roche, who had been given a raise since the turbine had been installed, suggested to Mayoral that he, Roche, might be able to help, and with the aid of a carpenter he set to work.[79] On April 29, 1856, Mayoral wrote Carlos Vives in Curaçao that the problem had been solved; Domingo Roche had installed the new wheel, and "it was functioning in full motion and with the greatest regularity."[80]

And so ended the period of furious construction. With its buildings, houses and barracks, and canals, Buena Vista was now not only an *estancia de frutos menores* but a fully fledged hacienda, manufacturing cornmeal from the corn it grew in its own fields. We should recall that it was the estate's profits on the sale of produce that brought about this transformation—a transformation that allowed Salvador de Vives to enjoy a share of local political power in Ponce, which up to that point had been dominated by military officers appointed by the governor or by sugar plantation owners during the constitutional periods. Salvador de Vives was mayor of Ponce three times: in 1840, in 1844, and in 1845 until his death on May 25 of that year.

CHAPTER THREE

The Flour and Cornmeal Market in Ponce

heat, rice, and corn have historically been the "daily bread" of the world's greatest civilizations.[1] Wheat has been the mainstay of the West, rice of the East, and corn or maize of the peoples of the Americas.[2] In Puerto Rico, from the pre-Columbian period to the nineteenth century, corn was one of the essential foods in the diet of its inhabitants. This cereal plant is a member of the grass family; it originated in the New World and was cultivated by the native peoples of the island they called Boriquén in plots across Puerto Rico. Upon the arrival of the Spanish colonizers and the increase in the island's population, the cultivation of corn became even more important, and this grain came to be one of the principal crops throughout the island's fertile coastal plains and lowlands.[3] Along with beans, plantains, and several varieties of sweet potatoes and other root vegetables, corn (roasted or as cornmeal) met the nutritional needs of the settlers and indigenes, and there was usually enough left over to use as fodder for hogs, horses, and poultry.[4]

In his *Memoria sobre la isla de Puerto Rico*, Alejandro O'Reilly notes that corn was bought and sold on the black market, mainly along the southern coast of the island. We know that when Ponce harbor was put in service as a port in 1813, the customs office there registered Puerto Rico's highest exports of corn.[5]

In the rich alluvial soil of the fields in the region around Ponce, corn grew quickly, easily yielding two crops a year. The land planted in corn increased rapidly from 1824 to 1864, from 340 to 769 *cuerdas*, for a total increase of 429 *cuerdas* (approximately 442 acres), with the fields producing some 1,900 *fanegas* per year. (1 *fanega* = 1.6 bushels in Spain, but was a measure of 500 ears of corn in Puerto Rico.)[6] In 1864, land planted in corn was exceeded only by land planted in sugarcane.

Similar growth had been experienced in the south-coast districts that lay to the west of Ponce: Peñuelas, Guayanilla, and Yauco. In the low-lying fields of Yauco, for example, there had been something of a boom in corn. Large landowners such as Pedro Antongiorgi, Francisco Mejía, Eugenio Rodriguez, Pastor Márquez, and the Olivieri brothers, among others, produced corn in great quantities.[7] The same happened in the district of Guayanilla, where land owned by the Rosaly and Ferrán trading company, Antonio Pascual, and Diego López produced corn in substantial amounts.

Corn at Buena Vista

From the beginning, Buena Vista grew a few acres of white and yellow corn.[8] The custom was to plant it in April and May, when the moon was waning, and during dry weather.

Above: Corn plant. (Singer, Holmyard, and Hall, eds., *A History of Technology*, vol. 3)

Right: Mill log, or account book, 1851. Note the names of the purchasing plantation or individual, the amount of cornmeal (*harina de maíz*, two left narrow columns in the center of the page), manioc meal (*mañoca*, next two columns), or straw (*paja*, right narrow column) purchased, and the price at far right. (BVA)

On April 20, 1856, Domingo Roche, one of the best overseers Buena Vista had ever had, described that season's plantings in the following way: ten *cuerdas* of old land planted in corn and bananas; twenty more *cuerdas* of old land in corn, sweet potatoes, and other crops; twenty of virgin land in corn, sweet potatoes, and plantains.[9] Two years later, a little more than forty-eight *cuerdas* of corn were planted.[10] But corn grew better on the flatlands along the coast than in the higher, wetter region around Buena Vista, so when the market for cornmeal expanded in Ponce, the administrators of Buena Vista decided to supplement their production of the crop by contracting to buy corn from other farms in Ponce and the surrounding cities and open land.[11] This practice was maintained for years, such that there were many providers of corn to Buena Vista, from several municipalities.

During the period from 1850 to 1876, the price of corn held at an average of 12 to 14 *reales* per hundredweight.[12] (A *real* was 12½ *centavos*.) Carlos Vives's will, notarized in 1872, estimates the store of corn in the warehouse at 13 *reales* per hundredweight.[13] In a single month, however, the price of corn from a single provider might vary from 1 to 2 *reales* per hundredweight.[14] The price Buena Vista would pay for shucked corn would depend on the quality, size of the ears (large or medium), time of harvest, condition (clean, dry, moist, weevily), time of year, and abundance or scarcity of corn on the market.[15] Bad corn yielded bitter cornmeal that was hard to grind, hard to sell, and apt to cause the administrators no end of headaches.[16]

In addition, if the corn was purchased outside the immediately surrounding area, in such distant places as the north-coast municipality of Isabela, a price much higher than the average might be paid, for the price would include off-loading of a shipment if it came by boat around the island and might also include cartage up to Buena Vista. For example, in April 1871, Carlos Vives made a deal with an Isabela grower named Domenech to buy 400 cwt. at a price of 15 *reales* per hundredweight; that price included delivery to Buena Vista.[17] The price would also be adjusted if the Vives family provided the sacks in which the ears of corn were shipped.[18]

Finally, unforeseen circumstances would also cause price variations. For example, when corn producers learned of the cholera epidemic that had struck the eastern part of the island in February 1856, they raised their prices, thinking they would make "brilliant profits."[19] On another occasion, in 1868, after several years of drought and then Hurricane San Narciso on October 29, 1867, followed by a series of terrible earthquakes that began on November 18 and went on for days, growers raised their prices to 20 *reales* per hundredweight.

To get the best prices, the administrators of Buena Vista would buy as early or as late as possible. Buying early might mean paying high prices, but buying too late might run the risk of buying old, even weevily corn, with the dreadful consequences that would have for the mills. What the management of Buena Vista had to attempt to do was buy corn and simultaneously sell the cornmeal that would be made from it; that was the secret to success.[20]

Lack of familiarity with the ups and downs of the market for the purchase of corn and the sale of the cornmeal brought misfortune and disgrace to administrators. This was the case with Joaquín Mayoral, who in early 1857 bought an unheard-of amount of corn, which he could not justify. To make matters worse, he paid an extremely high price for it, because he had received the mistaken report that there was a corn shortage in San Germán, Guayanilla, and Yauco.[21] Mayoral had to own up to his mistake, cancel his orders to several providers, and resign from Buena Vista and business in Ponce in general.

In contrast to the catastrophe in 1857 were the successful purchases of corn and sales of cornmeal in 1871. Early in that year, Antonio Navarro, administrator of Buena Vista, bought 2,541 cwt. of corn, which were sold before the year was out. He sold 2,318 of the 2,382 sacks of cornmeal that the mill produced.[22] In addition, as the money from the sale of cornmeal came in, the debt to the corn suppliers was paid off, with a net profit of 3,639 pesos.

Data available from the years 1850–71 show that purchases of corn increased at the time of the installation of the second corn mill (the turbine-driven mill) in March 1854 (see Table 3.3). Nevertheless, the average over each five-year period remained relatively constant during these years, al-

TABLE 3.1. Main Crops in Ponce, 1864

Crop	Cuerdas
Sugarcane	6,749
Corn	769
Coffee	500
Plantains	477
Rice	84
Tobacco	24

SOURCE: Agricultural Census, 1864, PMA.

TABLE 3.2. Corn Prices, Buena Vista, 1868

Amount of Corn Bought (cwt.)	Price	Total Amount (pesos)
1,281	15 reales (1.87 pesos)	2,401
1,145	18 reales (2.25)	2,576
728	16 reales (2.00)	1,456
685	20 reales (2.50)	1,712.5
215	14 reales (1.75)	374

SOURCE: Receipts, 1868, BVA.

TABLE 3.3. Corn Purchases per Five-Year Period, 1850–1869

Five-Year Period	Total Purchases (cwt.)	Average per Year (cwt.)
1850–54	16,580	3,316
1855–59	17,613	3,523
1860–64	16,039	3,208
1865–69	16,407	3,281

SOURCE: Account book, 1870, BVA.

though purchases decreased beginning in 1860 (and in spite of the fact that 1864 showed the highest purchases of the entire period) owing to the continued droughts of 1865–67, the impact of Hurricane San Narciso, and high imports of foreign cornmeal.[23] In 1871, purchases were down 740 cwt. from the previous five-year period (1865–69).

Day after day, oxcarts or mule trains toiled along the *camino real* between Ponce and Adjuntas with corn destined for Buena Vista. And even though the corn growers were in such far-off places as Isabela and transportation was slow and laborious, neither long distances nor deserted coastlines nor steep, arid terrain could slow the development of Buena Vista. Transportation to and from Buena Vista was, simply, one way or another, accomplished.

When the corn arrived at Buena Vista, the administrator or overseer, who would already be familiar with the quality of the product and its place of origin, would note on a slip of paper the name of the cart driver, the date, the amount of corn, and the selling price. To be sure of the correct weight of the sacks of corn, Buena Vista had three large scales.[24] If the load was accepted, the agreed-on price was almost always paid to the provider

on the spot, with the money sent back to him with the cart driver, but if for some reason the shipment did not satisfy the administrator, it would be returned. The costs of transportation would then be the responsibility of the provider or would be discounted from the amount owed him.[25]

Some providers reacted to this treatment by refusing to provide corn to Buena Vista. One such occasion was February 1873, when several providers from Guayanilla, chief among them Diego López, had a falling-out with Salvador Vives (the grandson) because Vives had complained that the corn had arrived in poor condition; the providers refused to assume the transportation costs for returning the shipment.[26] From that point on, there was always a certain amount of mistrust on the part of the López establishment with regard to transactions with Buena Vista, though they did continue to provide corn for Buena Vista's mills—with the proviso that they would collect the full amount due them for their shipments on the day of the shipments' arrival.[27]

Two-wheeled oxcart. The ox driver (*cuartero*) walked along in front of the oxen with his oxgoad or prod (*garrocha*). A wooden yoke (*yugo*) attached to the oxen's heads kept them together. A piece of canvas (*frontil*) protected the ox's forehead from being chafed raw by the rope (*coyunda*) that lashed the yoke to the ox's head (Rosa, *Lexicón histórico-documental de Puerto Rico*). (*Views of Puerto Rico*)

The Production of Cornmeal:
The Roasting Shed and the Mill

The process of grinding corn for cornmeal at Buena Vista began each day with an inspection of the mill. It was not to be started up, according to a list of instructions to the overseers, without first trimming its granite millstones, balancing them, adjusting them, and greasing the axles and the gudgeons that protruded from the center of the axles, because they were easily damaged. (Gudgeons are the rods, thinner than the axles though generally

Corn sheller. The machine could be turned by one or two persons or by another motive force when the gears were attached to a machine. It shelled fifty to sixty *fanegas* (2,500–3,000 ears) of corn per hour. (*Revista Agrícola Industrial* 1, no. 6 [December 1878])

made of iron, which bear the axles and on which the axles turn.) Everything had to be perfectly aligned and balanced.[28]

Let us look at how cornmeal was produced at Buena Vista. First, in the roasting shed the kernels of corn would be stripped off the ears by one of the several manual shelling machines. Shelling was exceptionally tedious work when done by hand using an unsharpened knife, as was done initially at Buena Vista, but after 1847 there was a shelling machine to do the work. After the corn was shelled, a worker would take it to the roasting room, where it would be heated; this process dried the corn, as it might be moist or have weevils.[29] This process occurred in a sort of tub set on top of a furnace; the corn would be stirred constantly so it would dry uniformly, with "no trace of black."[30] Because the corn could not be ground while it was still hot, grinding would be put off until the afternoon or evening.

From the roaster pan, the corn would be carried to the mill, which was located in another building, alongside the roasting shed. There, it would be dumped into a hopper, where it would fall through an opening into a slot that directed it between the millstones. Because the two interior surfaces of the millstones are not flat, when the upper stone turned (the lower stone was stationary), the corn would be pulverized.[31] Once ground, "with the greatest cleanliness possible," the cornmeal would be packed into 100-pound sacks or 196-pound barrels and then warehoused until dealers ordered it and picked it up.[32] In spite of these measures, if the corn was not ground soon enough, it got weevils; the cornmeal, too, might become infested.[33] Therefore, it had to be sold as soon as possible; if it were not, it would have to be sold at a lower price.

Once the two mills were in operation, and with plenty of corn and a good market, the production of cornmeal increased from 3,164 sacks in 1850 to 6,684 in 1855. This increase, however, was in part attributable to purchases of corn made during the cholera epidemic, so that Buena Vista would have a supply of corn in case things got worse and also because of the fear that imported cornmeal might transmit the dreaded disease.[34] When the cholera epidemic was past, production remained constant at something over three thousand sacks for the next few years, though there was little doubt that the market had begun to soften.

Cornmeal on the Ponce Market

Buena Vista cornmeal was an immediate success; its primary market was the sugar plantations in the region around Ponce. Cornmeal, inexpensive but rich in carbohydrates and protein,[35] was able to nourish human beings in the most extreme conditions and therefore became a staple food for slaves.[36] All the ingredients of corn are essential for good nutrition, and so long as there were slaves in Ponce, Buena Vista cornmeal would have a captive market. It was also the only bread ingredient for fieldworkers and hired laborers, whose diet consisted of four to five ounces of dried codfish, generally without oil, and eight ounces of cornmeal or, failing cornmeal, four plantains.[37] In his book *Las clases jornaleras* (The laboring classes), Salvador Brau made the following observations: "Sober more from necessity than from virtue, the campesinos satisfy their appetite with very little food. A piece of dried codfish, a bun or flat johnny-cake of boiled or roasted cornmeal, three or four hunks of boiled taro root, and a cup generally of coconut milk, or of coffee sweetened with honey, is the general daily nourishment of our starving poor."[38]

The white and yellow cornmeals of Buena Vista were known throughout the island for their quality. Within just eight years of the installation of the first mill to grind corn, Buena Vista's cornmeals won prizes at the second Public Exposition of Industry, Agriculture, and Fine Arts of the Island of Puerto Rico held in San Juan in June 1855. Carlos Vives received a gold medal for his "excellent" white and yellow cornmeals and for his manioc meal. The report on the exposition chronicled the award in the following way: "The jury unanimously agreed to bestow the gold medal on don Carlos Vives, resident of Ponce, who presented excellent samples of white and yellow corn meal and manioc meal, manufactured on his Hacienda Buena Vista." The report also called attention to the fact that the meals were produced by a turbine "which produces three barrels of 196 net pounds per

TABLE 3.5. Cornmeal Production at Buena Vista, 1850–1861

Year	Sacks of Cornmeal
1850	3,164
1851	2,407
1852	1,882
1853	3,405
1854	4,107
1855	6,684
1856	3,664
1857	3,316
1858	3,669
1859	3,209
1860	2,734
1861	2,708

SOURCE: Mill log, 1850–61, BVA.

Buena Vista cornmeal was awarded prizes at several expositions in Puerto Rico. In 1855 it won first prize, a gold medallion (17.95 grams, 31.2 mm × 39.2 mm (*above right*); in 1860, the silver (32.71 grams, 41.8 mm in diameter) (*above*); and in 1865, the gold once again (73.81 grams, 46.4 mm in diameter) (*facing page*). The coins now belong to the collection of José Luis Fernández Olalla, San Juan.

hour, and produced a total of some 1,500 barrels of corn meal." Regarding the sale of the product, the report notes that the price per barrel of cornmeal made from roasted kernels was five pesos, whereas meal from unroasted grains brought four and a half.[39]

Over time, the Buena Vista product was also awarded prizes at other agricultural fairs in Puerto Rico, such as those of 1860 and 1865. For the Paris Exposition of 1866, the Ponce city administration chose Buena Vista cornmeals to represent Puerto Rico.[40]

Local Competition

During the period from 1847 to 1873, the excellent quality of Buena Vista cornmeals made them reign supreme in Ponce. Although there were other mills producing cornmeal (such as those belonging to Ferrer and Gilbee, Juan Meylan, Francisco Manich, and Gerónimo Rabassa), they gave Buena Vista no real competition. In 1856, Buena Vista overseer Joaquín Mayoral summed up the competition in this way: The mill owned jointly by Ferrer and the English windmill engineer James Gilbee (founded during the 1850s on Hacienda Santa Rosa) had a huge waterwheel, and therefore showed great potential, but it did not function well because there was no way for the plantation to produce a good fall of water for powering the wheel. Another mill, leased by Juan Meylan from a Scotsman named Armstrong beginning in 1856, was about to start up production, but as a newcomer, Meylan presented no real competition to Buena Vista. Finally, the mill belonging to Gerónimo Rabassa produced too little cornmeal to have any impact on the market. Only the mill belonging to Manich, "the most im-

portant of the competitors," had substantial production, a good system of communication with plantation owners and the trading companies that sold the product, and a warehouse in the port of Ponce.[41] On March 28, 1856, Mayoral confessed to having been approached by Francisco Manich with a scheme to fix prices on cornmeal at eight pesos, so as to stop price erosion, avoid competing with each other, and mutually protect each other's interests.[42]

None of Buena Vista's competitors achieved the production level or quality that was consistently maintained at Buena Vista. In the long run, according to the Capital and Product Census for Ponce (1872–73), all the others disappeared, and the only cornmeal mill still in operation in 1873 was that belonging to the Vives family.[43]

Santander Flour and Foreign Competition

The other source of competition for Buena Vista cornmeal was wheat flour imported from Spain and the United States. Since the early nineteenth century, Spanish flour had monopolized the Caribbean markets of Cuba and Puerto Rico.[44] Flour from the Spanish province of Castile, exported by the merchants of the privileged port city of Santander (and known in Puerto Rico as "Santander flour"),[45] enjoyed extraordinary tax advantages, given that high tariffs were imposed on flour and cornmeal that came from countries other than Spain. The protectionist policy of the Spanish government was the result of a low yield of Castilian flour in comparison with the yield of other European countries,[46] and it also represented an attempt to keep U.S. flour and cornmeal out of Cuba, which was Spain's largest market.[47]

The purpose of the tariff reforms instituted by the Spanish government in 1835 and 1850, in fact, was precisely to further Castile's monopoly on flour exported through Santander to the Spanish Antilles.[48] In 1850, for example, the new tariffs on each barrel of Spanish flour were as follows: per barrel of domestic flour transported in a Spanish ship, a single duty of three pesos; on foreign flour transported in a Spanish ship, five; and on foreign flour transported in a foreign ship, seven.[49]

Still, at no time in the nineteenth century did the Santander merchants have enough flour to keep even their domestic and Caribbean markets supplied, much less take full advantage of the monopoly.[50] According to an 1809 report by Pedro Irizarri, civil mayor of San Juan, "There were times when a ration-card was needed for bread, and our poverty sometimes even reached the extreme of keeping back two barrels [of flour] in order to celebrate the holy mass in the Cathedral."[51]

In spite of the fact that by midcentury some 45 percent of all Spanish exports destined for Puerto Rico was flour, there were almost always shortages of flour on the island, and the lower classes were deprived of one of humankind's true staples—bread. In 1882, the Cuban-born Rafael María de Labra, a Liberal representative to the Spanish Cortes (Spain's legislative assembly) and severe critic of Santander's flour monopoly, observed that the annual consumption of bread in Puerto Rico was only fifty pounds per inhabitant, whereas in Spain the figure was at least four hundred pounds per person.[52]

From very early on in the nineteenth century, the shortages caused by this monopoly, and the consequent near famines, were denounced in no uncertain terms. But there was another problem, of local origin, that made supplying flour all the more difficult: local authorities fixed the price of the commodity and determined how it would be distributed, thereby creating artificial shortages in certain areas of the island.[53] This phenomenon, according to Governor Ramón de Castro himself (1795–1804), had in the past been "a source of scandal and a constant obstacle," and he promised that "during [his] administration it would never be said that there was any fraud or monopoly."[54] Years later, on July 15, 1809, when Ramón Power y Giralt was elected representative to the Spanish Cortes in Cádiz, he was instructed that one of his major responsibilities was to argue for free trade in flour.[55] On April 7, 1811, Power y Giralt stood before the Cortes to denounce the government's "crippling abuse" in taking upon itself the contracting and purchase of this article. In addition, he pointed out that this privilege had acted as a kind of bonus over and above the salary of the Spanish governors of Puerto Rico, for while the authorities reported that they paid eighteen pesos per barrel of flour, they secretly held the price at fifteen and pocketed the difference.[56]

During the first half of the nineteenth century, and in spite of the accomplishments of representative Power y Giralt (in 1811 the Cortes granted flour for public consumption absolute free trade), shortages of flour continued, and several governors were forced to undertake measures to alleviate the problem of supplying flour and cornmeal to the island.[57] Stormy conditions in 1817 led Brigadier Meléndez to order that flour for his troops be bought with Treasury funds; fourteen years later, on March 30, 1831, a shortage of Spanish flour led Governor Miguel de la Torre to temporarily suspend enforcement of the royal edict of November 7, 1830, and to authorize the importation of foreign flour and cornmeal; and in 1848, Governor Juan Prim, apparently moved by protests resulting from a lack of flour in San Juan, proposed a plan to establish a flour and cornmeal warehouse in the city, under the sponsorship of the City Council, that would be large enough to provide bread to the population for a period of four months.[58]

But none of these projects came close to solving the problem of flour shortages on the island, because Santander's monopoly, as we have seen, was favored by protectionist legislation, and so this situation continued unchanged throughout most of the nineteenth century. Thus it was that local Puerto Rican cornmeal, such as that produced cheaply and in abundance at Buena Vista, came to supplement the short Spanish supply of flour.

As early as 1832, George Flinter, traveling on the island, had noted that the price of foreign cornmeal was double that of cornmeal manufactured on the island. After observing that there were only two mills on the north coast of the island, he asked why there were not more.[59] Even at midcentury (1855), when Buena Vista began to expand its production, a hundredweight of foreign cornmeal was priced at 12.50 pesos (not including freight charges), while a ninety-six-pound sack of Buena Vista cornmeal was selling at between 2.40 and 2.75 pesos.[60]

In 1848, conditions for the Ponce cornmeal market improved when in order to underwrite the cost of the night watchmen in the city—men who carried a lance and a lantern and walked through the city singing out the hour and weather throughout the night—the Ayuntamiento imposed an additional tariff on each barrel of Spanish or imported flour entering through the port of Ponce.[61]

The Spanish flour monopoly was at last broken, if only temporarily, in 1868, when after years of drought, the terrible ravages caused by Hurricane San Narciso (October 29), and the earthquakes that followed (beginning November 18), there was such a drastic shortage of foodstuffs that Governor José María Marchesi was forced to commission a board composed of the island's most important merchants and landowners to look into the disastrous situation in an attempt to find a solution. Elías Iriarte, vice-chairman of the board, proposed that meat, salt meat, dried codfish, rice, and cornmeal be totally exempted from tariffs.[62] (It was cornmeal, in Iriarte's view, that sustained slaves and workingmen.) Governor Marchesi approved some of these measures, but it was not until the decree of January 5,

1868, issued by the newly arrived governor, Julián Juan Pavía, that imports of foodstuffs and consumer articles, including both Spanish and foreign (that is, U.S.) flour,[63] were declared to be tariff-free for one year.[64]

Governor Pavía's intention was to make flour and cornmeal cheap enough that the food shortage would be alleviated. But the Spanish importers and merchants of San Juan and Ponce were the ones who actually benefited from the measure, because even while no longer paying import duties, they kept the prices on their goods at the same level as before. Protests soon ensued, of course, and the months that followed this scandal (and others) saw the outbreak of a revolution aimed at the independence of the island. This rebellion took place in the municipality of Lares, in the mountains of the *cordillera central*, on September 23, 1868.[65]

A year after the failed uprising, Governor Pavía's order remained in effect. In Ponce, the Board of Agriculture, Industry, and Trade argued that the order be left in place indefinitely, not simply because it assured that there would be bread on workingmen's tables but also because in return for free trade on U.S. flour and cornmeal, the United States allowed island sugar an entrée into the U.S. market. The board saw the situation in this way: "Much greater sales will result from the discount offered by the government of that nation to our products in compensation for that discount which their own products receive in our ports."[66] The victory of the island sugar producers meant the beginning of the end, however, for the island's cornmeal manufacturers.

Sales: "Our Mill Sells Everything It Turns Out"[67]

Just as Buena Vista had when selling its plantains and other agricultural products, it carted its cornmeal in sacks or barrels to market in Ponce or to the sugarcane plantations in the region, though in some cases customers on the coastal plantations would pick up their orders at the mill itself. A great number of carts and wagons were needed for transporting the cornmeal, since the mill supplied more than fifty sugarcane plantations in Ponce (see Table 3.6), including the largest agro-industrial complexes in the area (those with more than one hundred slaves), but also the medium-sized (with forty to eighty slaves) and smaller plantations (twenty to forty slaves). The cornmeal would be bought by plantation owners, foreign, local, and Spanish merchants, and some functionaries of the Spanish government in Ponce. On a smaller scale the product was also shipped to warehouses belonging to the Aranzamendi trading house in San Juan and on a commission basis to other parts of the island. The bill would be settled up later. Cornmeal was supplied to all interested customers, but when there was a shortage, only orders from the largest and oldest clients would be filled.[68]

During the first twelve years of production at Buena Vista, the price of cornmeal ranged from four and one-half to eight pesos per 196-pound barrel, but as one might imagine, the price rose and fell on the basis of a number of factors: first, the abundance or shortage of the product on the local market; second, the freshness of the cornmeal (old meal was sold as "seconds" and more cheaply); third, any previous agreement on price; and fourth, the abundance of corn on the market. In the summer months, when the corn was harvested, it would be sold at a lower price than during the first months of the year when it was less readily available. Finally, the price of cornmeal depended on the competition, which according to overseer Mayoral was minimal: "Some people have complained of the price, but I ignore the complaints, because we have no competition and there are plenty of buyers."[69]

Let us look at the way two of Buena Vista's best customers, Ramón Tarrats and Juan Serrallés, went about making their purchases: Tarrats, a Catalonian, was the owner of a general store, La Puerta del Sol, that sold foodstuffs and hardware items on the town square in Ponce; he also owned Haciendas Feliz and Pastillo, both in the lowlands of Barrio Magüeyes, quite near Buena Vista. Employees of Tarrats's plantations would come to Buena Vista to pick up sacks and barrels of cornmeal and other foodstuffs they needed to feed the slaves and, from the 1850s on, the hired workers.[70] The Vives family sold to Tarrats on credit and, unlike the sugar factors and merchants of the town, expected to be paid in money, not sugar. The fact was, however, that Tarrats took his own sweet time paying what he owed Carlos Vives, so long that according to Don Carlos's last will and testament (1862), on September 29, 1861, the Tarrats estate owed him 2,580.11 pesos for merchandise sold by Vives to Tarrats over the course of several years.[71]

Another regular purchaser of Buena Vista cornmeal was Serrallés, the island's largest taxpayer and owner of the prosperous Hacienda Mercedita in Barrio Sabanetas in Ponce.[72] For example, from July 1874 to January 1875, Serrallés purchased fifty-three sacks of cornmeal at an average of three pesos per sack.[73] Unlike Tarrats, Serrallés paid his accounts promptly, and in June 1875 he owed Buena Vista only twenty-eight pesos.

Profits from the Buena Vista Mills, 1850–1870

The captive market for cornmeal in the sugar plantations of the south coast of Puerto Rico in the region in and around Ponce, combined with skillful and careful management, an abundance of cheap corn, and efficient mills, produced plentiful profits for Buena Vista. Within a year of the installation of the second mill (1855–56), when the cholera epidemic struck the island and purchases of local cornmeal rose in response to fears that imported

TABLE 3.6. Buyers of Buena Vista Cornmeal, 1854

Name	Hogsheads	Barrels	Sacks	Straw (barrels)
Agostini			2	
Alomar			49	
Arze			20	1
Aranzamendi		2		
Ahren			22	
Capril		4	294	
Cabrera			430	1
Dubocq		12	30	
Collazo	2	9	102	
Castaing			4	
Ferrer		16		
V. Font	5	6	40	
Fernández			69	
Fontainet			32	
Capó			26	
Davidson			96	20
Echeverne	1	19	26	
Hatch			8	26
Labarte		1	22	
Lacot		53	94	
Manfredi			91	
Mundet			20	
Newman		1	59	
Labau			59	
Oppenheimer			396	
Piris		4	90	
Quesada			42	
Pratt		4	12	
Plaja		8	28	
Salich			30	
Salomón		4	152	
Tarrats			77	1
Toro		8	27	

cornmeals might be infected, Buena Vista registered the highest profits in its history. The price per barrel of cornmeal rose to nine pesos, and profits totaled 10,740 pesos.[74] But once the emergency passed, growth tapered off and profits fell two-thirds: during the following nine years (1858–67), the mills brought in an average annual income of 3,742 pesos. In addition, the continued droughts of 1865 to 1867, combined with the impact of Hurricane San Narciso (October 29, 1867) radically reduced the corn crops and

TABLE 3.6 (continued)

Name	Hogsheads	Barrels	Sacks	Straw (barrels)
Moulin	1		12	
D. Torres	2	24		
Tricoche			4	
Villaronga			32	
Luchetti			16	
Quemado	3		142	
Esperanza		2	208	2
Sánchez		18	222	
Corona			16	
Dede		10	50	
Bayau		4	104	
G. Lucas	2	32	6	
Vestia			2	
Herrera			2	
Ortiz			4	
Efectivo	1		8	
Serrano			23	
Diana			48	
Vidal			2	
Molina			13	
León				2
Romero			4	
Victoria			2	
Barros			4	1
Mr. Vernus				1
Renta			4	
Ursulita			18	
Sabater C.			18	
Total	17	241	3,413	55

SOURCE: Mill log, 1854, BVA.
Note: A sack weighs 100 lbs.; a barrel weighs 196 lbs.

TABLE 3.7. Income from Mill, 1850–1870

Year	Income (pesos)
1850	3,464
1851	2,734
1852	2,441
1853	4,574
1854	5,500
1855	10,740
1856	3,100
1857	Not available
1858	4,858
1859	3,700
1860	3,417
1861	2,800
1862	2,905
1863	3,354
1864	5,542
1865	4,871
1866	3,700
1867	2,273
1868	1,788
1869	1,921
1870	3,639
Total	77,321

SOURCE: Simmonds & Co., Account book, 1850–70, BVA.

therefore the production of cornmeal (see Table 3.7 for a breakdown of the yearly profits). But once the crisis caused by the long drought had passed, production and sale of cornmeal began to rise once more, and although profits never equaled those of the previous decade, by 1870 they were once again considerable. During that year, Buena Vista invested 4,217 pesos in the purchase of corn, spent 800 pesos on operation of the mills, and had a gross income of 8,656 pesos, for a net income of 3,639 pesos.[75]

Extreme southern end of the Plaza las Delicias in Ponce. To the right is the city hall, inaugurated in 1843. To the rear, on the corner, with white awnings, is the Puerta del Sol, an import house owned by Tarrats y Revertier, with products brought to Puerto Rico from Spain, France, Germany, England, and the United States. (Olivares, *Our Islands and Their People*)

Profits on the sale of cornmeal for the twenty years of the mills' operation at Buena Vista totaled 77,321 pesos, enough so that at the time he made out his will (before the notary Francisco Parra),[76] Carlos Vives could declare, "I owe no one a cent," while he himself was owed 7,025 pesos in IOUs, promissory notes, and the like, and 9,063.26 pesos in accounts receivable from a large number of plantation owners in the municipality of Ponce.[77] In addition, Buena Vista was free of mortgage encumbrance, unlike the vast majority of the plantations in Ponce and across the island.[78]

During the same period (1850–70), the Vives family earned 48,569 pesos on fruits and other produce (pineapples, bananas, plantains, cacao, sweet potatoes, mangoes, avocados, and oranges), and from 1863 on it added to its holdings with the construction of six rental houses in Ponce.[79] Last, when in 1859 Carlos Vives sold forty-seven of his fifty-seven slaves for 36,000 pesos (766 pesos per slave, or 95 pesos more per slave than their market price), he realized his highest profit of all (see Chapter 4).[80]

In January 1869, the banking house of Murrieta and Company, whose

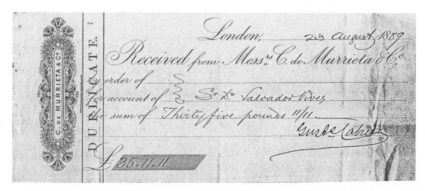

Top: Dividend checks such as these were received by the Vives family from the investment house of Murrieta and Co., London. (BVA)

Bottom: Envelope from Palmieri to Salvador Vives. Correspondence from Palmieri in Paris often brought news of profits on the sale of coffee in Europe or of Palmieri's investments on Vives's behalf with Murrieta and Co. (BVA)

clientele included members of the Spanish aristocracy and several American firms and which had good connections in the London market, advised Carlos Vives that the best way of investing his profits was in the consolidated funds of the English government,[81] whose bonds paid dividends at 3 percent per annum. Vives took his advice and invested 5,400 pounds sterling (31,320 silver pesos) in bonds issued by the English government for the English Orient Railway Line and the Entre Ríos Railway Line in Argentina.[82] For the next ten and seven years, respectively, dividends were collected by Murrieta on these investments and deposited in Carlos Vives's and his estate's bank accounts in Europe.[83]

Upon the death of Carlos Vives in 1872, his heirs (his wife Guillerma Navarro and his sons Salvador, Guillermo, and Carlos) instructed Murrieta and Company to remit two thousand pounds sterling to the firm of Palmieri and Company in Paris to be invested in consolidated funds of the French government at 5 percent interest. This capital, added to other capital that Carlos Vives had invested with Palmieri, allowed Salvador, Guil-

Map of the Entre Ríos Railway Line, Argentina, sent to Vives by Murrieta and Co. (1901) as a result of Vives's investment in the line. (BVA)

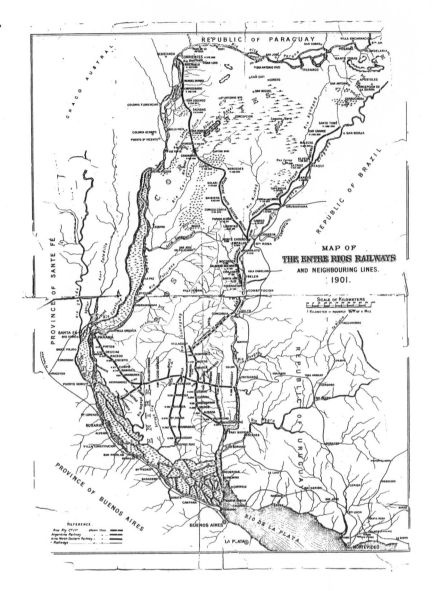

lermo, and Carlos to double their investment. By 1884, they had nineteen thousand francs invested with this house.[84] Over the years, Palmieri issued letters of exchange that paid for a wide range of things, from shells for Salvador's hunting rifles to medical school in Paris, Barcelona, and later Madrid for his younger brothers.[85] In fact, when Guillermo and Carlos arrived in Europe in 1877 to begin their medical studies, they went first to number 10, rue Cité Trévise to sign the agreements with Palmieri and Company that would provide them with their monthly allowance of seven hundred francs.[86]

CHAPTER FOUR

Buena Vista

A Village of Slaves, 1833–1873

ike many emigrants from Venezuela and the European colonies of the Caribbean, when Salvador de Vives disembarked in Ponce in 1821 with his Venezuelan-born wife, Isabel Díaz, and their son, Carlos, he was accompanied by two slaves.[1] They became part of the growing labor force of slaves that belonged to the Vives family from 1821 to 1873.[2] Indeed, from the founding of Hacienda Buena Vista in 1833, Salvador de Vives ensured the prosperity and growth of his estate by means of a predominantly slave labor force.

During the time of greatest success both of the cornmeal mill and the cultivation of fruits and vegetables for sale (1858), there were fifty-seven slaves at Hacienda Buena Vista. This is a considerable number in comparison not just with the other farms of the island but even with the large sugar plantations of Ponce and the rest of Puerto Rico. From one point of view, Buena Vista was a cornmeal manufacturing operation within a village of slaves. The history of slavery at Buena Vista is a paradox, because its slaves worked to feed other slaves in Ponce: "slaves feeding slaves."

From 1833 to 1864, Salvador de Vives and his son, Carlos, purchased thirty-two female and twenty-eight male slaves at an average price of 292 pesos per female and 270 pesos per male. It is worth noting that the price of slaves, both male and female, rose considerably after the cholera epidemic in 1856.[3]

The immense majority of the slaves bought were young farmworkers, though there were also purchases of skilled slaves, such as the forty-year-old creole Juana,[4] "intelligent in her work of cooking and ironing," who cost 300 pesos,[5] or the thirty-one-year-old creole José, who besides being a fieldworker also had skills in the sawmill and cost 375 pesos.[6]

Slavery at Hacienda Buena Vista was not simply a source of cheap, captive labor but also an investment in fixed capital.[7] Though Vives family members were not in any formal way slave traders, they did buy many more slaves than they needed and did sell the unneeded ones for high profits. The presence of slaves on Buena Vista was vital not only for the functioning of the farm but also for its profits; this state of affairs encouraged the buying and selling of slaves.

Don Salvador de Vives himself, in an official letter from the mayor's office (during his third term as mayor) to Governor Rafael de Arístegui on February 15, 1845, recommended the purchase of female slaves and also that the number of males be proportional to the number of females. He recommended in addition that the males and females be allowed to marry; permitting them to do so, he said, "would bring custom under law and achieve greater healthfulness among the slaves." And of course it would also insure the "desired increase in population."[8] The purchase of female slaves would

Registries of slaves owned by Salvador de Vives and Carlos Vives. (BVA)

be more than justified, therefore, because "strong arms were needed on all the plantations" of the island. In addition, the price of slaves was rising every day, so that for many, this sort of investment was not feasible.

The desirability of maintaining a proportion between the sexes for the purpose of procreation had been pointed out by George Flinter in 1832 when he said that "the planters of Puerto Rico having at the commencement only very small capitals, purchased for utility, and not for speculation, an equal number of male and female slaves, among whom marriages have been carefully promoted by the Spanish laws."[9] It is true that during this period the number of male slaves was not very much greater than that of females; in 1830, of a total of 34,374 slaves, 17,688 were male and 16,686 were female.

At Hacienda Buena Vista, Salvador de Vives's recommendations as to marriage between slaves were not followed, though many of the female slaves among his holdings did contribute to the "desired population increase." For example, the female creole slave Margarita, a fieldworker, gave birth to four children in the slave barracks of the farm: Rosalía, Francisco, Francisca, and Antonia.[10] In this way, the number of slaves increased and the children of the Buena Vista female slaves replaced those of African origin (the so-called *bozales*) and the earlier generation of Puerto Rican slaves, who were the oldest of the company. In 1867 there were only four of those *bozales* that had been bought as children and brought to the hacienda by Salvador de Vives: Felipe, the estate messenger, thirty-nine years old; Antonio, thirty-six; Pedro, thirty-one; and Rosa, forty (see Table 4.2). The rest of Buena Vista's slaves had been born on the grounds.

A Slave's Work at Buena Vista

A slave's day at Buena Vista began with a bell rung six times at daybreak. (Rung once, it called the owner; twice, the overseer; three times, the foreman; four times, the male slaves; five times, the females; and six times, everyone.) Because virtually all the adult slaves of both sexes were field-workers, they would pick up their hoes, picks, shovels, and the long, thin machetes known as *espadines* and head off to the field they were going to work that day.[11] There, they would clear land, cut down trees, weed fields, plant, or pick fruit, especially the plantains that, as we have noted, constituted Buena Vista's main agricultural crop until well into the second half of the nineteenth century.[12] So the slaves would have no excuse to leave the fields, they carried the water they would drink during the day; lunch would be taken to them by one of the female slaves.

Another, though smaller, group would work on jobs connected with the machinery and the canals. They would scour the countryside, gathering fallen palm fronds to be burned in the furnace of the corn roaster (and also to be sold), clean out the canals so the water could flow freely, and wash burlap and sew it into sacks for the cornmeal.[13]

Other slaves watched over the livestock in the pastureland, being sure no animals wandered off and giving them water twice a day, or they would yoke oxen to carts when goods needed to be transported. At night they would put the mules and horses that wandered around freely during the day in a corral.[14]

The slaves also worked diligently on constructing the farm's buildings. When the residences and cornmeal millhouse were built in 1845, it was slaves who split and trimmed the hundreds of shingles for their roofs: on December 16, 1845, six slaves split 700 shingles and trimmed or planed 450.[15] This carpentry work, plus the masonry that was also done by the slaves, explains why Buena Vista had a larger complement of slaves than virtually any other farm or sugar plantation in and around Ponce, in spite of its being "just a farm."

Other slaves, known as the "domestics," carried Buena Vista's cornmeal and other farm products to the marketplace in Ponce and to the surround-

Stamp of the slave registry. (BVA)

TABLE 4.1. Number of Slaves at Buena Vista, 1846–1872

Year	Number of Slaves
1846	50
1852	52
1858	57
1860	11
1862	18
1869	25
1872	21

SOURCE: Slave records, BVA.

Page from Census of Slaves at Buena Vista. (BVA)

TABLE 4.2. List of Slaves at Buena Vista, 1858

Name	Color	Age	Status	Origin	Job	Provenance
MALES						
Alejo	Mulatto	33	Single	P.R.	Lab.	Inherited from father
Rafael	Black	44	Single	Africa	Lab.	Inherited
Mariano	Black	30	Single	Africa	Lab.	Inherited
Hipólito	Black	30	Single	Africa	Lab.	Inherited
Agustín	Black	29	Single	Africa	Lab.	Inherited
Felipe	Black	25	Single	Africa	Lab.	Inherited
Martín	Black	22	Single	Africa	Lab.	Inherited
Pedro	Black	22	Single	Africa	Lab.	Inherited
Marcos	Black	23	Single	Africa	Lab.	Inherited
Antonio	Black	23	Single	Africa	Lab.	Inherited
Luis	Black	23	Single	Africa	Lab.	Inherited
Juan	Black	21	Single	Africa	Lab.	Inherited
Vicente	Black	25	Single	Africa	Lab.	Inherited
Reynaldo	Black	33	Single	Curaçao	Lab.	Inherited
José	Black	20	Single	P.R.	Lab.	Inherited
José	Black	32	Single	P.R.	Lab.	Inherited
Julio	Black	21	Single	P.R.	Dom.	Inherited
Simeón	Black	21	Single	P.R.	Lab.	Inherited
Narciso	Black	13	Single	P.R.	Lab.	Inherited
Ignacio	Black	13	Single	P.R.	Lab.	Inherited
Sirilo	Black	13	Single	B.V.	Lab.	Inherited
Domingo	Black	13	Single	P.R.	Dom.	Born at B.V.
Simón	Black	15	Single	B.V.	Lab.	Born at B.V.
Capnacio	Black	12	Single	B.V.		Born at B.V.
Florencio	Black	12	Single	B.V.		Born at B.V.
Eusebio	Black	12	Single	B.V.		Born at B.V.
Reymundo	Black	6	Single	B.V.		Born at B.V.
Tibursio	Black	3	Single	B.V.		Born at B.V.
Feliciano	Black	3	Single	B.V.		Born at B.V.
Bonifacio	Black	3	Single	B.V.		Born at B.V.
Donato	Black	2	Single	B.V.		Born at B.V.
Victorio	Black	3 mos.	Single	B.V.		Born at B.V.

ing plantations. The cart drivers and mule-train drivers carried a slip of paper on which the overseer authorized them to leave the estate, because they were forbidden to do so without that authorization.[16] From 1861 to 1871, Felipe, an African slave who had lived at Buena Vista for more than thirty-one years, was regularly sent with sacks of cornmeal to the sugarcane plantations on the coast,[17] while another slave, a fifteen-year-old creole, though sometimes reportedly a bit distracted by the *bombas* (songs and

TABLE 4.2 *(continued)*

Name	Color	Age	Status	Origin	Job	Provenance
FEMALES						
Celestina	Black	20	Single	P.R.	Lab.	Bought 1871
Abelina	Black	19	Single	P.R.	Lab.	Bought 1853
Merced	Black	39	Single	Africa	Lab.	Inherited from father
Rosa	Black	25	Single	Africa	Lab.	Inherited
Francisca	Black	25	Single	Africa	Lab.	Inherited
Catalina	Black	32	Single	Africa	Lab.	Inherited
Gregoria	Black	32	Single	Africa	Lab.	Inherited
Marcelina	Black	33	Single	Africa	Lab.	Inherited
Dionisia	Black	14	Single	P.R.	Lab.	Inherited
María	Black	17	Single	P.R.	Lab.	Inherited
Isidra	Black	17	Single	P.R.	Lab.	Inherited
Clotilde	Mulatto	49	Single	P.R.	Kitchen	Inherited
Sebastiana	Black	17	Single	P.R.	Lab.	Inherited
Sara	Black	17	Single	P.R.	Lab.	Inherited
Rosario	Black	31	Single	P.R.	Lab.	Inherited
Margarita	Black	19	Single	P.R.	Lab.	Inherited
Epifania	Black	13	Single	P.R.	Lab.	Inherited
Lorenza	Black	13	Single	P.R.	Lab.	Inherited
Paula	Black	10	Single	B.V.	Lab.	Born at B.V.
Gervasia	Black	9		B.V.	Lab.	Born at B.V.
Dolores	Black	9		B.V.	Lab.	Born at B.V.
Rita	Black	10		B.V.	Lab.	Born at B.V.
Victoriana	Black	9		B.V.		Born at B.V.
Matilda	Black	5		B.V.		Born at B.V.
Rosenda	Black	5		B.V.		Born at B.V.

SOURCE: Slave records, BVA.
Note: In 1858, Carlos Vives had a total of 32 male slaves. Of these, 12 had been born in Africa, 19 in Puerto Rico (P.R.) (10 on Buena Vista [B.V.]), and 1 in Curaçao. In 1858, Vives had a total of 25 female slaves. Of these, 6 had been born in Africa, 12 in Puerto Rico, and 7 on Buena Vista. "Lab." indicates a fieldworker, and "dom.," a domestic worker.

TABLE 4.3 Place of Birth of Buena Vista Slaves

Place of Birth	1858	1869
Africa	18	4
Puerto Rico	21	0
Buena Vista	17	21
Other	1	0
Total	57	25

SOURCE: Slave Census of Buena Vista for 1858–1869, BVA.

dances of African origin), would be sent out to deliver bananas, plantains, avocados, pineapples, and breadfruit.[18] Other slaves would occasionally be called on to go to the stores and factories on the coast or in town to pick up foodstuffs or construction materials for the farm.

Buena Vista also had slaves that performed very specialized work. One such was Margarita, a creole who was the farm's washerwoman. Another was Rosa, an African slave who had lived at Buena Vista since 1837, when

Francisco Oller, *La lavandera* (the washerwoman), ca. 1887–88. (Ponce Museum of Art)

she was nine, and who was the mother of Rodolfo, Dionisia, Ignacio, and Junco; Rosa cooked and picked coffee but also cultivated bananas on a little plot behind the house's kitchen garden. In time, this plot of land itself became known as "Rosa."[19]

Perhaps the most privileged slave had been Isidora, who was not only freed in consideration of her good service but also appeared in Salvador de Vives's will as the recipient of one-third of Don Salvador's worldly goods. This amounted to some three thousand pesos, and the will specified that Isidora was to receive that amount in payments of fifteen pesos weekly until her death.[20] Isidora herself, however, could not bequeath this inheritance, as upon her death the will instructed that it would revert to the estate's sole heir, Carlos María Vives. Even so, Isidora never received her inheritance,

The freed slavewoman Ma Leoncia in front of the roasting shed and mill. (1904, Grace Hartzell Collection, GAPR)

because when Don Salvador died, his widow, taking advantage of the powers given her within the will itself, did not ratify that clause. Out of Carlos Vives's compassion, however, Isidora did receive some sums of money.[21]

There were also slaves owned by other haciendas who were hired by Buena Vista to be "day laborers," or slaves owned by Buena Vista sent out to do work outside the estate. One such Buena Vista slave lived in the Vives house at the corner of Atocha and Vives Streets in Ponce. Slaves hired from other haciendas lived in the slave barracks on the estate, where they worked as day laborers but received the same treatment as the other slaves. Those were the conditions of contract, for instance, between Carlos Vives and the plantation owner José Alomar for the "rental" of the creole slave Julio.[22] His salary was to be seventeen pesos per month, to be paid the slave's owner.[23]

Finally, some slaves were used occasionally to defend the Vives interests. In March 1843, the Ayuntamiento of Ponce was planning to construct a new

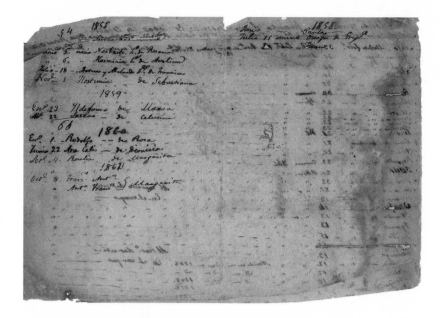

Left: slaves born on Buena Vista from 1858 to 1861; *right*: deaths. (BVA)

road from Buena Vista to the municipality of Adjuntas. Salvador de Vives did not look kindly on this project and so ordered his slaves to block the road to keep people from crossing his property.[24] Five years later, however, Carlos put several slaves to work building a highway and repairing more than thirty *cuerdas* of the *camino real* that passed through the hacienda and went on to Adjuntas.[25]

At sundown all the slaves would return to the hacienda's main plaza to turn in their planting sticks and other tools, be counted, and eat their evening meal.

The slaves' diet at Buena Vista must have been among the best in the Ponce region. It was made up of dried codfish (the most important source of protein), rice, cornmeal, and the great variety of produce that was grown on the farm, especially taro, sweet potatoes, and plantains. Unlike the cane-cutter surrounded by miles of sugarcane, the Buena Vista slave worked among acres of bananas, oranges, pineapples, mangoes, apples, avocados, acerolas, guavas, rose apples, soursops, and root vegetables of all kinds—any of which he or she might pick and eat at any time. In addition, the largest budget item in the maintenance of the slaves at Buena Vista was always "food." For example, in 1870 the estate spent 129 pesos on codfish, 72 pesos on forty-eight changes of clothing (two for each slave), 40 pesos on a doctor and medicines, and 12 pesos on blankets.[26] An uncommon expenditure was bread, as illustrated by the fact that from December 4 to December 17, 1871, the estate bought 161 loaves of bread (from one-half to one *real* per loaf) for its twenty slaves, though bread shows up at no other time in the estate's record books.[27]

After their dinner, some of the slaves might chew a wad of tobacco that the overseer gave them.[28] Finally, they would say their prayers before going into the barracks, a wooden building just sixty-two feet from the family's residence.

The Vives family was careful to follow the rules and regulations established in the Puerto Rico Slave Regulations issued by Governor Miguel de la Torre, who ordered that the sexes be separate within the barracks.[29] A guard would watch over the barracks during the night.[30] In spite of the fact that Buena Vista was virtually a village of slaves, its barracks, housing fifty-seven slaves, was quite small, especially in comparison with the owner's house. The slave barracks was only one-third the size of the "big house," which was occupied only by the master or perhaps in addition by one or another family member on rare occasions.[31]

In 1870 the Vives house was valued at 4,600 pesos, while the slave quarters were valued at only 480. Nevertheless, this wooden building with its galvanized-iron roof was better than the typical *bohíos*, or huts made of palm branches with thatched roofs, that existed on some of the haciendas along the south coast. There can be no doubt that the slave quarters at Buena Vista were a far cry from those described by the Irish military man Flinter, who had reported that the island's huts were built on tall stilts, had wooden floors, and were roofed with tightly woven palm fronds or "a strong dry grass resembling hay."[32]

The Cholera Epidemic at Buena Vista, 1855–1856

In his report on "The State of Slavery in Ponce" (1845), Salvador de Vives had observed that the sugarcane plantations of the municipality had infirmaries or "hospital rooms" and that a doctor visited frequently—daily, in fact, if necessary. In addition, the plantations were "visited by the authorities any time the authorities were called upon, being subject to the rules and regulations that governed them."[33]

At Buena Vista, when a slave fell sick, measures were immediately taken to ensure that he or she was quickly restored to health. During Carlos Vives's administration of the estate (1845–72), the sick man or woman would be quarantined, to avoid "any sort of disorder."[34] Three or four times a day the patient would be visited to find out how he or she was doing and to administer whatever home remedy or food might be thought needed. When the illness was a serious one, the slave would be sent at once by mule, cart, or stretcher to the doctor in town.[35] If the weather was bad and the overseer feared putting the slave on the road, a doctor would be asked to come to the estate.[36]

Between 1855 and 1869, a physician named Moringlane visited the estate

on many occasions to treat sick slaves, bandage them, and operate on them.[37] Dr. Moringlane was also the Vives family doctor. In one year, 1859–60, he attended the slaves at Buena Vista twenty-two times and billed the family for forty-four pesos.[38] Another doctor that often visited the estate was Dr. Ignacio Cornet, who operated on and treated the slaves during this same period.[39] In September 1862, he operated on a slave child (what the record lists as a *mulecón*, or "pickaninny") to set two fractures and treated him afterward, charging thirty-four pesos, which he later reduced to seventeen.

In addition to these measures for keeping the slaves healthy, there were times that called for extraordinary measures, such as when the slaves at Buena Vista were quarantined to save them from the terrible cholera epidemic that took the life of more than 26,820 persons in Puerto Rico in 1856. Of these victims, 5,469 were slaves.[40]

In late 1855, Joaquín Mayoral, Buena Vista's highly competent administrator, learned that the cholera epidemic that had struck other areas of the Caribbean some twenty years previously had now entered the offshore island of Vieques, devastating its population.[41] In spite of the many measures taken by the government to keep the dread disease out of Puerto Rico—measures ranging from the most elementary rules of public and private hygiene to a special watch over all foodstuffs (particularly foreign), such as flour—within days the disease appeared on the island, first making itself known in the municipality of Naguabo.[42]

During the next several months, cholera spread in all directions across the island, first toward the northwest and then in the summer of 1856 toward the southwest, through Yabucoa, affecting mainly the slaves and free blacks on the coastal plantations.[43] It was their inadequate nutrition and the terrible sanitary conditions in which they lived that caused the slaves to be the most terribly affected, and in spite of all the special precautions that Governor Juan Lemery decreed be taken on the plantations.[44] The slaves' good luck of 1833 had abandoned them.[45] In July it was learned that the epidemic had reached Arroyo, Guayama, and Coamo and was headed for Santa Isabel, the municipality bordering Ponce.

Mayoral wrote, "We are filled with fear, and more scared than ever."[46] And with good reason: within days the news came that cholera had struck the slaves on Hacienda de Capó.[47] At that, Mayoral, who complained of being "as though on the moon" for lack of news, ordered his overseer, Domingo Roche, the moment there was word of a single case in Ponce, to cordon off Buena Vista to the north, bordering Barrio Guaraguao, and to let no one pass.[48] The slaves were his first concern, he said; he feared it would not be possible to escape the disease, especially with the rainy season upon them. Nevertheless, with the increasing demand for cornmeal and fresh fruit being made on Buena Vista, the hours of work were doubled on the estate.[49]

In spite of the fact that the municipality had been cordoned off, by September 1856 cholera was widespread in Ponce, attacking slaves and free residents alike.[50] The sugar-growing barrios of Quemado, Capitanejo, Canas, and Bucaná, where there were a great number of slaves, were worst hit. From September 9 to September 30, 589 people had contracted cholera, 222 of them, including 132 slaves, eventually dying. By November 1, 476 slaves had died.[51]

Eduardo Neumann Gandía tells us in his *Verdadera y auténtica historia de la ciudad de Ponce* (True and authentic history of the city of Ponce) that to contain the epidemic two emergency hospitals were set up in Ponce, one in the port area, in the warehouse belonging to the Catalonian merchant Juan Lacot, and the other in La Perla Theater in town.[52] By the last quarter of the year, several cemeteries, both in town and in the countryside, had been opened especially for cholera victims. Dr. José Gassol, one of the bravest doctors in the municipality, died combating the epidemic.[53] Some wealthy whites, who had so far been spared by the disease, died during this time, and the epidemic threatened to expand into the upland barrios of the municipality.[54] In Barrio Magüeyes, where Buena Vista was located, the Tarrats plantation was invaded by the disease and eight slaves died; on Catalina Sabater's plantation, her nephew was killed by the disease.[55]

Since the dread disease was now close by, Mayoral ordered Buena Vista closed off completely. A few days later, he chose his twenty best slaves and

TABLE 4.4. Deaths Caused by
Cholera in Ponce, 1855–1856

Barrio Deaths	Number
First	13
Second	39
Third	27
Fourth	28
Fifth	57
Sixth	52
Machuelo Abajo	78
Machuelo Arriba	42
Cerrillos	31
Coto Laurel	95
Maragüez	32
Real	53
Guano	56
San Antón	59
Bucaná	85
Sabanetas	66
Vayas	97
Capitanejo	119
Quemado-Matojal	108
Playa	86
Canas	103
Pastillo	60
Magüeyes	80
Marueños	39
Quebrada Limón	45
Guaraguao	22
Portugués	53
Tibes	84
Total	1,709

SOURCE: Fortuño, *Album histórico de Ponce*, p. 18.

sent them to Joaquín Tellechea's plantation, where according to Mayoral no one had come down with the disease in a long time. Eight other slaves he sent to the beach, where there had been no victims for at least a month.[56] The rest, some twenty-nine slaves, remained on the estate.

With fewer slaves in the barracks, the quarantine was easier to bear. In early December it was learned that the epidemic had hit hard in Barrio Marueños, which bordered Buena Vista on the east, and had come as close as Barrio Guaraguao and Barrio Tibes, directly north and west of Buena Vista, respectively.[57] The cholera had crossed Magüeyes from south to north, taking the lives of eighty people, while Buena Vista continued free of the disease.[58] In fact, despite the death of 1,709 people in Ponce, whose slaves were the worst hit on the entire island, Buena Vista had not a single case of cholera, either among those sent into the lowlands or among those who remained on the estate.[59] A few days later, when the cholera epidemic had passed, Mayoral said that he would never have believed that they would be spared this terrible disease, and that the slaves were very happy.[60]

Runaway Slaves in Ponce, 1853–1865

Even before the epidemic there had been a great deal of discontent among the slaves at Buena Vista. We know that the estate had two sets of shackles and chains and a stocks for those who turned rebellious. On June 3, a short while before the terror of cholera struck in Ponce, a group of slaves ran away from the estate. When they were brought before the administrator, Mayoral, they complained of the overseer, who at this time was Domingo Roche.[61] And not a week earlier another slave had run away because of a dispute with Roche, as the overseer himself admitted.

Protests by slaves against their overseers were common in Puerto Rico during this period. The number of overseers murdered increased during these years, higher even than the number of slave conspiracies.[62] But in spite of the seriousness of this matter for the entire island, in Mayoral's opinion the slaves had nothing to complain of, and he threatened to punish them "if they came back with more tales of this sort." The overseer himself complained that one could "no longer punish a servant without his running away or wandering off."[63]

Interestingly, no Buena Vista slaves seem to have run away after the terrible cholera epidemic. From 1850 to 1864, according to reports to the Ayuntamiento, there were at least eighty-five runaway incidents involving a total of ninety-eight slaves in the municipality of Ponce, yet none of them involved Buena Vista slaves (see Table 4.6).[64] Since most of the Buena Vista slaves had been born in the barracks and had not had much exposure to the libertarian ideas of the African-born slaves along the coast ("the most

TABLE 4.5. Slave Deaths in Ponce, December 1855–November 1856

Owner	Number	Owner	Number
Ferrer	39	Van Rhyn	8
Plaja	17	Mundet	2
Torruella	8	Alvizu	3
Alomar	10	Cabrera	3
Mandri	16	Font	10
Archebald	36	Fernández	9
Caño Verde	9	Tarrats	8
Gallagher	2	Pámpanos	6
Gerardo	12	Quemado	22
Esperanza	11	Montalvo	1
Oppenheimer	43	Roubert	5
Jesús Colón	5	Renta	1
Pietrantoni	2	Ma. Sánchez	4
Serrallés	9	Salomón	9
Foces	24	Salich	1
Lacot	14	Dede y Overmann	10
Quesada	8	Gandía	3
Romero	2	León	3
Pratts-Vayas	21	González	3
Pratts-Matilde	46	Tricoche	1
Constancia	8	Zalvez	1
Piris	2	Ortiz	1
Castaing	2	Maro	3
Leandri	1	La Gastón	4
Daniel Rivera	5	Total	473

SOURCE: Letter from Joaquín Mayoral to Carlos Vives, Ponce, November 26, 1856, BVA.

rebellious slaves in the country"), so far as can be determined there was never a slave conspiracy on the estate, either before or after the cholera epidemic.

The 1859 Sale of Slaves

In the cholera epidemic of 1856, José Alomar, an old and frequent purchaser of Buena Vista cornmeal and owner of Hacienda Santa Isabel in the neighboring municipality of the same name, had lost many of his slaves, and so in mid-May of 1859 he visited Buena Vista to look over the slaves on that estate. He found them to be in excellent condition and offered to buy forty-

TABLE 4.6. Runaway Slaves in Ponce, 1853–1865

Owner	Slave's Name	Age	Date of Escape
Hac. Bordaverry	Juli	50	Jan. 14, 1853
Hac. Fortuna (Ferrer and Gilbee)	Tohanis	39	Feb. 12, 1853
Hac. Vayas	Tiburcio	25	Apr. 13, 1853
Hac. Serafina Van Rhyn	José	35	Apr. 16, 1853
Hac. R. Muñiz	Tomás	40	Oct. 14, 1853
Hac. Rita Begona	Mónica	45	Nov. 28, 1853
Hac. Juan Prieto	Jacinto	32–40	Feb. 6, 1854
Hac. José Gillivan	Facundo	30	Feb. 8, 1854
Hac. José Zaldo	José Estalisnao	45	May 3, 1854
Hac. Paolo Manfredi	Orián	60	May 3, 1854
Hac. Juan Fontenit	Baldomero	18	May 21, 1854
Hac. Muñiz	3 slaves		May 22, 1854
Hac. Muñiz	4 slaves		May 29, 1854
Hac. Josefa	Raymond	18	June 14, 1854
Hac. Fortuna	Jacinto		June 17, 1854
Hac. U. González	Soledad		July 27, 1854
Hac. Playa Hermosa	Juan	23	Nov. 27, 1854
Hac. Juan	Isidro	25	Dec. 4, 1854
Hac. Jac. Mauri	Luciano	35	Dec. 4, 1854
Hac. J. R. Soler	Miguel	24	Dec. 3, 1854
Hac. Van Rhyn	Guillermo	24	Feb. 14, 1855
Hac. Francisco Prieto	Castro	24	Feb. 20, 1855
Hac. J. M. Fornie	2 slaves	40	Mar. 19, 1855
Hac. J. Barnes	Alejandro	21	Mar. 29, 1855
Hac. Torruella	Carlos		Mar. 24, 1855
Hac. De Becerra	Francisca	14	Apr. 12, 1855
Hac. L. Tillet	Ambrosio	25	May 10, 1855
Hac. Quemado	Juana Aibonito	18	May 29, 1855
Hac. Aguaprieta (José de Jesús)	Francisco	35	June 19, 1855
Hac. Plaja (C. Cabrera)	3 slaves		June 19, 1855
Hac. Hacob (Juan Mandri)	Guillermo (English)	25	July 6, 1855
Hac. Margarita (Juan Laborde)	José	24	July 20, 1855
Hac. Goicochea	Magdalena	28	July 28, 1855
Hac. J. Barnes	Manuel		Aug. 13, 1855
Hac. Quemado (Hmos. Laporte)	Francisca	18	Aug. 25, 1855
Hac. Barnachea	Juan Angel	22	Aug. 30, 1855
Hac. Destino	Juan	60	Sept. 19, 1855
Hac. Ferrer/Gilbee	Tomás	44	Oct. 25, 1855
Hac. Ferrer/Gilbee	León	35	Nov. 12, 1855
Hac. Fco. Carreras	María	24	Nov. 19, 1855
Hac. Santiago	Pedro		Jan. 3, 1856

TABLE 4.6 *(continued)*

Owner	Slave's Name	Age	Date of Escape
Hac. Consuelo (Serrallés)	Julio-Curaçao		Jan. 9, 1856
	Aquilino		Feb. 1, 1856
Hac. Citrona (Archebald)	Estevan		Feb. 27, 1856
Hac. Overmann	Luis		Mar. 3, 1856
Hac. Bronce (Rodríguez)	Victoriana	20	May 20, 1856
Hac. Juan Fouti	Bautista		June 6, 1856
Hac. E. Quesada	2 slaves		June 13, 1856
Hac. E. Quesada	Celestino		July 21, 1856
Hac. Juan Mandri	Enrique	35	July 26, 1856
Hac. Dede and Overmann	José		Sept. 26, 1856
Hac. L. Becerra	Licen		Nov. 19, 1856
Hac. Becerra	Bonifacio		
Hac. Davidson (F. Pasarell)	Francisco		Nov. 24, 1856
Hac. T. Davidson	Manuel Soan		Oct. 23, 1856
Hac. Josefa (Fonteni)	Raymundo		Oct. 31, 1856
Hac. Peoli Casau	Ramón	15	Apr. 11, 1857
Hac. Sta. Rita (E. Quesada)	José		Mar. 10, 1857
Hac. Davidson	Consuelo		May 26, 1857
Hac. S. Plaja Herm.	Antonio		Sept. 1858
Hac. S. Plaja Herm.	Calixto	34	Sept. 13, 1858
Hac. Flor de Oro (M. Ferrán)	Alejandro		Jan. 29, 1858
Hac. Conuco (J. Arecai)	Pedro	26	June 9, 1859
Juan Rivera	Francisco		July 19, 1859
Hac. Víctor More	Eduardo		Oct. 1, 1859
Hac. V. Cuiro	Ana	16	Oct. 10, 1859
Hac. Estrella (J. Franceschi)	8 slaves		Apr. 24, 1860
Hac. Restaurada (F. Vivas)			May 21, 1860
Hac. Sánchez	1 slave	42	Aug. 7, 1860
Hac. Becerra	2 slaves		Apr. 1861
Hac. Becerra	Caimito		July 1861
Hac. Bocachica	Tomás		Dec. 23, 1861
Hac. Corinao (Catalina)	Benito		Apr. 5, 1863
Hac. Becerra	Miguel		Apr. 18, 1863
Hac. D. Palmieri	Eusebio		July 22, 1863
Hac. J. Rivera	Máximo		July 28, 1863
Hac. Oppenheimer	Tomás		Sept. 9, 1863
Hac. Victoriano (M. Serra)	Unknown		Nov. 1863
Hac. de León	Juan de Dios		Apr. 1, 1864
Hac. Serrallés	Miguel		Aug. 5, 1864

SOURCE: Legajo 241, "Asuntos varios," box 229, "Archivo en que se anotan los esclavos prófugos que se entregan a ocurrencias notables," no. 931, PMA.

El cimarrón (the runaway slave), an engraving based on the oil painting by Patricio Landaluce. (Moreno Fraginals, *El ingenio*)

seven of the fifty-seven. We do not know whether Carlos Vives had put the slaves up for sale or whether Alomar's splendid offer of 36,000 pesos—an average price of 765 pesos per slave[65]—was so tempting that he simply sold them, but however it was, Vives agreed to Alomar's offer. It may have been that because construction on the millhouses had been completed and Buena Vista now bought most of its corn, there was no longer any need for so many slaves, and thus the offer "made good business sense." As an additional persuasion, Alomar guaranteed his debt to Vives by waiving his rights under the Privilege of the Indies, which prevented creditors from foreclosing on land to collect bad debts; under the conditions of their contract, Vives could legally take over Alomar's plantation if he reneged on his payments.[66]

Yet another reason that might explain the sale was that at this same date Carlos Vives was beginning construction on a new residence in Ponce (Ponce's fourth-largest private house, designed and built by the famous architect Juan Bértoly), which was going to cost him thirty-six thousand pesos—the same amount he received for the slaves.

In one fell swoop, then, the slave population of Buena Vista was reduced to eleven, though when several children were born to Margarita (four) and Abelina (one) and five more were bought,[67] the number of slaves rose to twenty-one, just at the twilight of the institution of slavery in Puerto Rico.

Top: On the left, the Vives family's permanent residence in Ponce, designed by the Italian architect and builder Juan Bértoly in 1859. The house on the right also belonged to the family. (*Puerto Rico Herald* [newspaper], October 1901)

Bottom: Vives Street in Ponce. The street was named by proclamation of the City Council in 1863 in honor of the city's deceased mayor Salvador de Vives. This is a view of a union demonstration marching past the Vives family's residence. (Postcard, BVA)

After 1870 two slaves, Alberto and Esteban, were born, but the law that paved the way for the abolition of slavery (the Moret Bill of July 4, 1870) freed them because they were born to slave mothers and had been born after September 17, 1868.[68] But freedom came to all the slaves three years later, on March 22, 1873, when the abolition of slavery in Puerto Rico took effect.[69]

CHAPTER FIVE

Coffee at Buena Vista

The Farm Becomes a Coffee Plantation, 1868–1898

n the waning years of the nineteenth century, coffee was king in the Puerto Rican economy. It had been introduced to the island as a commercial crop a little more than a century earlier, and it had quickly become one of Puerto Rico's major products. Coffee production grew steadily, until in 1896 it reached the highest level in history, with exports of 58,656,826 pounds—fueling expectations of even greater numbers, perhaps 80 million pounds, in the years to come.[1] The export value of this burgeoning crop was 13,864,341 pesos, 10,129,771 pesos more than sugar, the former monarch of the Puerto Rican economy.[2] And with the expansion of coffee cultivation, the central mountain range, or *cordillera central*, became one of the most densely populated areas of the island. Its forests were felled to make way for coffee: 122,399 *cuerdas*, upward of 120,000 acres, were planted in coffee trees by the end of the century. Forty-one percent of the cultivated land in Puerto Rico was given over to the coffee bean.[3]

Coffee beans had been used to make a beverage since time immemorial. The plant, *Coffea arabica*, is of the Rubiaceae family, native to Ethiopia in western Africa, but as early as the fifteenth century it had spread prolifically throughout the fertile lands of Yemen, in Arabia. From there it had been brought to Europe by the Dutch and later by the Italians. And as in Mocha, the port city in Yemen that gave the finest coffee its name, coffeehouses soon sprang up in all the main cities of Europe.[4] The first coffeehouse in London opened in 1652, and twenty years later there was a coffeehouse in Marseilles.[5]

The Dutch took coffee to their fertile colony of Java, in the Indian Ocean, and to their New World colony of Suriname; in 1698, when their war with France ended, they presented Louis XIV with two coffee trees, which he sent to have planted in the Jardin des Plantes in Paris. In 1720, when all the cacao trees in the French colony of Martinique were destroyed, the governor of Martinique, naval captain Gabriel de Clieux, requested on a visit to Paris that he be allowed to take some of the coffee trees in the botanical garden back with him to his island in the Caribbean archipelago, to replace the trees that had been lost. From Martinique, coffee trees soon spread to other French colonies in the Caribbean: the islands of Guadeloupe and Saint-Domingue (Haiti), the French portion of Hispaniola.[6] From Haiti the trees made their way to Cuba and from there, in 1736, to Puerto Rico. In Puerto Rico, with the help of Captain-General Felipe Ramírez de Estenós (1755), who had experience with the tree in Cuba, coffee made rapid progress.

On June 8, 1768, a royal decree exempted from payment of taxes for five years all those persons who dedicated themselves to the cultivation of

Coffee. (Heck, *The Iconographic Encyclopaedia of Science, Literature, and Art*)

coffee. This measure, combined with opportune purchases by the Compañía de Asiento de Negros (which preferred coffee to tobacco), trade with the Danish black market on neighboring St. Thomas, and the fact that coffee could be grown and harvested with very few resources on small plots of land, led to production levels of 7,280 cwt. in 1770, followed by even higher numbers—11,000 cwt.—in 1776.[7]

The Rise of Coffee in Ponce, 1775–1898

In his *Historia geográfica, civil y natural de la isla de San Juan Bautista de Puerto Rico*, published in 1788, Fray Iñigo Abbad noted that coffee was Ponce's main crop, being grown all along the coast on prosperous plantations. Abbad went on to say that the cultivation of coffee required little labor and was therefore a favorite among the Ponceños.[8] He noted that there was a good market for the coffee that came from the islands of the Caribbean, which was valued above all other New World coffee for its quality. In 1797, the French naturalist André Pierre Ledrú led an expedition into these waters, later describing Ponce as an important municipality not so much for its population size (5,733) as for its harvests of coffee, which totaled some forty-seven thousand *fanegas*.[9] These climatic, market, and harvest conditions were clearly very favorable to the growth of the Ponce coffee industry, as were other events that occurred in the early nineteenth century, such as the rise in the price of coffee attendant on the destruction of the Haitian coffee plantations and the emigration from Haiti of Frenchmen who brought their technical skills and knowledge about the crop to Puerto Rico. Yet the droughts that struck southern Puerto Rico during the first half of the nineteenth century momentarily slowed the development of the nascent industry.[10] In addition, those people who had some capital to invest realized that sugar was a better investment than coffee. In 1840, while the price of coffee had dropped, sugar was at a high, and there were good markets for it in the United States, England, and France. The land on the south coast, known for its fertility, was ideal for growing sugarcane, though not so good for coffee.[11] And one should add that many of the wealthy foreigners who came to Ponce from the various countries of Europe and the New World already had experience with sugarcane and thus were predisposed to grow that crop rather than learn the new skill and techniques necessary for coffee. In 1863, there were 7,642 *cuerdas* planted in sugarcane, while only 497 were in coffee.[12]

The growing and processing of coffee in Ponce suffered a severe blow on the night of October 29, 1867, when after several years of drought the island was hit by Hurricane San Narciso. Not only did this hurricane, "the most terrible hurricane that had hit the Island so far," wipe out most of Ponce's

TABLE 5.1. Coffee Production in Puerto Rico, 1864–1896

Year	Exports (pounds)	Value (dollars)
1864	16,874,231	1,012,450.86
1865	18,960,252	1,137,615.12
1866	14,924,810	895,488.60
1867	19,220,194	1,153,211.64
1868	16,063,431	963,805.86
1869	15,736,163	944,179.68
1870	17,406,762	1,045,005.70
1871	20,822,229	1,249,337.94
1872	18,335,133	1,101,307.90
1873	25,884,033	1,550,431.98
1874	17,769,195	1,066,151.70
1875	26,162,600	1,569,761.40
1876	20,826,390	1,249,583.40
1877	15,843,387	3,010,338.53
1878	17,051,486	3,325,390.77
1879	67,161,383	5,189,743.17
1880	48,032,296	3,077,304.00
1881	47,748,210	7,077,304.35
1882	29,788,671	3,391,285.40
1883	37,555,117	4,779,742.10
1884	26,025,690	3,317,451.48
1885	47,670,440	6,067,185.72
1886	36,742,010	4,693,055.96
1887	27,611,652	3,514,210.28
1888	51,095,847	6,503,007.80
1889	37,952,398	4,858,306.04
1890	43,822,794	5,577,166.56
1891	41,623,716	5,297,563.88
1892	47,264,988	9,452,999.60
1893	49,124,374	11,611,215.72
1894	50,401,309	11,912,038.26
1895	40,159,358	9,492,212.08
1896	58,656,826	13,864,340.88

SOURCE: "Balanza Mercantil de Puerto Rico" [annual trade summary], 1864–98, CHR.

coffee plantings, but it also destroyed buildings and razed to the ground most of the corrals and outbuildings in the municipality.[13] A few days later, there was great alarm at the advance of the ocean, and the residents of the town fled to the nearby hilltop known as El Vigia. And on November 18, before the island had even begun to assess its losses, much less rebuild, it was

TABLE 5.2. Coffee Production in Ponce, by Barrio, 1863

Barrio	Number of Cuerdas
Tibes	100
Marueños	76
Machuelos	56
Real	47
Guaguao	43
Quebrada Limón	38
Portugués	30
Mameyes	30
Magüeyes	16
Guaraguao	2
Total	438

SOURCE: Legajo 119, box 112b, Agricultural Census, 1863, PMA.

TABLE 5.3. Main Coffee-Producing Municipalities in Puerto Rico, 1897

Municipality	Number of Cuerdas
Utuado	15,075
Las Marías	10,969
Maricao	8,622
Ponce	6,259
Lares	6,098
Mayagüez	6,050
Yauco	4,452
San Sebastián	4,158
Juana Díaz	3,551
Añasco	2,768
Others	60,455
Total	128,457

SOURCE: Carroll, *Report on the Island of Porto Rico.*

hit by a series of earthquakes, and the ground seemed to rumble constantly for several days thereafter.[14]

But after San Narciso, coffee production recovered, and during the next twenty-five years, more than 5,762 *cuerdas* (from 497 in 1863 to 6,759 in 1897) were planted in the "new" crop in and around Ponce, mainly in the northern barrios of Marueños, Machuelos, and Tibes (see Table 5.2). The municipality, which was already the island's largest sugar producer, became one of its most important coffee producers as well, standing fourth on the island in terms of land planted in coffee, behind only Utuado, Las Marías, and Maricao.

The burst of expansion in coffee growing in Ponce (and the rest of the island as well) during the last quarter of the century was due to several factors. First, coffee adapted successfully to the virgin, moist, shady highlands of Puerto Rico's western mountains (between 650 and 2,500 feet elevation) and the springlike climate of the region—much like the climate of Yemen, in fact.[15]

Second, coffee could be grown on very small plots of land; clearly, this made it attractive to small landholders, for whom families were the major source of labor. Nor did cultivating coffee prevent small farmers from growing subsistence crops such as rice, plantains, bananas, sweet potatoes, and corn, for these crops could be planted alongside coffee or even among and under the coffee trees.

Third, there was an abundant, cheap labor force, which, though not composed of slaves, still tended to live within the confines of the coffee plantations and to be dependent on it.[16] On each of the coffee plantations in the municipality of Yauco, famous for the quality of its coffee, there lived from twenty to thirty families of sharecroppers.[17] Two-thirds of the population of Puerto Rico, in fact, was dependent on coffee in one way or another.

Coffee pickers, in the beginning "almost always women," were paid by the amount of coffee picked, generally measured in *almudes* and always in *fanegas*. Earnings, therefore, would vary from week to week and would be higher at the beginning of the harvest than toward the end, when there were fewer and more-difficult-to-reach beans.[18] Earnings would also vary depending on the many agreements the workers would have with their employers and on the "benefits" (clothing, housing, food, seeds) that the coffee pickers received in return for work.[19] On many plantations, pickers would be paid with nonprecious metal tokens called *riles*, which were issued by the plantation owner and had value only on the plantation that issued them. But some workers never received hard payment, whether legal tender or *riles*, because they would be deeply in debt even before the harvest began and their earnings from this week would go to pay last week's bor-

rowings. One can imagine the profits pocketed by the plantation owners, who sold coffee for gold and paid their workers with tin tokens!

Fourth, expansion resulted from tremendous consumption of coffee in Cuba, Puerto Rico's sister Spanish colony, where Puerto Rican coffee could be imported without the burden of tariffs and where, therefore, excellent coffee could be bought for a low price.[20] The War of Independence (1868–78) that had broken out in Cuba's Oriente Province had interrupted the production of Cuban coffee, as coffee plantations had become the *mambises'* battlefields and many stands of coffee trees were totally destroyed.[21] But the Cuban coffee industry had been in a decline since midcentury, when capital investors, first in Occidente and then Oriente Province, decided to replace coffee with sugarcane, a crop that would yield much larger profits for them.[22] This situation allowed Puerto Rico to export more than a quarter of its coffee production to Cuba during the last third of the nineteenth century.

The fifth factor was the growing demand for Puerto Rican coffee in the Spanish Peninsular market, and especially in Barcelona. Spain gave Puerto Rican coffee preferential tax treatment, and the importer paid only for transport, not import duties; this made Puerto Rican coffee cheap on the Peninsula. While "foreign" (that is, non-Spanish colonial) coffee paid fourteen centavos per pound in import taxes, Puerto Rican coffee paid only

The bustling area of the wharves in Ponce, from which more coffee was shipped than any other on the island. Merchandise about to be shipped out, on its way through customs, or about to be picked up by its owners was stored in the large open shed on the left, known as the *tinglado*. (Olivares, *Our Islands and Their People*)

"Coffee Pickers, Porto Rico," ca. 1920. (CTPR)

four and one-half centavos.[23] And to Spain, as to Cuba, Puerto Rico generally exported its run-of-the-mill-quality coffee, not its "superior" brands.

Sixth was the international situation that favored increased production. Brazil, the world's largest exporter of coffee, had been hurt by a number of factors: drought, yellow fever, low slave-assisted production and the eventual abolition of slavery in 1888, old and exhausted tree stocks, and the advent of the republic in 1889.[24] The Dutch colony of Java had a shortfall at the same time, so that supplies of coffee plummeted on the European market, and this temporary crisis in turn led to price increases that inspired Puerto Rico and other coffee-producing regions to rush to fill the void.[25] In the last two decades of the century, prices rose astronomically. The pound of coffee that had sold for fourteen centavos in 1868 sold for thirty-two centavos in 1894—the highest price Puerto Rico had ever received for its coffee.

And the last factor influencing expansion of coffee growing in Ponce was the truly excellent quality of the superior grades of Puerto Rican coffee, with its large beans, its polish, and its gleam. Puerto Rican coffee had no trouble finding purchasers in the major European cities, and it brought the highest prices on the market. According to José de Diego, coffee was a "luxury product, whose incense-like aroma rose from the tables of the wealthy and whose beans, like pearls, fetched the price of jewels."[26] Branches of island coffee-exporting houses were opened in such key cities as Le Havre, Genoa, Hamburg, and Bremen, and their presence was a great ally to the placement of high-grade Puerto Rican coffee in the European market.[27] Another factor that favored Puerto Rican coffee in the European market (except Spain) was that the monetary systems of all European countries were at the time based on the gold standard, whereas Puerto Rico's was based on silver. By virtue of the exchange rate, island coffee merchants received extraordinary prices in the local currency.

At the end of the century there were more than 102 properties in Ponce, with 6,259 *cuerdas* of land, planted in coffee. Every year the coffee growers bought more land and grew larger crops. As one father, the Ponce merchant Vendrell, confided to his children, given that the money invested in coffee was quickly recovered, coffee growers could take out loans that far exceeded the value of their properties, for their crops, which were "as good as gold," could be used as collateral. Several merchants, having now become coffee factors, he said, "were proud to extend credit to the coffee-grower from Ponce or any other town whose coffee might be exported through their port, and their vaults were standing open to them whenever they should need them." All—coffee growers and coffee merchants alike—"were in the same coffee-boat."[28]

Thus at the end of the nineteenth century there were many in Ponce whose entire fortune depended exclusively on coffee. Most not only covered the expenses of growing the aromatic bean but enjoyed profits that allowed them to travel the world and build magnificent houses replete with every comfort. Eduardo Neumann Gandía, a contemporary chronicler, echoes Vendrell, but goes on to describe the mansions in this way: "They are elegant structures built of brick and mortar, or of good solid stonework, adorned with lovely architectural elements and decorated inside with true luxury, embellished with lovely gardens, filled with comforts such as electric lighting, bathrooms, running water and all the improvements that speak of a comfortable life, one in which a 'man's home may truly be his castle.'"[29]

In the end even such Ponce sugar magnates as Serrallés, Cortada, Barnés, Torruellas, and Rosaly invested in this most promising industry—so promising that it even threatened to displace sugar as the island's largest export product.

By 1890 coffee export houses and warehouses such as Sobrinos de Mayol, Fritze and Lundt, Felici and Company, and Cortada were specializing in the final phase of processing: husking and polishing. And the port of Ponce registered the highest exports of any island port during this period.

TABLE 5.4. Coffee Prices, 1839–1894

Year	Price (pesos/cwt.)
1839	11
1846	6
1854	9
1860	12
1868	14
1875	16
1884	17
1887	21
1893	28
1894	32

Note: These are average prices, which varied depending on the quality of the coffee.

TABLE 5.5. Coffee Exports, by Port, 1888

Port	Pounds Exported
Ponce	8,654,482
Mayagüez	5,864,984
San Juan	5,271,541
Aguadilla	1,774,847
Arecibo	289,784
Total	21,855,638

SOURCE: *RAIC* (July 1888).

A trading house in Ponce.
(*Harper's Weekly*, February 1899)

Other important coffee growers, such as José Pina, Sauri y Subirá, Bregaro and Company, and E. Salazar, also opened small processing plants in Ponce where they husked and polished their coffee; some used blueing to turn it a deep, gleaming black.[30] These plants were the most advanced mechanical operations of the time, for even though they were turned by oxen and only sometimes by steam engines, they represented a great advance for the island's agricultural industry and were a considerable improvement over other such installations.[31]

It was here that the coffee was also graded, "a long, demanding operation, and therefore extremely costly." Coffee was graded into the following categories: *first grade*, which is a healthy, robust, whole, clean bean, also known as *café selecto*; *second grade*, or *triache*, which is made up of small beans that have turned black from having been picked from the tree early; and *third grade*, or "broken," which was just that—broken and split beans.[32]

Skilled women and girls usually graded the coffee, though there was also a machine, known as the Smout separator, that was sometimes used. This machine consisted of a large wire-mesh cylinder through which the beans were passed, falling as they did into separate bins according to size.

Then the coffee would be graded on the basis of quality, depending on its size, color, aroma, taste, and place of origin. The "Yauco" brand was the top grade, followed by "hacienda" and then "common." For example, in July 1887, the *Revista de Agricultura, Industria y Comercio* informed its readers that the select coffee grade "Yauco" was selling for 20 to 21 pesos; "hacienda," from 18 to 19; and "common," from 16 ½ to 17 ¼.[33]

Finally, the beans were put into crates, barrels, or burlap sacks stencilled with their grade and the name of the port to which they were destined—Le Havre, Barcelona, Hamburg.[34]

A view of Ponce harbor. Ships did not tie up at the docks but rather anchored farther out in the harbor; scows transported merchandise and passengers to and from the ships. (Olivares, *Our Islands and Their People*)

The Planting of Coffee at Buena Vista
under Salvador Vives (1872–1898)

In the 1830s, when Salvador de Vives bought the Buena Vista lands, he did not purchase the most desirable or most fertile land in Ponce for growing coffee. Droughts were constant along the coast, and although the estate was fairly high, the coffee variety that was grown on the island, *Coffea arabica*, needed a great deal of rain, humidity, and altitude.[35] In addition, it was hard, though not impossible, to grow the large, high-grade bean on Buena Vista that was grown at higher elevations, where the heat of the coastal zone was never felt.[36] The main buildings at Buena Vista are located just five hundred feet above sea level, where the droughts were worst.

The city of Ponce, by Juan Ríos, 1855. At the end of the nineteenth century, Ponce had the largest population (24,654 inhabitants) and geographic area (660,000 m²) of any town on the island. (PMA)

And yet it is at precisely that point that the land begins to rise and the steep uphill climb to Adjuntas begins. From Buena Vista to Adjuntas, the land rises to fifteen hundred feet (or even slightly more) above sea level, and that altitude is reached even on some Buena Vista land. It was there, on the wet, shady slopes of the rising hills, that the estate's coffee was planted during the boom period of Puerto Rican coffee.

This time it was the grandson, also named Salvador, who developed the Buena Vista land, now as a coffee plantation.[37] We should recall that even in the time of Salvador de Vives, from 1833 to 1845, coffee had been planted on Buena Vista and that in 1837 the first ox-turned machine was installed for depulping the beans. The annual production of coffee during the period from 1847 to 1866 was approximately 15 cwt., though the importance of that crop was overshadowed by the immensely profitable production of cornmeal. The documents of the estate contain occasional news clippings about coffee, snatches of information about the increase of prices during the 1850s, or a note about the deterioration of the pulping machine during the 1870s.[38] But coffee never received the attention that cornmeal did, even though its harvest rose as high as 19 cwt. in 1861, when only five *cuerdas* were planted in coffee trees. During the next nine years, and under the impact of Hurricane San Narciso in 1867, which destroyed two-thirds of the estate's new as well as old plantings, production fell to 10 cwt.[39]

Left: Coffee cullers or graders. The success of Puerto Rican coffee lay in its quality, its size, and the cleanliness and shine of its bean, which was picked over by women such as these in this photograph, who would discard any beans that did not "come up to standard." (*Harper's Weekly*, February 1899)

Above: Certificate of residency, Salvador Vives Navarro, January 7, 1880. (BVA)

From 1876 on, which coincided with the boom in Puerto Rican coffee, new fields were planted on the estate. Stands of coffee trees, which by 1880 totaled some ninety-four *cuerdas*, would be planted among fields of bananas, plantains, sweet potatoes, mangoes, avocados, and shade trees such as the *guamá* or so-called sweetpea tree (very often used to shade the coffee), the *moca* or "dog-plum" tree, the *capá prieto*, and the *búcare* or "swamp immortelle." The larger trees not only shaded the sensitive coffee trees (which were trimmed and kept short so that the coffee-bearing branches could be reached more easily) but also protected them from erosion, storms, and hurricane winds.

The main coffee "plot" on Buena Vista was known as San Carlos, and it lay more than a mile from the central plaza at Buena Vista. One had to go up the steep San Carlos road that crossed the estate to get there. Dirt roads, footpaths, and narrow trails branched off from this road toward the farthest corners of the estate, linking all the fields to the main plaza. During the 1880s a section of the San Carlos road was replaced by the state's new *camino real*, or "carriage road," which connected Ponce and Adjuntas and ran through the center of the estate. Although people who had nothing to do with the work of the estate, including thieves, were thus allowed to cross the property every day, the new road did bring the coffee fields closer to the machines.[40]

The virgin lands of the estate were intensively planted with the new coffee trees. Seedlings, usually about fifteen inches high, would be planted in June or July, just before the annual rainy season, when new branches were beginning to appear on the seedlings.[41] This was the most delicate operation in the entire cycle of cultivation, when the seedlings were gently transplanted from the nursery to the coffee field. In 1886, on the San Carlos

Photograph of Salvador Vives Navarro (1848–1937). (Donated by the Vives family to the CTPR)

TABLE 5.6. Losses at Buena Vista from Hurricane San Narciso, 1867

Type of Destruction	Cost (pesos)
Complete loss of plantains and bananas, old and new plantings, 30 *cuerdas*	1,800
Loss of two-thirds of old and new plantings and one harvest of coffee	400
Loss of some palm trees, other trees, and almost all fruit trees	600
Destruction of part of canal to cornmeal mill and roofs torn off	600
Landslides near the house, preventing traffic inside the estate, exit from estate, requiring large outlays for clearing away rubble and reconstructing road toward Guaraguao and Adjuntas	1,100
Total losses	4,500

SOURCE: Carlos Vives, "Manifestación de los perjuicios que ha sufrido la Estancia Buena Vista, Ponce, November 19, 1868," BVA. Loss to coffee totaled four hundred pesos.

plot, more than 2,200 new trees were planted, followed by 1,300 on the Quemado plot, 950 on the Cedro plot, and 900 on the Corcho plot (see Table 5.7).[42] These four fields were contiguous, and since the beginning of that year *alquilados* had been hard at work clearing and cleaning the land and making the furrows for the new trees.

That year, 8,600 seedlings in all were planted, and in following years new plots of land on the slopes of the hills were constantly being cleared. For example, on April 20, 1890, clearing began on a plot of land called Jacana, and two months later the furrows were cut and then the seedlings were planted; planting continued until the following year. The same thing occurred days later on the plots of land known as Corozal (where 458 seedlings were planted), Corcho, and Quemado. In 1893, according to Salvador Vives, these fields together totaled some 110 *cuerdas* planted in coffee, although, as was customary, the fields also contained shade trees, plantain and banana trees, and other crops.[43]

While planting of seedlings continued, beans from the producing trees would be picked constantly. "Producers," as they were called, had to be scrupulously cleaned (so as not to get strangled by vines and the other parasitic climbers of the tropics) and looked after, as the new trees would not

Advertisement for Querejeta y Hermanos foundry and blacksmith shop, offering "manufacture and repair of all types of cast-iron parts for steam engines and sugar mills, such as rims, hubs, rollers, firegates and doors for boilers, conical gears of all sizes, balconies for houses and mausoleums, ingots of all shapes and sizes, sluicegates and other gates for steam equipment, etc." Querejeta also advertised a stock of "pulleys, iron pipe, accessories for steam engines, picks, shovels, machetes, cold chisels, rubber for packing, oakum, American, English, French, and Spanish plows, paint, iron bars and sheets, hoes, and other assorted articles" always on hand. (*Boletín Mercantil de Puerto Rico*, October 3, 1879)

bear fruit until their sixth or seventh year. It is this cycle that explains why the account books of Buena Vista evidence such care and precision in their notations of the exact number of trees on the estate, distinguishing between the new plantings and the old. One must remember that coffee, unlike corn, plantains, and sugarcane, cannot be harvested the same year it is planted but must pass through a period during which the tree is coming to maturity.

After about ten years, the patient wait would be rewarded with extraordinary results. The production of 10 cwt. of coffee per year became a thing of the past; by 1882, production had risen to 62 cwt. and during the next fifteen years (1882–97) continued to increase, reaching 335 cwt. in 1897, the year of highest production in the estate's history (see Table 5.8).

The Five Steps in the Processing of Coffee at Buena Vista

While new trees were being planted on the higher slopes of the estate and production increased, Buena Vista's machines—located at the entrance to the estate, on its main plaza—were going through important changes. In October 1878, several parts were replaced on the old pulping machine, which was now in a very deteriorated state. Among the new parts was the axle for the drum, with the gudgeons and handles that connected to it; they were manufactured by the very well known Ponce foundry Ferretería Sobrinos de Querejeta.[44] The new pulping machine, like the old one, was installed between the roasting shed and the cornmeal mill and was driven by the old waterwheel.

As each day's harvest of coffee was brought in, processing would begin immediately. First the coffee would be taken to the machine shed, where it would be weighed; then it would be dumped into a hopper filled with water, which would help prepare the "cherries," as the picked fruit was called, for the pulping process.[45] From this hopper the cherries would roll down a chute into the pulping machine, which was basically a drum made of solid wood covered with a thin sheet of copper with rivetlike buttons[46] that turned against a wooden piece to which two iron blades were attached.[47] As the drum rotated, it squeezed the cherry against the blades; as the cherries tried to pass along the drum, the bean would be separated by pressure (though not enough pressure to cut the bean) from the pulpy outside part of the cherry.[48] The pulp would be thrown to one side, while the bean, now divided into its two halves, would fall into a trough that carried it to a cement tank filled with water, where the process known as "maceration," or soaking and softening, began.

This second stage in the process separated the slimy mucilaginous matter that covered the bean (in Spanish called *baba*, or "drool") from the bean it-

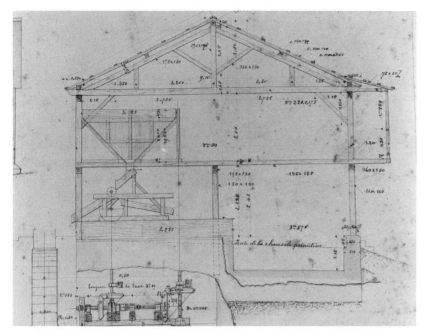

Depulping shed. Design for the wooden bench for the depulping machine, 1886. (BVA)

TABLE 5.7. Replanting of Coffee Trees on Buena Vista, 1886

Plot	Number of Trees Planted
San Carlos	2,200
Quemado	1,300
Cedro	950
Corcho	900
Tallón	750
Cacao	600
Gracia	400
Jobo	400
Meléndez	350
Aquilino	200
Granadillo	200
Capás	150
Guardarraya	150
Coco	50
Total	8,600

SOURCE: Account book, April 1886, BVA.

Note: The size of these plantings indicates that Buena Vista must have had a good nursery. From germination of seed to a two-inch seedling that could stand up to transplantation took fourteen to eighteen months. It was necessary to plant twice the number of seedlings as trees desired, because fully half the seedlings died before reaching maturity.

self. The mucilage must be removed from the coffee bean before drying because it prevents the bean from drying thoroughly and uniformly. The process at Buena Vista lasted from ten to twelve hours, or until a slight fermentation was noted. This was the most delicate of all the coffee-processing operations, as the chemical reaction that caused the fermentation of the mucilage had to be monitored carefully by the coffee grower or the worker in charge.[49] When the mucilage was fermented or "digested," water would be turned into the tank and the beans would be washed several times,[50] then drained and turned out onto the glacis or drying terrace to dry. The beans would be laid out on canvas tarpaulins so that if a sudden rain came (a frequent event in November and December, when the cherries were harvested), the beans could be gathered up quickly and moved under shelter.

In 1887, Buena Vista's former slave barracks was converted into a building that housed a system of huge drawers, twenty-four in all, that could be rolled out onto the drying terrace on a stepped series of iron rails. The drawers themselves had iron wheels that fitted the rails, much like enormous flatbed railroad cars, and the length of the rails increased from upper to lower drawer—the drawers were staggered so that when they were rolled all the way out of the shed, they would not cast shadows on the drawers below. Twelve drawers emerged from each end of the shed. If the day was sunny, the drawers would be rolled out and coffee beans would be spread out to dry. But at night or if it rained, the drawers would be rolled back inside.

The old slave quarters (far right) were turned into drying sheds for the coffee when several enormous "drawers" were installed in them. These drawers, with screen or mesh-wire bottoms and wooden railings all around them, could be rolled in and out of the building on iron rails, thereby allowing the coffee to be exposed to air and sun and protected if rain threatened, or at night. (BVA; photograph donated by the Vives family to the CTPR)

Table 5.8. Buena Vista Coffee Production, 1861–1897

Year	Hundredweights
1861	19
1870	10
1882	62
1893	273
1897	335

SOURCE: Account book, 1861–97, BVA.

The drying process, which made such a difference in the quality of the finished coffee, was a long and tedious one; during the rainy time in December it might take more than five days for the beans to dry thoroughly. But however tedious, the process at Buena Vista was very similar to that used for drying coffee on virtually all the island's coffee plantations at the end of the century.[51]

By century's end, some plantations and urban operations had begun changing over to drying machines.[52] In the Ponce Agricultural and Industrial Exposition of 1882, Bauzá de Mirabo exhibited a machine for drying coffee by means of currents of hot air.[53] But the drying machine that was best known through magazines, journals, and the Puerto Rican press was that which had been patented by José Guardiola, under patent series L133, John Gordon Company, engineers, and manufactured in London, England.[54] One of these machines was imported by Francisco Blanes in 1886 and installed in the municipality of Lares on the gigantic coffee plantation owned by Suau and Company (see illustration, "Guardiola's Patent Coffee Drying Machine"). The machine was powered by two fifteen-horsepower Westinghouse steam engines, six feet long and six feet in diameter, and it dried the coffee uniformly in less than fourteen hours by evaporating the water that still remained in the bean.[55] But it was a very expensive machine; in addition, it gave Puerto Rican coffee an "off" flavor and failed to impart to it the rich color the sun gave beans dried on the drying terrace. These factors were important to the quality of a coffee that was by now recognized internationally.

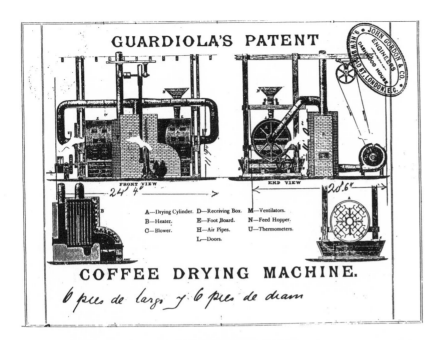

Top: Illustration of a "Guardiola's Patent Coffee Drying Machine," ordered from London by Salvador Vives. Handwritten notes as to machine's dimensions. (BVA)

Bottom: Section drawing of the drying shed, with drying apparatus installed, 1886. The *tahona*, which is the bin with two vertical rollers just under the roof, can be seen in more detail in the following illustration. (BVA)

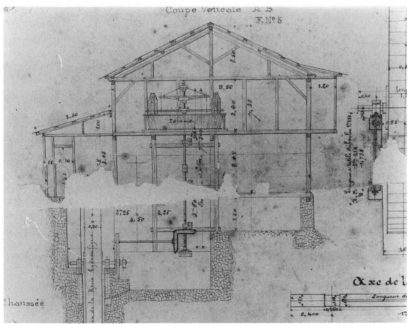

Drying machines were also manufactured at the Ponce blacksmith shop and foundry owned by the Scotsman Robert Graham, who had worked for many years with Puerto Rican sugar plantations and was now a specialist in the construction of coffee-processing machinery.[56] But although Graham frequently visited Buena Vista to see to its machinery or install new parts and machines, he never installed a drying machine for Salvador Vives.[57]

Until 1893, Buena Vista coffee was depulped, its mucilage was removed, and the beans were washed and dried, but the parchmentlike husk and silvery inner skin were not removed before the beans were sold to exporters in Ponce.[58] Exporters would buy the coffee still in its parchment or silvery covering, husk it, and polish it. Obviously, by selling unhusked coffee the Vives family received a lower price than for husked; there were times when Buena Vista did husk and polish its coffee at a husking mill belonging to another coffee grower, but of course it had to pay for the service.[59] All this changed in 1892, when a group of carpenters and masons began work on a *tahona*, as the husking mill is called in Spanish, for removing the parchment skin from the Buena Vista bean (see the schematic drawing of the husker).

The husking mill was built in the same place as the former corn mill had been, and it used many of the axles and gear mechanisms of that installation. The old waterwheel was strengthened by giving it a new axle with special braces and three brass bearings (the most expensive parts of the entire machinery complex) and by installing a new flange for the gear wheel. Carpenters also reinforced and repaired the interior of the old millhouse with new beams and braces. The water of the Canas River, which for more than forty years had turned the wheel that powered first the old mill and later the pulping machine, now supplied power for the husking mill. Paradoxically, only three years earlier, basing its argument on the recurring droughts that parched the southern areas of the island, the Agricultural Society of Ponce had petitioned the government to be allowed to build a series of canals or aqueducts to bring water from the powerful rivers on the northern side of the island to the south coast.[60]

Buena Vista's husking mill was made of the hardest wood then available. It was thirteen feet in diameter, with a trough in the bottom; around the trough ran two wooden wheels, attached to an iron axle yoke that was in turn attached to a post or axle that rose through the center of the construction. As the central axle (linked by a conical gear to the main gear wheel) turned, the wheels rolled around the trough. The downward pressure of the running wheels, the friction between one bean and another, and that between the beans and the floor and walls of the trough, together husked the coffee. The beans would then be winnowed, to separate the light parchment from the heavier beans. By going through this process, Buena Vista prepared its coffee (and that of other coffee growers in the vicinity) more thoroughly and could receive better prices for it. (There is no documentation whatsoever that blueing, which gave coffee the appearance of being fresh even if it was not, was ever used at Buena Vista.)

When the processing of the beans had been completed, oxcarts would be loaded up with sacks of coffee and driven to the port of Ponce. But in distinction to the cornmeal and other products that Buena Vista sold, which

Facing page: Schematic drawings of the *tahona*, or coffee-husking apparatus, showing the circular bin or trough into which the coffee was placed, the two vertical rollers that removed the husk by friction, and the various gears and gear wheels that eventually connected to the waterwheel. (HAER, drawing by Richard H. Howard, 1977)

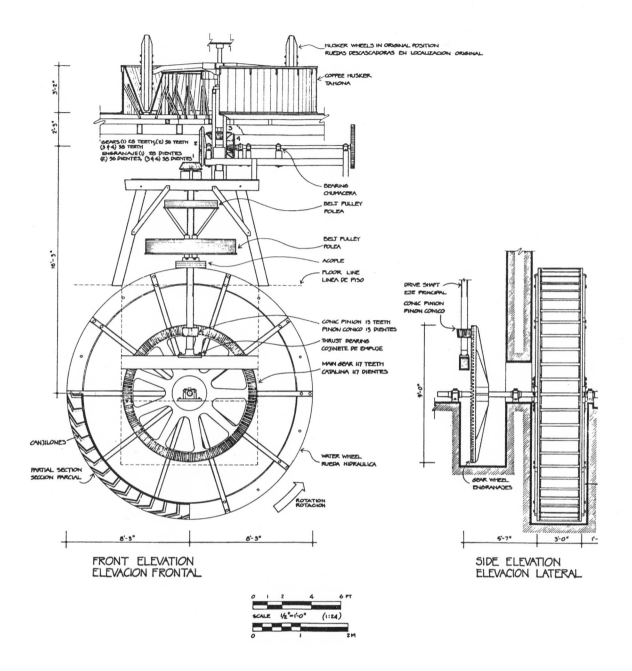

FRONT ELEVATION
ELEVACION FRONTAL

SIDE ELEVATION
ELEVACION LATERAL

HUSKER WHEELS IN ORIGINAL POSITION
RUEDAS DESCASCADORAS EN LOCALIZACION ORIGINAL.

COFFEE HUSKER
TAHONA

GEARS (1) 28 TEETH, (2) 56 TEETH
(3 & 4) 38 TEETH
ENGRANAJE (1) 28 DIENTES
(2) 56 DIENTES, (3 & 4) 38 DIENTES

BEARING
CHUMACERA

BELT PULLEY
POLEA

BELT PULLEY
POLEA

ACOPLE

FLOOR LINE
LINEA DE PISO

DRIVE SHAFT
EJE PRINCIPAL

CONIC PINION
PINON CONICO

CONIC PINION 13 TEETH
PINON CONICO 13 DIENTES

THRUST BEARING
COJINETE DE EMPUJE

MAIN GEAR 117 TEETH
CATALINA 117 DIENTES

CANJILONES

PARTIAL SECTION
SECCION PARCIAL

WATER WHEEL
RUEDA HIDRAULICA

ROTATION
ROTACION

GEAR WHEEL
ENGRANAJES

SCALE ½"=1'-0"   (1:24)

would be destined to the marketplaces or plantations along the south coast, the sacks of coffee would be exported to the main markets in Europe.

Sales to exporters would be made in a more or less piecemeal fashion, by *partidas* or "lots," as they were called, as the harvesting and processing of the coffee progressed through the harvest season. From October of one year to July of the next, lots would be sent down to the coast. For example, in 1892 nine lots were sent out, for a total of 271 *quintales*, or hundredweight.

In addition to selling his coffee directly, Salvador Vives also sold (as evidenced in the Buena Vista correspondence) to exporters in Ponce such as Fritze and Lundt, Fernández, Morales, Kraemer, and Mayol. Sometimes, too, the Vives family would ship coffee directly to Europe, without intermediaries. In Barcelona, for instance, consignment houses such as Comas y Miracle and Juan Amell y Milá would take Buena Vista's beans,[61] and in London the Murrieta banking house would do the same. This Spanish firm, which as we have seen had charge of the family's investments in Europe, regularly sent them notes addressed to "our friends in Puerto Rico," telling them of the magnificent prices paid for Puerto Rican coffee in London, the demand for it for the past two weeks, the sales, and, from time to time, after auctions, requesting new shipments of the product that was selling for some of the highest prices on the market.[62] During the decade from 1870 to 1880, in fact, the price paid for Puerto Rican coffee of the superior grade was exceeded only by that paid for the favorite coffee of the English, Costa Rican.[63]

CHAPTER SIX

Hired Workers, 1873–1898

n March 23, 1873, by unanimous vote of the National Assembly of the Spanish Republic, slavery was abolished in Puerto Rico, bringing to an end four centuries of that mournful institution on the island.[1] In the municipality of Ponce, where most of the slaves on the island were to be found, there were citywide marches, and fiestas took place on the large Oppenheimer and Cabrera plantations. A Te Deum was even sung.[2] The famed Puerto Rican abolitionist Ramón Baldorioty de Castro, invited by the Englishman Guillermo Lee to attend a celebration at Lee's Hacienda La Ponceña, exhorted the former slaves there to "interpret this law as a sacred obligation to labor."[3] And indeed, in spite of the immediate abolition of slavery, the Spanish government ensured that the newly emancipated slaves, now to be known as "freedmen" and "freedwomen," would be obliged for the next three years to enter into individual labor contracts with those who had once been their masters, with other persons, or with the state.[4]

Forty-five-year-old Rosa, born in Africa, a coffee picker and fieldworker; thirty-eight-year-old Antonio, African, canal cleaner and fieldworker; and twenty-year-old creole Estefanía, also a coffee picker, were three of the sixteen freedmen and -women who hired on in the aftermath with Buena Vista.[5] In the language of the estate, they became *alquilados*, or "hired workers."[6]

These sixteen former slaves joined four other hired workers who had been living at Buena Vista for some time, in a wooden house located to the north of the slave barracks. Up until this time there had always been very few hired workers at Buena Vista, because from the estate's founding in 1833 it had owned a labor force of more than fifty slaves. Even after the sale of forty-seven of its fifty-seven slaves on May 15, 1859, the Buena Vista labor contingent on the eve of abolition consisted of only four hired workers, along with nineteen slaves.[7] It is possible, as the administrator Antonio Navarro observed, that there were so few hired workers because it was so hard to find any at all.[8]

As had occurred during the period of slavery, most of the freedmen and -women were assigned to agricultural work: clearing land, felling trees, picking produce, and cultivating garden plots. A smaller group cleaned the canals, kept the sluice gates working, and attended to other chores of the like; another kept the machinery aligned and in trim, processed coffee, roasted and ground corn, ginned cotton, processed rice, or cleaned palm fronds used for thatching. Other workers were carpenters, drove the carts and wagons that transported the crops to market, cleaned sacks, made charcoal and rope, broke up rocks, or looked after the livestock. Finally, some workers cooked, washed and ironed, and performed various other kinds of domestic work in the owner's and overseer's houses (see Table 6.1).

Although there were several skilled *alquilados*, most of them had dual re-

sponsibilities—they worked on both the agricultural and the industrial jobs that needed to be done on the estate. It was the rare *alquilado* who did only a single job, for all types of work on the estate sometimes had to be done at the same time, during the appropriate season. For example, the mill mechanics and the man who cleaned out the canals worked all year long, but the coffee picker worked only from the end of August to December and thus had to have employment at other seasons.

The account books for the period from 1870 to 1886 show that there were ten hired workers, although this number doubled or tripled (1887–98) when the "months of uncertainty" ended, the coffee bean turned red, and the coffee harvest began.[9] At that point, an army of workers who lived on the estate and worked at other chores either in the fields or in the house would all pitch in to pick coffee.[10]

The coffee pickers were almost all women. Apparently, women were more careful than men and would take care not to disturb the still unripe green beans as they picked the red ones. November 1874 was a typical coffee-picking month at Buena Vista: the women—Dionisia, Belén, Matea, Andrea, Genara, Rosa, María Gracia, Guadalupe, and Josefa—picked 88 percent of the bean crop; the rest was picked by the men—Pedro, Esteban, and Ramón. Andrea alone picked more coffee than all the men together (see Table 6.2). Still, women were excluded from the coffee-processing operation that went on at the main plaza of the estate. It was invariably men who pulped, fermented, washed, dried, and husked the coffee.

TABLE 6.1. Jobs Done by Hired Workers at Buena Vista, 1873–1904

GENERAL AGRICULTURAL
Making new plots ready (clearing and digging holes)
Planting
Replanting
Burning
Weeding
Felling trees
Picking coffee, corn, plantains, bananas, gathering eggs, digging up sweet
    potatoes, etc.
Pulling old, dry palm fronds off the palm trees
Gardening (both flower garden and kitchen garden)

LIVESTOCK
Pasturing
Fattening
Docking tails
Breeding
Cleaning corrals

MACHINERY AND CANALS
Cleaning canals and clearing tunnel
Opening sluice gates
Adjusting and aligning machinery, trimming stones, greasing axles, checking all
    chocks, etc.
Watching for leaks in canals and sluice gates
Trimming gear teeth, etc.

CORNMEAL MILLS
Shucking corn
Shelling corn
Weighing shelled corn
Roasting or drying corn (making fire with dried palm leaves)
Grinding corn
Weighing cornmeal and sacking it
Carrying firewood

COFFEE
Weighing the cherries
Pulping the cherries and fermenting the beans
Drying the beans
Packing
Stirring and washing pulped beans
Husking the beans in the *tahona*, then winnowing

OTHER GENERAL WORK
Transporting produce and products (cart drivers and mule drivers)
Rope making
Washing sacks

TABLE 6.1 *(continued)*

Mending old sacks
Trimming millstones
Cooking, washing, ironing, and other domestic work in the residences
Making charcoal
Making and installing roofing shingles
Collecting guano
Fertilizing fields
Working on the fences and corrals
Security
Stripping leaves off branches
Making levers and handles
Pruning trees
Cleaning the fields of coffee trees and the other crops
Gathering dry palm fronds for ovens
Gathering firewood

Unfortunately, the Buena Vista account books for 1891–1900 do not list the names of those who worked on the estate, but beginning in 1887, when the names were still listed, one can see an increase in the number of men and a drop in the number of women, in spite of the fact that production was higher.

Once the coffee was picked, workers brought it down from the hillsides to the main plaza of the estate in baskets, where each *almud*, as it was called, was weighed in the old roasting shed. (An *almud* was a unit of volume used for the coffee beans, equivalent to twenty liters of volume, about twenty quarts; it would contain approximately twenty-eight pounds of cherries, which usually yielded about five pounds of prepared coffee beans.) During the 1880s, pickers were paid eight *reales* (one peso) per *almud* of ripe coffee beans, men and women equally. But although the period between 1884 and 1894 saw the price of coffee rise from seventeen to thirty-two pesos per hundredweight, the price paid per *almud* of picked beans was increased from eight to only nine *reales* during that same period.[11]

In November, the hired workers' earnings would be higher than at other times because there was a great deal of coffee to be picked, but as the harvest neared its end and there were fewer coffee beans on the trees, earnings would fall while the work would become harder and harder.[12] And there was another factor: many of the coffee pickers no longer lived on the estate as they had in the past but were brought in from outside year after year by an agent named Justo Cale. The agent was paid one *real* per coffee picker he could find during the harvest season.[13]

The hired workers' earnings depended on the work they did. The over-

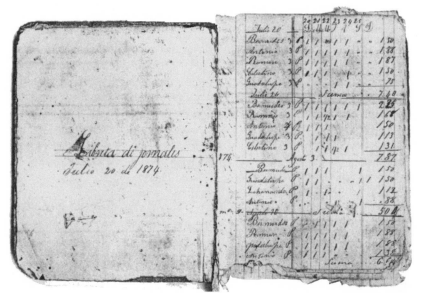

TABLE 6.2. Coffee Pickers at Buena Vista, 1874

Men (N = 3)	Number of *Almudes*	Women (N = 9)	Number of *Almudes*
Ramón	4	Guadalupe	14
Esteban	3	Rosa	29
Pedro	24	Belén	4
		Matea	27
		Andrea	72
		Dionisia	27
		Genara	15
		Josefa	18
		María Gracia	24
Total	31 (12%)		230 (88%)

Grand total = 261 *almudes*

SOURCE: Account book, November 1874, BVA.

seers were always the best paid; as on other large coffee plantations in Puerto Rico during the period from 1874 to 1894, they earned from twenty to twenty-five pesos per month (see Table 6.5).[14] They were also given a very simple house in which to live, consisting of one bedroom and a living room, on the main plaza of the estate, along with the necessary kitchen utensils.[15] Their salary was not only higher than that of any other employee but also generally as much as a quarter of all the hired workers' earnings

TABLE 6.3. Coffee Pickers at Buena Vista, 1890

Men (N = 20)	Number of *Almudes*	Women (N = 14)	Number of *Almudes*
Felipe León	8.5	Elvira León	11.75
V. Chamorro	12.5	Carmen Martínez	12.5
G. Hernández	23	Luisa Arroyo	15.5
Juan Elisea	43.75	Matilde Laboy	10.75
José Arroyo	12.25	Julia Laboy	14.15
Justo Cale	17	Fausta Serrano	10.5
Genaro Lugo	11.25	Elena Torres	11.75
Juan La O	35.75	Juana Guzmán	5
Vicente La O	15.75	Isabel Guey	3.75
Mateo Colón	11.25	C. González	27.5
Eleuterio Méndez	25.75	Magdalena	5.5
Antonio Aponte	1.75	Segunda Medina	2.25
Cornelio Aponte	17.75	Ana Guey	7.75
Elías Román	13	Rosa	1.25
Lorenzo Bay	9.75		
Domingo González	2.5		
Juanito Rodríguez	3.5		
Gabriel Rosario	14.75		
Francisco Padín	7		
Ignacio Lugo	2		
Total *almudes*	288.75 (67%)		140.75 (33%)
Grand total = 429.5			

SOURCE: Book titled "Café," 1887–90, week of November 15–22, 1890, BVA.

taken together (see Table 6.6). Of course, a great deal was expected of the overseer in return. Among other things, he was expected to supervise the work on the estate, watch over the welfare of the hired workers (as he had previously done with the slaves), recognize the freshness of the corn, know how to make good sales of cornmeal and the estate's other produce, watch over the warehouse and mechanical areas, keep all the machinery used in the processing of coffee and cornmeal in good running order, and know something about carpentry; he also had to be honest.[16] The overseers were, in a word, responsible for everything. For example, when the cornmeal was found to have weevils in July 1872, and two months later all the pastures, plantain and banana trees, and coffee trees went to pot and their fruits were stolen, the person responsible, according to administrator Antonio Navarro, was the overseer, Blas Casandia. Although Navarro knew that Casandia's neglect was due to his wife's being ill, Navarro recommended that Salvador Vives "fire him."[17]

Account book noting coffee pickers, Buena Vista, 1887. (BVA)

TABLE 6.4. Payment to Coffee Pickers per *Almud* of Coffee Picked at Buena Vista, 1874–1894

Year	*Reales* per *Almud*
1874	8
1884	9
1894	9

SOURCE: Account book, 1874, 1884, 1894, BVA.

Other privileged workers on the payroll of Buena Vista were the masons and carpenters. These two types of workmen did not live permanently on the estate but were called in when necessary. During the restoration of the waterwheel and the changeover of the mill from cornmeal to coffee grinding (from December 1892 to May 1893), masons were paid 8.75 pesos for a five-day workweek, and carpenters, among them the freedman Esteban Vives, were paid 7.50 pesos for six days, whereas a worker supervising the livestock was paid 2.50 pesos for six days, a gang foreman 2.50 for four days, and the cook 0.80 for four days.[18]

Hired workers might be paid per unit of work, per job, or per day. For example, in May 1876, the hired worker Vicente Martínez cleaned four *cuerdas* and was paid 18 *reales* per *cuerda*; for cleaning three *cuerdas* of fenceline he was paid 12 *reales* per *cuerda*; for cutting wood he was paid 12 *reales*, or 1.50 pesos, per day; and for other jobs, he was paid 4 *reales* per day.[19]

Per-job payments to the hired worker Saturnino Pabón, who had been overseer in 1874, are another example. In June 1878, when Saturnino worked on the completion of clearing and planting plantains on a plot of land called El Cedro, he was paid 7.50 pesos per *cuerda* and was given the seed, but when he later weeded the plot called El Jobo (which had been cleared that same month), he was paid only 22 *reales* (2.75 pesos) per *cuerda*.[20]

Another case in which the same worker was paid different wages for dif-

TABLE 6.5. Overseers at Buena Vista, 1872–1878

Name	Years	Months Worked	Salary (pesos)
Blas Casandia	1872–73	11	250
Saturnino Pabón	1874	12	300
Agustín Dorato	1875	10	200
Agustín Dorato	1876	6	120
Agustín Dorato	1877	2	40
Agustín Dorato	1878	11	250

SOURCE: Account book, 1872–78, BVA.

TABLE 6.6. Salaries at Buena Vista for All Hired Workers (approximately 10), 1875

Month	Total Salary Paid (pesos)	Overseer Salary
August	85.71	20
September	70.95	20
October	92.58	20
November	108.35	20
December	99.37	20

SOURCE: Loose sheet of paper, "Expenses, Hacienda Buena Vista, 1875," BVA.

ferent jobs is that of the cook Margarita (1874). As a cook, she earned twenty-five *reales* per week, but as a coffee picker she earned eight *reales* per *almud*.

Let us look at some of the main jobs and the wages that would be paid per job or day of work as they appear in the Buena Vista account books for the year 1873–74. A worker, for a day of various jobs, would be paid the following: 4 *reales* for planting a *cuerda* of land; 1.25 pesos for cutting down plantains; 1.05 for weeding; for pasturing livestock, 12 *reales* per day; for roasting corn, 4; for bringing in firewood to the oven, 28; for making rope, 1 *real* per dozen feet; for cooking, 2 *reales*; for picking coffee, 9 *reales* per *almud*, or less if the coffee beans were green; for grinding it, 6 *reales* per barrel, depending on its class—first-class, "color," or low-grade; and for transporting it to the port, 4 *reales*.

At Buena Vista, earnings therefore depended on several factors: agreements the worker reached with the administrator, the kind of work assigned, the amount of work done or produce harvested, and so forth. The administrator paid the workers every week, and unlike the case with other

plantations in the Ponce area and on the rest of the island, he paid in *Mexican* currency, silver pesos.[21] There is no evidence of paying the workers in scrip or in tokens—unofficial metal coins that the plantation itself issued, called *riles* in Spanish[22]—as many coffee and sugar plantations in Puerto Rico did during the last third of the nineteenth century.

Still, at Buena Vista as at other coffee plantations on the island, there were few hired workers (whether field hands, artisans, or overseers) who were not in debt even before the harvest began.[23] At Buena Vista the day laborers would almost always ask for an advance against their earnings because "they were in a tight." The advance would be paid in cash, though also sometimes in codfish, bananas, plantains, sweet potatoes, or other fruits and vegetables.[24] The advances would be subtracted from the worker's wages at the end of the week or at the end of the agreed-on time. A typical

In time, Cale went farther afield to find hired workers for Buena Vista. (Olivares, *Our Islands and Their People*)

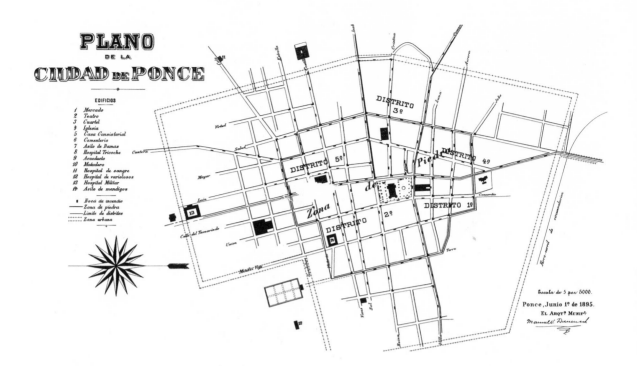

Map of Ponce by Manuel Domenech, municipal architect, 1895. (BVA)

example of a man in debt with Buena Vista is that of Corcino Colón, a day laborer who worked as a coffee picker and grinder, seasonal livestock man, weeder, and so on. For weeding twelve *cuerdas* in July 1878 he was paid 38.78 pesos, but he had already had an advance of 26 pesos, so his "take-home pay" was 12.78 pesos. A month later he was advanced 48.84 pesos in cash and then worked from August to November and earned 38.73, thus being left with a debt of 10.11 pesos. In December he began to work again, and by June he appears on the Buena Vista record books with a debt of 57.13 pesos.[25]

he Spanish-American War broke out in April 1898. On July 25, the day of the celebration of the Feast of St. James, the patron saint of Spain, after several months of combat in Cuba, the U.S. warship *Gloucester* entered the unprotected bay of the little town of Guánica. A skirmish followed the disembarkation of troops, and after a few hours the invaders took possession of the municipality of Yauco. The town itself, in the heart of coffee-producing country and the seat of the most recent separatist conspiracy (1897), fell the following day.[1]

As news of the event spread through the south coast region, the neighboring city of Ponce, which in the words of Guillermo Vives had "not a fort, not a miserable cannon," mobilized battalions of volunteers and its mounted guerrillas. The marketplace was deserted. A group of people congregated up on the summit of El Vigia, alongside Juan Rosa's lime kiln, to watch the movement of the American troops down on the coast.[2] Some of the families that lived in town, fearing a bombardment (Admiral Sampson had bombarded San Juan on May 12), had already sought refuge in the highlands of Barrio Magüeyes or fled (as many Spanish soldiers likewise did) toward the interior.[3]

The next day, expecting an invasion by land, the Spanish forces dug trenches, one on the road through Barrio Canas on the Armstrong property and another on the Juan Pratts road, but the trenches proved futile, for on the morning of the twenty-seventh three large warships, the *Dixie*, the *Annapolis*, and the *Wasp*, pulled up offshore and aimed their guns at the municipality: two at the town itself and one at the port.[4] Lieutenant G. A. Merriam, threatening to bombard the city, demanded the immediate surrender of his feeble enemy. To forestall the bombardment, Fernando M. Toro (English vice-consul and chargé d'affaires for the United States in Ponce) and the rest of the consular corps—the German vice-consul and exporter Enrique Fritze, the Dutch consul and sugar and coffee grower Pedro J. Rosaly, and the Scottish manufacturer and foundry and plantation owner Robert Graham—all stepped in as mediators in the conflict.

After several hours of tension and uncertainty—there was no Spanish officer authorized to transmit an order through the mediators for the evacuation of the city—Commander Davis reached an agreement for surrender with Captain General Manuel Macías via telegraph. The next morning, July 28, 1898, twelve thousand U.S. troops and eighty pieces of artillery disembarked, and the American flag was raised over the customs house.[5]

Dr. Guillermo Vives, an ophthalmologist, who at the time was medical director of the Tricoche Hospital in Ponce and therefore traveled the length and breadth of the municipality, told his brother Salvador, the administrator of Buena Vista, of his amazement at the number of steamships of every

CHAPTER SEVEN

Buena Vista after the U.S. Invasion, 1898–1904

Movement of U.S. troops toward Ponce. (Olivares, *Our Islands and Their People*)

kind and size, from newspapermen's and tourists' yachts to the monitor ("like a whale") that had accompanied the invasion; there must have been fifteen or seventeen, Dr. Vives reported. He also reported the landing of the troops:

> All these steamships brought soldiers—26 or 27 thousand—over a period of several days, of course; thousands of mules; bales of hay for them by the boatload; provisions for the soldiers by the ton—biscuits, canned beef, etc.—all sorts of things; 2 or 3 thousand four-wheeled kitchen wagons for the Red Cross, etc., etc.; tents, cots, etc., etc., even lumber, even an iron pier, so they say; even carpenters (these, as I saw myself, reconstructed the old wooden storage shed in 24 hours for provisions and every sort of article one can imagine); engineers, blacksmiths, machineworkers, harness-makers, etc.[6]

Meanwhile, General Nelson Miles, accompanied by Commander Davis, took the city: at 10:00 A.M. the Spanish turned over the Ayuntamiento. Thus it was, foreshadowing what was to occur over the rest of the island, that Ponce was defeated without a single shot having been fired. Dr. Vives noted, "The transformation was like a dream, and the change seemed quite providential, there being none of the unfortunate occurrences that might be feared."[7]

Angel Rivero, a captain of the Spanish artillery in Puerto Rico at the time, relates that during the invasion and occupation many residents of Ponce, among them many ladies of society, took drives in their carriages down the road that led to the port. Ponce had the look of a city in the midst of a festival: there were parades and music, and the streets and squares were decorated with the bright colors of the American flag.[8] Merchants in town reaped a bonanza on the sale of souvenirs to American soldiers—Spanish fans, Spanish flags, the spats worn by the Insular police (the Guardia Civil), swords, dress swords, and all sorts of other uniform paraphernalia were in great demand.[9]

Dr. Vives was a witness to the way the people of the town, full of hope for the new period of change, peace, and well-being that was to come, turned over their weapons and cooperated with the invading forces. "Without this change, the ruin of the country looked to be inevitable." The changes that were hoped for included a lowering or elimination of trade tariffs, the coastal black market, and all sorts of payoffs and shady dealings. At this point, said Vives, "if a man wants a priest, he must pay for it out of his own pocket, [just] as he must [also] pay the foreigners brought in by Sanz as schoolteachers, and the ones Sanz did not bring in, too."[10]

The occupation forces set up camps around town: on Schuck's property, at the racetrack, at Hacienda Barrancas, at Quintana's hot springs, in Barrio Canas, at Armstrong's quarry near the place the trenches had been dug, at the Irizarry house, at another house near town, at the aqueduct, and, finally, on the hilltop in Melero's pasture.

Buena Vista during the U.S. Occupation of Ponce

During the war, Dr. Guillermo Vives and his family left their house in town and took refuge at Buena Vista to avoid any possible bombardments from the warships on the coast and any other "unruliness and rumor-mongering" that they feared might be mounted against the volunteers and the Guardia Civil. Dr. Vives was in charge of the estate at the time of the invasion, as Salvador, its official administrator, was in Europe on a pleasure trip, and he opened its doors to many people (among them, the brothers Arce) who wanted to stay. But on August 5, he and his family decided to return to their house in town, which now seemed safer than the countryside. As he himself reported, "outrages, even murder, are being committed against the Spanish."[11] As vengeance for perceived historical injustices, groups of Puerto Rican campesinos—*partidas sediciosas* (seditious gangs)—were persecuting Mallorcan, Canary Island, Corsican, and other Spanish mer-

Top: The occupation of the Ponce dock area by U.S. troops. (*Harper's Weekly*, September 3, 1898)

Bottom: General Miles's proclamation to the inhabitants of Puerto Rico. This copy was saved by the Vives family for the BVA.

chants, plantation owners, and soldiers in Ponce.[12] According to Dr. Vives, the soldiers were being made to pay for the part they had played during what was called the Componte, or reign of terror: "They [the *partidas sediciosas*] sought [soldiers] out in their houses and demanded that they turn over their weapons to the new command, they insulted them and beat them." The same thing was happening in Yauco, Adjuntas, Utuado, Las Marías, Mayagüez, and Lares, not only to soldiers but also to all representatives of the empire (including its merchants) on the island. The meek Puerto Rican peasant, the humble *jíbaro*, had turned.[13]

In Ponce, the spontaneous rebellion against the Guardia Civil and Peninsular government officials was brought on by the memory of those days of persecution, arrests, and evictions that had occurred during the administration of Governor Laureano Sanz (1868–70 and 1874–75) and the months of terror in 1887. In that latter year (and before, though to a lesser degree), the new government of Lieutenant General Romualdo Palacios González, egged on by conservative elements on the island, had unleashed a wave of brutal and arbitrary persecution against *autonomistas* (those who wanted Puerto Rican self-rule), *autonomistas* that were believed to be *independentistas* (a political option that was much more threatening to the empire than mere self-rule), and those who were neither, but merely suspected.

LAS DOS CONQUISTAS

1508. Juan Ponce de León á sus tercios españoles:—¿Veis á esas pobres gentes desnudas? Son los naturales del país. Dentro de cincuenta años......ni uno.

1898. El General Miles á sus soldados americanos:—¿Veis á esas pobres gentes indefensas? Son los naturales del país. Dentro de cincuenta años......ni uno.

The administration used the Guardia Civil to deal out "object lessons" in the form of beatings and tortures that employed sticks, knotted rope and chains, whips and riding crops, fists, and feet and to elicit "confessions" from those suspected of conspiracy against the Spanish regime.[14] In Ponce, one Corporal Barboza and his men terrorized the countryside with their maraudings. Many *jíbaros* fled the rural areas where the Guardia Civil suspected the underground existence (and machinations) of such secret societies as the Torre del Viejo.[15] Leaders of the newly founded Puerto Rican Autonomist Party—among them Antonio Molina, chairman of the local committee for Ponce, and Ramón Baldorioty de Castro, chairman of its board of directors and party delegation—were arrested and sent to the prison in the nearby town of Juana Díaz or, when the jails were full around Ponce, to the dungeonlike cells of El Morro Fortress in San Juan.[16] Ponce was under what amounted to martial law, administered by virtually the entire roster of the Guardia Civil and the Valladolid Battalion. And it was in that state of affairs that Governor Palacios González made the menacing statement that in the happy city of Ponce, "those who amuse themselves today may well find themselves weeping tomorrow."[17]

"The Two Conquests. *1508*: Juan Ponce de León to his Spanish followers: 'D'ye see those poor naked folks? They are the natives of this island. Within fifty years . . . not a one shall be left.' *1898*: General Miles to his American troops: 'D'ye see those poor defenseless folks? They are the natives of this island. Within fifty years . . . not a one shall be left.'" (*Puerto Rico Herald*, September 1903)

Buena Vista after the Invasion

Within just days of the invasion, a group of U.S. soldiers loaded down with cameras visited Buena Vista and made one another's pictures under the

aqueduct and sitting on a bench in front of the falls.[18] The harvest of coffee beans had just begun; this lot would consist of 8 cwt. of beans for the exporting concern of Bregaro and Company and would be followed by two further lots, and then six more through the next two months, for a total of 113 cwt.[19] Still, as on the rest of the island, where the production of coffee fell to 121,572 cwt. for the year 1900–1901, at Buena Vista some 289 cwt. fewer beans were sold in 1898 than in 1897.[20]

The next year, 1899, saw Buena Vista return to normal: the machines were cleaned and made ready, the cart drivers drove cornmeal down to the coast, and in August, as usual, hired workers made preparations for the first round of the harvest. But this normality was turned upside down when Hurricane San Ciriaco hit on August 8. This devastating hurricane, stronger than San Narciso in 1867, with winds surpassing eighty-five miles per hour, unleashed rains that lasted for more than six hours, dumping twenty-three inches of rain on the south coast. The storm hit land at Arroyo and headed more or less northwest, passing just to the north of Ponce and moving offshore northwesterly at Aguada; it left 3,369 dead.[21] Many people were drowned as a result of the unprecedented floods caused by the rain that fell over the *cordillera central*, especially around Utuado and Jayuya.[22] Many cattle were drowned, and fruit and vegetable, tobacco, and sugar crops were ruined. Coffee was hit worst of all. More than 250,000 people whose lives and livelihoods depended on coffee were reduced to the most pressing poverty, and 90 percent of the crop that year was lost.[23] The hurricane toppled or uprooted between 55 and 60 percent of the island's coffee trees and that many more shade trees. Hundreds of acres of hillsides planted in coffee trees simply ceased to exist; the devastation was "indescribable."[24] When final damages could be assessed, losses to the coffee in-

U.S. soldiers sitting beside the canal with the falls behind them, and at the base of the aqueduct, Buena Vista, 1898. (Browne and Dole, *The New America and the Far East*)

dustry were calculated to be more than $20 million.[25] It was the worst meteorological disaster ever to have hit the island.

In Ponce, the wind began to blow at eight in the morning and continued until four in the afternoon, when the eye of the storm passed over the region. Unsuspecting residents poured out into the streets, but minutes later the storm's fury began again, and many people died when they could not

The devastation caused by Hurricane San Ciriaco to the port of Ponce, 1899. (*Harper's Weekly*, 1899)

get back to shelter. During the night, the rains were torrential, and the Portugués River overflowed and flooded much of the city, ripping houses from their foundations and floating them through the streets like toy boats.[26] In Ponce, more than 283 people died in the disaster, most of them as a result of drowning. The distinguished Ponce merchant Fernando A. Vendrell recalled that "coffee-growers woke up the day after the hurricane ruined, because their estates had been wiped out." He described the way "the storm split, pulled up, and toppled trees with the fury of its winds. It was dreadful to see, all through the flatlands along the coast, the trees that had been carried down by the terrible avalanche of the rivers' water. . . . All one heard was wailing and lamentation at the disaster. The highlands had been devastated, their trees swept down to the flatlands, the coast, the ocean."[27]

Vendrell added that hundreds of landowners, who only days before had ridden or walked out over their properties to admire the beauty of the stands of coffee trees and the valuable harvest they bore, on the day following the storm had to clear away fallen trees and branches from the roads only in order to see the fruit of their years of labor lying spilled on the

The destruction caused by San Ciriaco to the town of Ponce, 1899. (*Harper's Weekly*, 1899)

ground. What had days before been a landscape like a garden now had no trees or even soil—the harsh, rocky subsoil was all that was left to see; the rest had been swept down the hillsides.[28]

Domingo Serra's Hacienda Boca-Burenes, in Barrio Tibes, had produced 1,000 cwt. of coffee a year before the hurricane; in 1899–1900 it yielded only 50. Losses to the coffee crop around Ponce alone were calculated at more than a million dollars.[29]

At Buena Vista, the storm caused virtually no lasting damage; the canals and buildings seemed to have withstood the wind and water. But on October 14, 1899, the carpenter Esteban Vives began some repairs, and as was to be expected after such a storm, the yield of many fruits and vegetables was considerably reduced. The first pass of the coffee harvest had taken place in late September, but most of what had been ready for picking in early October was lost to the hurricane. Only 82 *fanegas* and 75 *almudes* were finally picked, yielding 46 cwt. of net coffee.[30] A year later, production recovered a bit: 78 cwt. was sent to Fritze and Lundt in the port of Ponce.

But yet another and more terrible catastrophe was in store for Buena Vista and Puerto Rico in general—and this one could be seen coming: a drastic drop in the world price of coffee, owing to overproduction. The 1900 crop was quoted at only $12.00 per hundredweight, $2.40 less than the 1896 price of $14.40. In the next few years, the price would fall even further, to $11.00 per hundredweight.[31]

This price drop made the coffee-industry crisis all the worse, since banks and moneylenders, unable to collect on their notes, were not willing to lend

TABLE 7.1. Coffee Production,
Buena Vista, 1893–1900

Year	Amount (cwt.)
1893	273
1897	335
1898	159
1899	46
1900	78

SOURCE: Account book, 1893,
1897–1900, BVA.

more money to a dying operation. Neither land nor crop was good collateral. Foreclosures (on mortgages totaling some $4.8 million) were the order of the day.[32] And to make the problem of lack of capital even more pressing, on January 20, 1899, President William McKinley devalued the Puerto Rican peso, which had been one-for-one with the American dollar, to sixty cents on the dollar; this reduced circulating capital still further.[33] No other sector was as affected by the virtual abolition of the provincial currency as were the coffee growers, because until this time they had reaped handsome profits simply on the favorable exchange rate.[34]

The sharp drop in coffee prices was due to huge coffee output from Brazil, which after years of serious political and economic problems had begun to plant new coffee plantations on virgin land worked by immigrant laborers and to open the interior by a new system of railways, which made quick marketing of their product feasible for the first time.[35] Per-acre yield in Brazil was very high, much higher than in Puerto Rico. And in Puerto Rico, production costs (calculated in dollars) were higher than in Brazil;[6] the production cost for a hundredweight of coffee in Puerto Rico was almost as high as the selling price, a situation that greatly reduced the coffee grower's possibility of profit. In New York, Brazil's Río #7 was quoted at less than six cents a pound ($6.00/cwt.), while it was impossible to *produce* coffee in Puerto Rico for less than seven cents.[37]

Ironically, then, Puerto Rico reached the point of importing coffee from the United States—free of tariff charges, since the Foraker Act of 1900 had removed all import-export tariffs between Puerto Rico and the United States—in order to satisfy the local needs of Puerto Rico.[38] The coffee that was imported would come from Brazil, Venezuela, Java, and Tampico and might have been imported legally or even illegally by New York importers.[39] To give the coffee a better look and to make it more closely resemble island coffee, it would generally be husked (and sometimes even reexported) as though it were, in fact, Puerto Rican–grown.[40]

The situation in the coffee industry could not have been more difficult for many coffee growers, for even more problems occurred during the first years of the century: first, the irretrievable loss of the Cuban market from 1898 to 1902 when Spain gave up its Caribbean colonies and an end came to the preferential tariff treatment that Puerto Rican coffee had received in Havana;[41] second, a new tariff of 12.80 pesos per hundredweight with which Spain replaced the old freight charge, making Puerto Rican coffee more expensive on the Spanish market; third, the closing off of European markets to Puerto Rican coffee because of the change of sovereignty, because the United States was not a coffee-producing country and thus had not been a signatory to any of the trade agreements that included coffee;[42] and fourth, the resistance on the part of the American market (the largest in the world)

Coffee plantation. (Olivares, *Our Islands and Their People*)

to changing its consumer habits and abandoning a cheaper, less flavorful coffee in return for a shiny, robust-flavored, and of course more expensive bean.[43] One of the major U.S. coffee concerns, Francis Leggett and Company, declared from the very outset that it was interested in buying Puerto Rican coffee at market prices, which meant in its natural unhusked state, because in the company's view the polishing was the great drawback.[44] What the New York market wanted, Merchor, Armstrong, and Dessa reported, was a dry, flat bean of a yellowish or greenish color, and unpolished, not the dark, gleaming Puerto Rican bean.[45]

Puerto Rican coffee, even though produced on U.S. soil, enjoyed no tariff protection whatsoever and so had to compete with the cheapest of the foreign brands, such as those from Brazil. It was a difficult situation, because during the years of the coffee boom the United States had bought only 1 percent of the island's production.[46] In 1896, of the 580,000 cwt. of coffee exported from Puerto Rico, only 1,899 were sent to the United States, which consumed the inferior grades of Brazilian coffee and the superior grades of Mocha and Java coffee exclusively, with no "in-between." And the country was not going to upset its trade relations with all other coffee producers in the world simply to make a few people in Puerto Rico happy.[47] On

Printed bylaws of the Ponce "Tramline Company" (1878) (top), the Ponce "Electric Light Corporation" (1897) (bottom), and the Banco Crédito y Ahorro Ponceño, or Ponce Savings and Loan Bank (1894) (facing page).

the contrary, roasting companies included Puerto Rican coffee among their cheaper brands or even went so far as to mix it with beans of lesser quality.[48]

But there was better news for coffee growers when on June 22, 1903, President Theodore Roosevelt notified the governor of Puerto Rico, William H. Hunt, that Puerto Rican coffee was the only kind used in the White House and that he and his family were quite pleased with that arrangement.[49] From that point on, advertising agencies used the president's words to promote Puerto Rican coffee as "the only coffee used in the White House" or "the coffee that made the White House famous."[50] But in the long run, the ads went for naught, because during the next ten years purchases of island coffee in the United States remained at only about 1 percent of the island's total coffee exports.

Finally, all the laudable efforts of the Puerto Rican House of Delegates to secure a public loan from the U.S. War Department to reconstruct the island's coffee industry failed, time after time. The island military governor, George W. Davis (1899), and, following his lead, his U.S. advisers saw no need for such help, a fact that led Mateo Luchetti to say that so far as the Americans were concerned, "our local crisis is no more than a tempest in a coffee pot."[51]

Given this situation of plummeting prices and unfavorable treatment in every other way, many former coffee growers abandoned their stands of trees and sought to make their living in other branches of agriculture, where they might find not only decent prices but also some interest on the part of American markets. Between 1900 and 1909, 44,646 *cuerdas* of land were lost to coffee production on the island as a whole; in Ponce, a little more than 1,000 *cuerdas* were lost.[52]

For many people, tobacco began to look to be the way to go, because in 1900 the U.S. tobacco trust opened an island branch, the Puerto Rican–American Tobacco Company, which bought tobacco from growers to manufacture cigars and cigarettes for export. The company also acquired some of the island's largest cigar and cigarette factories. Tobacco growers could count on ample credit possibilities, high demand for their product, and wide advertising.[53] For coffee, there was no large trust, no credit, no demand.

But despite the lure of tobacco, some coffee growers converted their estates to orange groves.[54] It has been estimated that from 1898 to 1904, more than six thousand *cuerdas* were planted in orange trees across the island; several packinghouses were opened in Mayagüez and Ponce.[55]

Buena Vista followed this route. Although some oranges had been grown on its land since its founding in 1833,[56] it was not until 1898 that Salvador Vives, aware of the promising New York market for this fruit, new possibilities for credit, the availability of crates, wrapping paper, and intermediaries, and interest on the part of American firms, increased production to the point that oranges became one of his estate's main crops. After looking into several U.S. firms that were interested in marketing his product, he chose Sgobel and Day and later R. S. Hammond for this important work; both specialized in citrus crops from Cuba, California, Florida, and Puerto Rico.[57] Because of their quality and freshness, the first harvests of oranges sent to New York found a ready market and generated demand for more.[58]

Orange growing gave Buena Vista a new lease on life, even though the coffee crisis had been far from a mortal blow, because the livelihood of the younger brothers Guillermo and Carlos (the first, a prominent ophthalmologist) did not depend on profits from Buena Vista.[59] Still, we should recall that the earnings were important in the years they were studying medicine in Europe. Their older brother, Salvador, who after the death of their father (1872) had remained on the island to oversee the administration of the estate, was a clever businessman. He had invested his fortune in stock: the Ponce Tramline (1878), the Ponce Electric Light Corporation (1897), and the Banco Crédito y Ahorro Ponceño (the Ponce Credit and Savings Bank) in 1894.[60] Salvador Vives, in fact, was a founding partner and later president of the Banco Crédito y Ahorro, and in the other corporations he held positions on the boards of directors.[61] In addition, the Vives brothers received some income from rental properties on Atocha and Vives Streets in downtown Ponce.

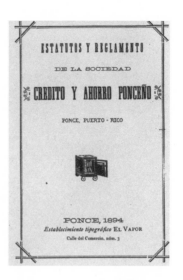

Cornmeal after the Invasion

As we have seen, the immediate success of cornmeal from the Buena Vista mills was owed in large part to its consumption by slaves on Ponce sugar plantations. So long as slavery continued to exist, Buena Vista cornmeal had a captive market. But from March 1873 on, with the abolition of slavery in Puerto Rico, the bottom dropped out of the market for cornmeal, and Buena Vista production was cut back drastically. Three years later, Salvador Vives observed that despite the power of his mills (especially the turbine-driven mill) and the good production of corn in Ponce and the neighboring region, there was demand for no more than about nineteen hundred barrels per year.[62] The years of growth in the Ponce sugar industry had come to an end, as well, and from 1871 on, sugar production began to decline. In 1898 only fourteen thousand hogsheads were produced, twenty-one thousand less than in 1871.[63] Many plantations went bankrupt, and to pay their debts they were forced to sell off their lands piecemeal. In 1886 only twenty-two sugar plantations were left.[64]

At the same time, the tariff advantages that had allowed Buena Vista cornmeal to prosper disappeared at the end of the century, because while

Ponce physicians. Dr. Guillermo Vives Navarro is standing at the far right, ca. 1904. (BVA)

tariffs remained high on flour, the Spanish government's monopoly on imports to Puerto Rico ended. We have seen how the protectionist policies of the Spanish government discriminated against foreign flour, especially that from the United States, creating constant shortages. As a consequence, prices rose tremendously, and the resulting high prices prevented most Puerto Ricans from purchasing and consuming flour. But at the end of the century, U.S. flour (that product that brought in the most foreign-trade money to the United States and played a major role in the country's ability to pay off its foreign debts)[65] replaced the Spanish product on the Puerto Rican market. In August 1891, Spain passed a trade agreement with the United States that halved import tariffs on flour and cornmeal to the Spanish Caribbean.[66] As a result, U.S. flour and cornmeal displaced the much more expensive Spanish product, and large amounts of both flour and cornmeal entered the island market. Spanish ships almost entirely ceased to anchor in Caribbean harbors.[67]

In 1896, of the 173,078 barrels of flour imported to Puerto Rico, 157,259 were from the United States, while only 15,288 were from Spain, and these, quipped a contemporary, were also from the U.S. "The funniest and yet bitterest thing about it is that no true *Spanish* flour comes in. What passes for flour from Barcelona or Santander is genuine, 100% authentic, U.S. flour, which goes first to Spain and then is exported to Puerto Rico as a Spanish product, with the traders making a modest profit off the turnaround."[68] In these late years of the nineteenth century, the new abundance of U.S. flour allowed island entrepreneurs to establish four new cracker factories and several noodle manufactories in Ponce.[69]

With U.S. dominion over Puerto Rico in 1898 came even more imports, since now U.S. flour could enter the island with no difficulty whatsoever. High protectionist tariffs were a thing of the past. The United States reduced the tariff from $1.86 to just $0.45 per hundredweight of U.S. flour.[70]

It was these three factors—the end of slavery, imports of U.S. flour under Spanish rule, and the change of sovereignty in 1898—that caused the production of Buena Vista cornmeal to drop from more than 2,000 sacks per year in 1871 to 1,281 sacks of ninety-five or one hundred pounds in 1904.[71] Formerly, the cornmeal had been sold to plantations along the coast, but now it was sold to the large trading concerns in Ponce. To sell its product retail, Buena Vista began packing its cornmeal in small paper bags and selling it out of the storeroom of the Vives family residence in Ponce. And because the local market had shrunk so drastically, Salvador Vives began sending several sacks of cornmeal to be sold on consignment from the San Juan warehouse of the American merchant Andrés Crosas.[72]

Logo used to identify cornmeal products from "Buena-Vista Mills." (BVA)

During these first years of the century, and as a consequence of the trying market situation, there was a considerable reduction in the estate's purchases of corn. Such suppliers as Gustavo Jordán and Eugenio Rodríguez from Guayanilla continued to be the largest suppliers, though there were also lots bought from Guayama, Lajas, Arroyo, and Aguadilla. These latter shipments would be sent to Ponce by the new railroad, which had been opened in 1892, and then carts from Buena Vista would pick up the produce after weighing it at the train station. Corn would also be ordered from several trading houses in San Juan, such as Baquero y Gándara, which imported provisions from all over the world.[73] The two parties would stay in touch by mail and telegraph, and once an agreement had been reached, Salvador Vives would place his order, which would immediately be shipped by barge or steamship around the island to the port of Ponce.[74] As always, Vives demanded the highest-quality goods: the grains all had to be the same size and be dry and free of weevils. These demands could be justified by Baquero y Gandara's selling price—$1.45 per hundredweight, not including shipping or other charges.[75]

Hired Workers after the Invasion

During the Spanish-American War in 1898, the day laborers or hired workers at Buena Vista continued their work on the estate. Little or nothing
changed, though one of the workers, Luis, had gone off with the volunteers
to fight the Americans in the mountains of Aibonito.

The labor force had shrunk somewhat; it now consisted of twenty-five to
thirty steady hired workers, but during the months when the beans, oranges, avocados, and coffee were picked and pineapples harvested, it might
swell considerably.[76] During the coffee harvest, for example, there might be
more than fifty day laborers at Buena Vista on any given day.[77] Most of
these workers picked and weeded the coffee trees—jobs that were done
constantly and simultaneously from August to December each year—but
unlike former years, when most of the coffee pickers were women, in 1904
there was only one woman among them: Isabel Aponte.[78]

From 1900 on, more care was taken in the picking of oranges than had
been the custom. Now the oranges were cut from the tree with scissors,
graded by hand, and wrapped in tissue paper and put into crates for export.

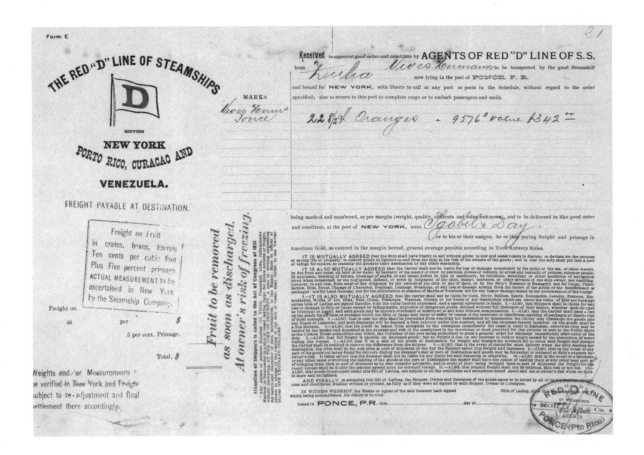

The production of cornmeal, which as we have seen dropped off sharply, required only five or six workers, of whom two were roasters (those who dried out the corn before grinding), two fed the hoppers, and the rest were cart drivers. There were other workers, fewer in number, who did specialized work, such as Carmelo Gilbee, who oversaw the coffee pickers; José Rivera, who picked avocados and gathered the palm fronds that were used in the roaster furnace, for thatching, and for other purposes on the estate; Ramón Méndez, who ran the *tahona*; Juan Díaz, the estate mule driver; Esteban Vives, the estate carpenter; and Albino Torres, who looked after the livestock. Still, it was the rare worker who did only a single job. For example, one of the workers, Candelario Maldonado, had picked *yautía* and other root vegetables during the week of October 16–22, 1904, but the following week he picked coffee on Monday, roasted corn on Tuesday and Wednesday, planted coffee on Thursday and Friday, and on Saturday went back to the cornmeal mill.[79] Much the same thing happened with Juan Cruz, who on Monday, October 30, picked coffee, on Tuesday and Wednesday planted coffee (half a day Tuesday and more than half a day on Wednesday), picked beans all day Thursday, on Friday spent three-fourths

Papers on shipment of "Vives Hermanos" (Buena Vista) oranges through the port of Ponce to Sgobel and Day, New York, 1906. (BVA)

of the day planting beans, and on Saturday picked coffee again for half a day.[80]

The fieldworker continued to be the lowest-paid employee on the estate. The coffee picker and weeder, the person who felled trees on new land, the bean and root-vegetable picker were all paid thirty cents a day. (Coffee pickers were no longer paid by the amount picked but by the day, and all pickers were paid equally.)[81] The men who worked at the ovens where the corn was roasted earned thirty-five cents a day, while cart drivers and guards earned forty. Two of the gang bosses were paid fifty cents a day. The estate's full-time carpenter, Esteban Vives, earned more than anyone else: one dollar a day. Finally, in some cases workers were still paid by the job, that is, by the amount picked, as with José Rivera, who picked avocados and earned seven cents per five hundred avocados, and Milton Marteles, who earned fifteen cents for each load of palm fronds that he brought in.

CHAPTER EIGHT

Conclusions

he history of Buena Vista—farm, cornmeal manufacturer, and coffee plantation—is a unique episode in the social and economic history of Puerto Rico. Although most histories of enterprises such as these examine trade or the production of sugar or coffee, the history of Buena Vista reveals ways of accumulating capital during the nineteenth century that were "different." It all began when a Catalonian emigrant who had lived in Venezuela, Don Salvador de Vives, an accountant by training and education, came to Puerto Rico and in 1833 founded what we might call a "truck farm," growing fruits and vegetables for sale at the marketplace in Ponce. His son, Carlos, transformed that farm into a cornmeal mill (1847), and later, his grandson Salvador converted the operation into a coffee plantation, though he never abandoned the cultivation of the fruits and vegetables that had started it all, nor the manufacture of cornmeal.

Between 1833 and 1847, the plantain was the farm's main crop and most profitable product. It was grown to supply food to the sugar haciendas along the southern coast and, to a lesser degree, the vendors at the *plaza de mercado* in the town of Ponce, never to supply the tables of the United States and Europe as was the case with sugar, coffee, and tobacco. And plantains were necessary to the south coast because commercial agriculture, dedicated to sugarcane, had pretty thoroughly replaced subsistence farming along the coast around Ponce; therefore, the mountains nearby were cleared and cultivated not for coffee growing, as in other places in Puerto Rico, but for growing fruits and vegetables.

In addition, Salvador de Vives's prosperous farm opened the doors to local political power, which until 1840 had been the domain of military officers appointed by the governor during absolutist periods or of sugar plantation owners during the constitutional periods. Don Salvador was mayor of Ponce for three terms—beginning in 1840, 1844, and 1845—and was remembered as one of those who made the greatest contribution to the wealth and welfare of the municipality. In the words of the nineteenth-century chronicler and historian Eduardo Neumann Gandía, Vives was a "progressive" mayor and a "man of integrity."[1]

Four years after founding Buena Vista, foreseeing that many of the farm's products would have no commercial future unless they were processed, Salvador de Vives installed the farm's first machinery: a coffee pulper, a rice huller, a cotton gin, and a corn mill. This last piece of machinery was his best investment. When two new mills were later installed, the former truck farm was suddenly an important cornmeal mill. Cornmeal was developed as an alternative to Spain's endless monopoly on flour in Puerto Rico. With abundant corn, low production costs, and a virtually

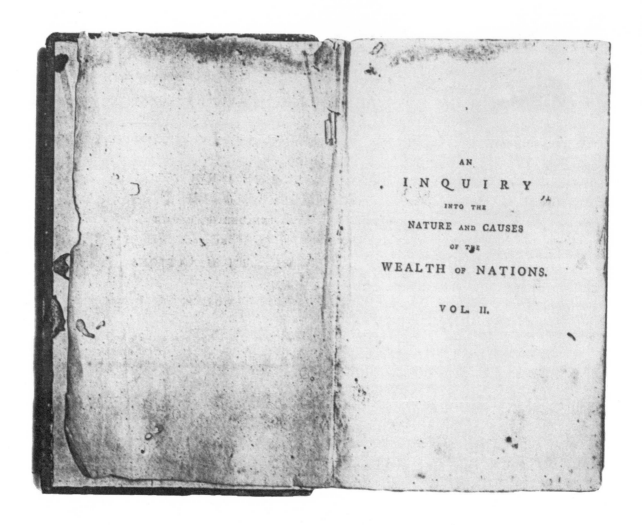

AN
INQUIRY
INTO THE
NATURE AND CAUSES
OF THE
WEALTH OF NATIONS.

VOL. II.

Among the treasures of the Buena Vista Collection are the books that belonged to the Vives family. One is this copy of *The Wealth of Nations*, 8th ed., vol. 2 (1796). This volume discusses, among others, a topic that must have been of particular interest to the development of the Buena Vista cornmeal factory: the corn trade in England.

captive market in the sugarcane plantations along the Ponce coast, Buena Vista quickly prospered.

During the first forty years of Buena Vista's existence as farm and cornmeal mill, slavery provided the estate's main labor force. In 1858 Buena Vista was a village of fifty-seven slaves, a number larger than that of most of the sugarcane plantations on the island. The purchase of slaves was the most expensive and prolonged investment Vives made and one of his principal sources of profit. In addition to working in the fields and picking fruits and vegetables, the slaves also worked as carpenters, masons, woodworkers (to produce the shingles used for roofing on the buildings on the estate), livestock workers, and cart drivers. After the abolition of slavery in Puerto Rico on March 22, 1873, most of the slaves remained on the estate, taking their former owners' last name but becoming "hired workers," semienslaved laborers—for, like many others, they would be in debt to the Vives family even before the harvest started. Nevertheless, unlike many day labor-

The Vives family subscribed to many kinds of technical journals and were in the habit of requesting catalogs from off-island manufacturers, among which were the French firm Decauville, the U.S. firm of Geo. L. Squier, and the English firm of Blackstone and Co.

ers on island coffee plantations, Buena Vista laborers were paid in legal tender and not with *riles*.

In the mid-nineteenth century, Puerto Rico was a backward agricultural colony that still allowed slavery and semislavery, lacked a stable monetary system, had no banks, and had only rudimentary manufacturing operations. The tools used by workers in the outlying country "were worthy of being included in a museum of prehistoric curiosities."[2] Many areas of the

View of the Buena Vista plaza. To the left are the old slave barracks that were later turned into the drying shed and storage house for coffee. At the right rear, the roasting shed with its smokestack, and beside it, the millhouse. The freedwoman Ma Leoncia (with cane) is to the right, walking toward the camera. (Photograph, 1904, Grace Hartzell Collection, GAPR)

island were isolated by lack of roads. And yet the history of Buena Vista, like that of many island estates, shows that its proprietors and administrators kept abreast of the latest advances in European and American science and technology and were not unaware of the fundamental laws of capitalist finance. Within twelve years of the patenting of the reaction turbine by the Scotsmen Whitelaw and Stirrat (1841), Carlos Vives ordered one, though considerably modified, from the famous West Point Foundry in Cold Spring, New York.[3] The magnet of technology led Carlos and his oldest son, Salvador, to request catalogs from the most prestigious manufacturing companies and to travel to the United States, England, and France in search of machines. But they also employed immigrants such as the engineer Robert Bennet and the blacksmith Mateo Rabainne to design, install, maintain, and improve the machines they already owned.

The overshot waterwheel and the reaction turbine that were installed at Buena Vista's mills belong to the period in which European and American capitalism demanded the greatest efficiency possible from its machinery in order to increase profits and avoid the problems of worker exhaustion, livestock maintenance, pollution, and despoliation of land. Although Buena Vista was in what was clearly an "underdeveloped country," it managed to keep up with the technological and financial advances of Europe and the United States.

In the absence of banks and with a constant monetary crisis on the island, Buena Vista's profits were reinvested in Europe through trading and investment houses in London, Paris, and Barcelona, which not only performed transactions among themselves on behalf of the Vives family but also issued letters of credit, negotiated higher dividends (which were sent to

the family every six months), and advised them on investing their funds in bonds.

The decline and eventual death of the Buena Vista cornmeal operation during the period from 1880 to 1904 was the result not of inefficiency but of the loss of the local market owing to the abolition of slavery in Puerto Rico in March 1873, and especially to importation of U.S. flour at the end of the nineteenth century. U.S. flour soon came to dominate the market, and with the U.S. invasion of Puerto Rico in 1898, the market became even more flooded with it.

But Buena Vista was spared complete disaster by the coffee boom of 1880–98. Beginning in 1880, hired workers cleared forest on Buena Vista to plant new stands of coffee trees, and Salvador Vives Navarro made coffee the estate's primary crop. He also improved old machines and installed new ones, yet he never overlooked the fruits and vegetables that had started his grandfather's business.

Diversification had always been the key to the estate's success, and thus when the first crisis in Puerto Rican coffee occurred between 1898 and 1904, Buena Vista did what many other former coffee plantations did: it became an orange grower for the New York market. This enterprise also prospered, because unlike the case of coffee, a grower could obtain credit on his orange crop, and there was a growing demand for the product in the United States.

But the history of Buena Vista was much more than the deeds of the Vives family. It would not be possible to conceive the history of the estate without examining the contribution of trusted administrators such as Domingo Roche and Agustín Dorato, who knew every aspect of the estate and its operation; engineers such as Robert Bennet, who designed machinery and advised the Vives family on the purchase of the best machines possible for their needs; manufacturers, blacksmiths, and other craftspeople such as Mateo Rabainne, the Sobrinos de Querejeta, and Robert Graham, who not only made machines and parts but also oversaw their operation; slaves and hired workers who among their many jobs picked fruits and harvested crops, ground cornmeal, and processed coffee; carpenters, masons, and plasterers who built the structures in which the machines were installed; and artisans who cut and trimmed the millstones and kept the machinery in good running order.

he "golden age" of Hacienda Buena Vista came to a sudden end at the turn of the century. As we have seen in Chapter 7, coffee was no longer as important as it had been, though the estate maintained modest production until the 1950s. Cornmeal, which had been king before coffee, lost its market altogether when it was unable to compete with the U.S. flour that filled the market in Puerto Rico. But Buena Vista continued to produce the fruits and vegetables it had always grown (plantains, bananas, corn, avocados, and so on), though on a smaller scale than previously.

Salvador, Guillermo, and Carlos Vives Navarro (the last generation of the Vives family to be discussed in this book) and their descendants decided to leave commercial agriculture and follow other paths, although they did continue to visit Hacienda Buena Vista as a "weekend farm." Hunting within the shadowy forest was one of their favorite pastimes.

There is a great deal of the fascinating collection of documents in the Buena Vista Archives still to be studied, especially those documents that pertain to the first half of the twentieth century. Unfortunately, they are not as rich in detail as those used here; most are account books, which one day will give us a good idea of the period during which Buena Vista began to languish.

Unlike what happened to other estates in other parts of the island, Buena Vista was never divided up because of financial reverses or constant haggling over inheritances; it remained whole until 1958, with the same amount of land as at its founding, and with the same factory buildings, machines, houses, barracks, and canals that had been built in the years of the cornmeal boom.

Buena Vista, then, was still intact that year when the Administration of Social Programs of the government of Puerto Rico expropriated most of its land to divide up and redistribute. The Vives family kept eighty-seven *cuerdas*, which included all the buildings around the main plaza—land the Conservation Trust of Puerto Rico was to purchase twenty-six years later in order to restore the buildings and grounds and establish the island's first Living Museum of Art and Science.

Recent view of a part of the old entrance to Buena Vista from the *camino real*, or colonial highway, that crossed the island. At the rear is the first millhouse, where the coffee mill is today, and beside it, the roasting shed. To the right can be seen the rails on which the coffee-drying drawers roll out. (Photograph, Jorge Carbonell, 1988)

1821	Salvador de Vives, his wife, Isabel Díaz, and his son, Carlos, disembark in Ponce after their voyage from Puerto Cabello, Venezuela. They are accompanied by two slaves.
	Salvador de Vives appointed to the clerk's office of the municipality of Ponce.
1833	Buena Vista founded, at first as a farm on which plantains, sweet potatoes, bananas, cacao, and other fruits and vegetables, especially root vegetables, are grown.
1837	Purchase of first machinery for Buena Vista: rice huller, cotton gin, coffee pulper, corn grinder.
1840–45	Salvador de Vives mayor of Ponce for three terms (1840, 1844, 1845).
1845	Death of Salvador de Vives; his only son, Carlos, becomes administrator of the estate.
1845–47	Construction of owners' residence, slave barracks, warehouse, first cornmeal millhouse, roasting shed, and canal for water to power mill.
1847	Governor Arístegui authorizes Carlos Vives to take water from the Canas River, later to return it to the streambed.
1850–73	The bonanza years of Buena Vista cornmeal.
1851	Construction completed on Buena Vista aqueduct.
1853	During the summer, Carlos Vives travels to New York, later ordering a hydraulic turbine from the West Point Foundry in Cold Spring. James Finlay, representative of the Whitelaw patent in the United States, along with the inventor himself, take part in the design, construction, and installation of the turbine.
1854	In January, the turbine, cornmeal mill, and all other necessary parts arrive in Ponce.
	In July, construction of turbine shaft and turbine housing completed, along with second millhouse.
1855–56	Cholera epidemic: 476 slaves die in Ponce; slaves at Buena Vista not affected.
	Year of greatest profits on Buena Vista cornmeal.
1855–60	Buena Vista cornmeals win prizes at Puerto Rican Exposition.
1859	Sale of forty-seven of the estate's fifty-seven slaves for thirty-six thousand silver pesos.
	New family residence built in Ponce; value, thirty-six thousand silver pesos.
1867	Hurricane San Narciso strikes Puerto Rico; damage to Hacienda Buena Vista estimated at forty-five hundred pesos.
1868	Independence movement in Lares fails.

1869   Carlos Vives's first investment of capital with Murrieta, London; Vives family investments will be made with several investment houses in Europe.

1870–90   The coffee years. Planting of coffee trees on a larger scale at Buena Vista; Buena Vista no longer a farm, now becoming a true hacienda.

1872   Death of Carlos Vives; his oldest son, Salvador, assumes control of the estate.

1873	Abolition of slavery in Puerto Rico. Buena Vista frees twenty slaves but immediately hires sixteen freedmen and -women. Freed slaves and other day laborers become *alquilados*, or "hired workers."
1878	Several pieces of the old pulping machinery are replaced.
1882	New pulping machinery, manufactured by Sobrinos de Querejeta, Ponce, installed.
1886	Hurricane San Felipe.
1887	Reign of Terror against autonomists, *independentistas*, and suspected autonomists and *independentistas* in Ponce.
	Old slave barracks converted to coffee-drying shed.
1892	Commercial coffee mill built; first cornmeal mill eliminated.
1893	Coffee production totals 272 cwt.; one decade earlier, production had been 100 cwt.
1897	Coffee production increases to 335 cwt.
1898	Buena Vista continues to produce more than forty commercial agricultural products: diversification is the key to its success.
	Spanish-American War.
	United States invades Puerto Rico at Guánica; three days later, American troops disembark in Ponce. Vives family moves to the estate to protect themselves from the bombardment; no radical changes at Buena Vista.
	Three American soldiers photographed at Buena Vista.
1899	Hurricane San Ciriaco wipes out 60 percent of the island coffee crop.
1900	After San Ciriaco catastrophe, Buena Vista produces only 78 cwt. of coffee.
	Price of coffee drops precipitously; recovery of Puerto Rican coffee industry is made very difficult.
	Puerto Rican cornmeals cannot compete with U.S. flour; market shrinks drastically.
1904	Cultivation of oranges for the U.S. market begins on a large scale at Buena Vista.

Accounting of existing items in the large residence

No. Article

2 Mahogany beds in good condition
1 Iron bed
3 Mattresses
4 Cot frames
1 Chifforobe
2 ?, one in good condition
4 Three boxes and one trunk (one with newspapers)
28 Wicker chairs
1 Wicker rocking chair
11 Wooden chairs, including one child's chair
1 Complete kerosene lantern
1 Candlestick with globe [chimney] (i.e., danger) [sic, probably for "dangerous"]
2 More ditto
1 "Guardabrisa" [sic, probably globe for lamp]
1 Crystal [or glass] globe (that looks like fermenter)
1 Portrait of His Holiness the Bishop
1 Magnifying mirror on stand
1 and another on tin tube
1 Wall clock
7 Mining tools
1 Bellows
1 Small dressing table with the good [?, sic]
1 Desk
3 Small wicker trays
1 Small drawing compass
1 Pair of scissors for trimming wicks
1 Set of checkers
5 Tables
1 Sideboard

1 Washbowl
1 Water filter and stone, with all necessaries
1 Sofa
8 Pictures in parlor
2 Round mirrors
1 and square
2 Tin spittoons
1 Wooden bathtub
1 Small fine sieve [perhaps sifter]
1 Canvas hammock [probably stretcher] for the sick
2 Vases
1 Roll or piece of screen for sieve
1 Rosary, with several silver medallions
1 Bell
   Several bottles of medicine

Miscellaneous

4 Wineglasses
4 Small glasses
1 China sugar bowl
1 and one crystal
7 White cups
7 Small saucers
1 Butter dish
1 Large cup
1 Soup tureen
8 Plates
3 Serving bowls
3 Serving plates [or platters]
1 Crystal bottle
10 Full bottles of liquor
2 Large bottles of candy
1 Small ditto
2 Cans of sardines
2 Books of cigarette papers
2 Buckets

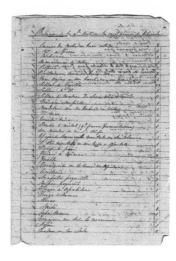

1   Coffeepot
2   Castile pots [?]
1   Mortar
1   Wooden oven spatula
1   Small funnel
2   Danesas [?]
     One barrel and one grater

Overseer's room

4   Large silver spoons
1   Shotgun
1   Duster
1   Lamp
1   Cask of Epsom salt
2   Large files [for filing metal, etc.] and a level
1   Coping saw
1   Iron tool for scraping barrels
1   Machete
9   Plates for the ———
2   Glasses
1   Washbowl
3   Cups and saucers
1   Book of medicine
1   Ditto confessional
1   Sugar bowl
1   Punch bowl
1   Seal for marking plantains
1   Cord for measuring land
1   Table with two tablecloths

Kitchen

2   Large pots
2   others, smaller
2   others, small
2   Coffeepots, one with top
2   Mortars with pestles
1   Table

Animals

30   Draft oxen
2   others, calves
11   Large mares
3   Fillies
1   Foal
2   Burros, one small, one large
1   Female ditto
3   Male

Machinery and warehouse

2   Machines, with accessories, for grinding corn
3   others for shelling corn, one iron
1   other, for hulling rice, iron
3   Large platform scales, complete
1   and another small one
2   Jacks, for raising millstones, with all necessaries
1   Winnower, with five sieves [or sifters]
24   Hammers for trimming millstones
6   Hogsheads of white coffee
1½   Barrel and a half, coffee *en collor* [?]
1   Large table (portable), complete
1½   One and a half sheets of roofing iron
22   Pine planks
6   Large pine timbers
1   Large tin funnel
3   Grain-stirring poles
1   One washtub with tin scoop for cornmeal
2   Old sieves from the machinery
2   Small fine sieves in wood frame
3   Burlap tarpaulins for laying out coffee

Carts, wagons

3	Wagons, with wooden sides
1	other, with palings
1	Sideboard for wagon with palings
4	Wagon chains
9	Yokes
1	Chain for chaining up dog
1	Mule collar, with chain
38	Metal axle rings for wheels
14	Rims
2	Mahogany iron tools [*sic*] for pulling screen
2	Shackles, one with chain
9	Bars, iron
2	Small planks [or perhaps sheets of metal] to use as tops for bins
1	Millstone in bad condition
1	Seal for marking Salvador Vives's animals, and another small one, Carlos Vives, for marking horns

Carpentry tools

2	Large saws, one new
1	Crosscut saw
2	Hacksaw in good condition
2	others, old
1	more, small, thin
1	Half wood-plane
1	Small plane
2	½-inch drill bits
1	and another 1 ¼ inches
2	Wrenches
1	Pair pliers
2	Hand adzes
1	Mason's hammer
1	Sawhorse
2	Clamps
1	Chisel
1	Cooper's blade

1	New farming adze
1	and another old one
1	Hand axe
1	Brush
1	Drawing compass
1	T square
1	Carpenter's line
	Several instruments or mining [*sic*] mentioned at beginning
1	New millstone
1	New pair scissors

Tools

11	Hoes in use
20	others, old
14	Machetes in use
20	others, old
8	Axes
3	Large mallets [sledgehammers?]
4	Picks
10	Shovels
1	Hooks for weighing barrels
3	Peacocks
7	Ducks
2	Guineas
	Roosters and several hens
1	Coffee-shelling machine, middling condition
1	Press, not in use
	Other machines not in use
3	Men's saddles
3	Pairs of saddle baskets, good
2	Half *almudes*

Entered as existing in accord with statement of this accounting—

Man. Hernández
March 13, 1863

FOREWORD

1. Archaeological reconstruction was first used to study the lives of slaves and former slaves in the British Caribbean. See, for example, Mintz, *Caribbean Transformations*, pp. 157–79; Handler and Longe, *Plantation Slavery in Barbados*; and, more recently, Douglas V. Armstrong, *The Old Village and the Great House*. In Puerto Rico, this type of work has been carried out by Díaz Hernández, *Castañer*, and O'Neill, *La industria cafetalera de Puerto Rico*.

2. My own *Capitalism in Colonial Puerto Rico*, although compiled in a very different way from Baralt's, falls in this category. Picó, *1898: La guerra después de la guerra*, opened the way for the examination of local reactions to the change in sovereignty in 1898 that continues to this day.

3. Rigau-Pérez, "The Introduction of Smallpox Vaccine in 1803," and Camuñas Madera, *Epidemias, plagas y marginación*.

INTRODUCTION

1. Letter from Carlos Vives to the City Council [Ayuntamiento] of Ponce, April 8, 1847, BVA.

CHAPTER ONE

1. The surname used for this first generation of the Vives family in Puerto Rico will be "de Vives," as was customary during the period. By the time his children reached majority, however, they were known as "Vives," and I will use that surname throughout the rest of the book. [Trans.]

2. The "municipality of Ponce" is, in Spanish, the *partido de Ponce*. The term *partido*, according to de la Rosa Martínez, *Lexicón histórico-documental de Puerto Rico*, was used from the early years of the colony to refer to the two major divisions of the island: the Partido de Puerto Rico on the eastern half of the island, and the Partido de San Germán on the western. Later, however, the term was used to refer to the various further subdivisions that were under a single municipal, ecclesiastical, or electoral jurisdiction; clearly, these were not "municipalities," "counties," or "parishes" in the English senses of those words, but a government division that has no clear English synonym. By the time Vives and his family arrived, the term was being used to refer to the area governed by the municipal government, even though this might not be a "town" or a "city" in the centered and concentrated way we tend to think of "municipalities" today. The term *partido* has generally been translated as "municipality," and I have chosen to follow that practice, while reminding the reader that it was a division of island government that does not fit the general U.S. divisions of city, county, state, and so forth. I will not use the word "municipality" in any but this restricted technical way; where other, less specific Spanish words referring to areas or regions occur, I will use the less technical words "area," "region," and so on or, if to cities and towns, those words. [Trans.]

3. In the late eighteenth century, the lands of the municipality of Ponce were made up of *cotos*, *criaderos*, and *hatos*, which were both communal and individually owned. All these words indicate parcels of land on which cattle roamed more or less freely. Scarano

(*Sugar and Slavery*, p. 40) reports that the *hatos* could not legally be fenced off. A beater and his dogs would watch over and check the cattle and deliver them when called upon to their respective owners. From the time of the Real Cédula (royal decree) of 1778, which ordered the redistribution of land and allowed those who had worked land owned by the Crown to hold clear title to it, these holdings began to be abolished, a practice that made possible (after a period of conflicts between the small, generally communal landholders and the new owners of the large haciendas) the development of the thriving and land-hungry Puerto Rican sugar industry at the beginning of the nineteenth century. See Fray Iñigo Abbad y Lasierra, *Historia geográfica, civil y natural de la Isla de San Juan Bautista de Puerto Rico*, p. 142; Córdova, *Memorias geográfica, histórica, económica y estadística de la isla de Puerto Rico*, 2:160; Neumann Gandía, *Verdadera y auténtica historia*, p. 68. Scarano gives a brief overview of the changes brought by the 1778 Cédula Real in *Sugar and Slavery*, pp. 113–15.

4. Lee, *An Island Grows*, pp. 11–12.

5. Eugenio María de Hostos, *Obras completas*, 14:334.

6. Ponce was declared a municipality in 1692. At that time it was one of the three administrative subdivisions of San Germán.

7. Charles, *La economía haitiana y su vía de desarrollo*, p. 30. The virtual halt of sugar production in French Saint-Domingue (Haiti) created a tremendous shortage of sugar on the international market and a consequent increase in price. The lack of production in Haiti was due to the slave revolution that broke out in 1789 and culminated in independence for Haiti in 1804.

8. Cole, *Wholesale Commodity Prices in the United States, 1700–1861*, vol. 1. The prices quoted are the average price for the decade on the Philadelphia market.

9. Valle, *Memoria, presentada a la Junta Calificadora*, p. 4.

10. Muscovado sugar, or "moscovado," as Scarano terms it in *Sugar and Slavery*, is raw or "crude" sugar, before refining—the first solid precipitate formed in the sugar-boiling process. The sugar as sold would generally be centrifuged to remove liquid, though it would still have a very high moisture content, but the term "muscovado" could also refer to uncentrifuged sugar.

11. Francisco Scarano, "Inmigración y estructura de clases: Los hacendados de Ponce, 1815–1845," in Scarano, ed., *Inmigración*, p. 27. For an excellent description of the development of sugar cultivation and production in Ponce, see Scarano, *Sugar and Slavery*.

12. Córdova, *Memorias*, 2:261.

13. Scarano, *Sugar and Slavery*, p. 26.

14. Flinter, *Account*, p. 176.

15. Scarano, "Inmigración," p. 25.

16. Córdova, *Memorias*, 2:252.

17. Ultramar, Legajo 1069, expediente 22, March 12, 1843, NHA.

18. Córdova, *Memorias*, 2:252. This was impossible because sugarcane had been cultivated for more than two hundred years in Ponce. For example, in the early eighteenth century, Sgt. Miguel de Miranda installed a *trapiche* (a cane press) on his farm in Barrio Bucaná, where he had a small stand of sugarcane. In 1702, Críspulo Toro brought another molasses mill to Barrio Pámpanos. See Gil-Bermejo, *Panorama histórico*, p. 124.

19. Flinter, *Account*, p. 30.

20. Ibid. Córdova makes the same observation (*Memorias*, 2:252).

21. Córdova, *Memorias*, 2:252.

22. "Balanza Mercantil de Puerto Rico" [annual trade summary], 1839, CHR. In 1839, 113 of the 208 ships that anchored in Ponce were of U.S. registry, and only 41 were Spanish.

23. "Charles de Ronceray al Honorable Lewis Cass, Secretario de Estado, EEUU"

[Charles Ronceray to the Honorable Lewis Cass, secretary of state of the United States], San Juan, January 16, 1860, *Despachos de los cónsules norteamericanos en Puerto Rico*, doc. 250, 1:425, CHR.

24. James Bandinell, *Some Accounts of the Trade of Slaves from Africa*, p. 148. For the history of the slave trade in Puerto Rico and its abolition, see Morales Carrión, *Auge y decadencia de la trata negrera en Puerto Rico (1820–1860)*.

25. Lee, *An Island Grows*, p. 13.

26. Darío de Ormachea, "Memoria acerca de la agricultura, el comercio y las rentas internas de la isla de Puerto Rico, 1847," in Fernández Méndez, ed., *Crónicas de Puerto Rico*, pp. 429–34.

27. Scarano, *Sugar and Slavery*, pp. 145–55; Pérez Vega, *El cielo y la tierra en sus manos*, p. 99.

28. Obras Públicas, Memorias Descriptivas: Ponce, June 30, 1846, José E. Ortiz, mayor, GAPR. For the English names of the trees listed here, see the standard work in the field: Little, Wadsworth, and Marrero, *Arboles comunes de Puerto Rico y las Islas Vírgenes*. Drawings by Frances W. Horne.

29. Ilustre Ayuntamiento de Ponce, March 17, 1844, Salvador de Vives, BVA. This order was based on a previous one dated August 4, 1824, and issued by the governor-superior of the Island of Puerto Rico, Don Miguel de la Torre (Circular no. 493).

30. Caja 4b, January 4, 1876, PMA. Here, we see that in 1876 the Ponce delegation to the Philadelphia World's Fair took samples of certain island trees—the *capá blanco* and *capá prieto*, the *húcar* (oxhorn bucida or "bullywood" tree), the *guanábana* (or soursop, a fruit tree), the *guayacán*, the *almácigo* (the West Indian birch, turpentine tree, or naked-Indian tree), and the *jobo* (either the ambarella [golden apple] or the hog plum tree, both fruit trees, though the former is the most popular in Puerto Rico)—to be exhibited as trees good for burning to make charcoal.

31. In 1828, there were 171 such artisans in Ponce, 150 in Mayagüez, 117 in Guayama, and 112 in Arecibo.

32. Fortuño Janeiro, *Album histórico de Ponce*, p. 112; García and Quintero, *Desafío y solidaridad*, pp. 19–22.

33. Cruz Monclova, *Historia de Puerto Rico*, 1:79. In addition, this decree exempted immigrant landholders for ten years from all personal tax and from the tax on slaves, at the end of which period they would pay only one peso per year for each slave.

34. See, in this regard, Scarano, *Sugar and Slavery*, pp. 86ff.

35. The given names of these men appear here in Hispanicized form because this form is used in all the official and in most unofficial records of the time.

36. "Cuaderno de Riqueza Agrícola de Ponce, 1848," PMA. In 1847, there were fifty-two sugar haciendas in Ponce, with their respective cane-crushing equipment. Of these, forty-three had crushing wheels turned by oxen and four by the scanty water energy of the valley; only the haciendas of the foreigners Oppenheimer, Voigt, Gilbee, and Dubocq had steam-driven grinding equipment.

37. Scarano, "Inmigración," p. 54.

38. See Pérez Vega, "Las sociedades mercantiles de Ponce."

39. Legajo 518, expediente 366: "Población del partido de Ponce," PMA.

40. Córdova, *Memorias*, 3:437.

41. Marazzi, *Impacto de la inmigración a Puerto Rico*, p. 56.

42. Córdova, *Memorias*, 3:437.

43. Brau, *Fundación de Ponce*, p. 34.

44. Ormachea, "Memoria," p. 437. A decree of June 18, 1813, made the use of the Venezuelan currency, the *macuquina*, legal, although it had been used for some time already on the island. The *macuquina* was a more or less round gold or silver coin minted

with the seal of the Royal Treasury. Its intrinsic value varied considerably, however, because it did not have beaded edges and thus could be easily "trimmed," or altered.

45. Pérez Vega, *El cielo y la tierra en sus manos*, pp. 73–83.

46. Porrata Doria, *Estado actual de Ponce: 1899*, p. 20; William Armstrong, *Manuscrito sobre algunos pueblos de la isla*, p. 187.

47. *El Ponceño*, September 11, 1852.

CHAPTER TWO

1. Visit of Governor Méndez Vigo to Ponce, March 27, 1841, BVA. At the urging of the mayor of Ponce, who at this time was Salvador de Vives, Méndez Vigo ordered the Magüeyes road and bridges rebuilt.

2. An *estancia*, or "farm," differed from a *hacienda*, even when they both grew corn, coffee, or sugarcane, in that an estancia had no machinery or equipment for processing its products into cornmeal, finished coffee, or molasses or sugar, whereas a hacienda did. An *estancia de frutos menores* was what has generally been called a "truck farm" in the United States, though of course the fruits and vegetables grown were quite different.

3. "Don Carlos Vives al ilustre ayuntamiento de Ponce," n.d., BVA, copy. In this letter, Carlos Vives points out that this paved road, twelve *varas* wide and twelve miles long, was built by his slaves.

4. The Canas River rises in the island's central mountain range, in the place known as Yagrumo, from several springs. Its main confluence is in the upper region of Barrio Guaraguao, from which it descends through Corral Viejo and Barrio Magüeyes. At the end of the nineteenth century its mouth was at Boca de los Meros, between Haciendas Reparada and Matilde, on the south coast.

5. Map of Barrio Magüeyes, 1873, PMA. The description included in the text is drawn from that map. In 1821, Magüeyes was one of twenty-two barrios into which the municipality of Ponce was divided. Magüeyes is to the east of Barrio Marueños, south of Barrio Guaraguao, and west of Barrio Tibes. At the end of the nineteenth century its land area was 4,362 *cuerdas*, or approximately 4,231 acres. See also "Pretendientes del camino a Magüeyes," December 18, 1837, BVA.

6. Salvador de Vives was born in 1784, the legitimate son of Quirse Vives and Ana María Rodó. The province of Gerona is located at the confluence of the Ter and Ona Rivers on the road from Barcelona to France (Isidro Colón, *Nociones de geografía universal*, p. 69). According to Estela Cifre de Loubriel, Gerona was home to the third largest number of Spanish emigrants (*La inmigración a Puerto Rico durante el siglo XIX*, p. lxxvi).

7. "Real Certificación para poder empezar estudios de Filosofía," Royal University of Toledo, November 24, 1804, BVA. He graduated in 1808 (notary attorney Atanasio García, Secretary, Royal University of Toledo).

8. "Hacienda Nacional de las Provincias de Venezuela," José Ramón de Gorbea, October 31, 1822, BVA. Copy.

9. Ibid. In 1814 Vives had been part of the Squadron of the Constitution organized in 1813 to defend the Spanish flag.

10. Certification signed by Luis Linares, lieutenant of justice, Villa de Cura, Venezuela, April 20, 1821, BVA.

11. "Don Julián de Ibarra, Ministro Principal de Real Hacienda y Guerra del Ejército Pacificador de estas provincias de mando de Venezuela Excelentísimo General en Jefe, don Pablo Morillo, Certificación," April 27, 1820, BVA. Copy.

12. Ibid.

13. "Gobernadores Españoles: Concesión de Licencias de José Aleutiza[,] Contador y

Decano Propietario de Cuenta del Distrito de la Villa de Cura, interinamente, 27 de junio de 1821, a don Salvador de Vives," GAPR.

14. Diego de Alegría, Ponce, December 29, 1825, BVA. Offices were sold at public auction to the highest bidder. In this case, the price was twenty-seven hundred pesos, of which Vives paid twenty-two hundred, leaving a debt of five hundred. See de la Rosa, *Lexicón histórico-documental de Puerto Rico*, p. 101, s.v. "*remate.*"

15. Documents of Salvador de Vives, "América septentrional, Isla de Puerto Rico," June 30, 1841, BVA:

Date of Purchase	*Cuerdas*	Seller
Aug. 19, 1833	100.	Ramón Luna
Sept. 13, 1833	133.	Tomás Román
Apr. 5, 1834	30.	José Guadalupe
May 7, 1834	58.	José M. Rodríguez
July 9, 1834	37	Ramón Luna
Dec. 16, 1834	42.	Manuel de Jesús
Dec. 3, 1834	36.5	Ramón Luna and Rosa Alvarado
Aug. 21, 1835	30.	Cayetano de Ribas
Sept. 9, 1835	16	José Santos Rodríguez
Total	482.5	

16. Legajo 119, caja 112b, 1863, PMA. Magüeyes and Pastillo were the two barrios that paid the least amount of agricultural tax to the Ponce municipal government in 1863.

17. I stress the fact that he *bought* the land, because he might have acquired it from the Junta de Terrenos Baldíos, or Vacant-Land Board, which under the Cédula de Gracias of 1815 granted land to foreigners who brought capital with them when they immigrated to Puerto Rico.

18. These were not the long, relatively sickle-shaped bananas known to nontropical consumers but rather a native type called the *mafafo*, a short, thick, stubby banana with a heady, distinctive flavor and a thin skin that makes it unsuitable for long-distance transport.

19. Renato de Grossourdy, *El médico botánico criollo*, vol. 1, pt. 2, p. 139; RAIC, no. 8 (March 25, 1892): 93.

20. "A large Relation of Port Ricco Voyage; written as is reported, by that learned man and reverend Divine Doctor Eglambie," in *Hakluytus Posthumus, or Purchas His Pilgrims*, by Samuel Purchas, p. 95. The organization of the volumes in this edition of *Purchas* causes Layfield's relation (included in "Doctor Eglambie") to be in volume 16, whereas the title page indicates that this text is chapter 3, section 4, of the sixth book of the second part of the entire work *Purchas His Pilgrims*.

21. "Carta del Obispo de Puerto Rico don Fray Damián López de Haro, a Juan Diez de la Calle, con una relación muy curiosa de su viaje y otras cosas. Año 1644," in Fernández Méndez, ed., *Crónicas de Puerto Rico*, p. 165.

22. Ledrú, *Relación del viaje a la isla de Puerto Rico*, p. 113.

23. Fray Iñigo Abbad, *Historia*, p. 234.

24. Annual report, 1845, BVA. At Buena Vista, as on many haciendas in Puerto Rico, a cultivated plot of land was called a "lot," or *pieza*. On the Schomburg map of Buena Vista in the Introduction, these *piezas* are denominated by the abbreviation *pza*.

25. Córdova, *Memorias*, 2:257.

26. "Fondo Municipal de Guayama, Libro de Actas," March 2, 1843, GAPR.

27. Baralt, *Esclavos rebeldes (1795–1848)*, pp. 91–100. Although this collective challenge by the slaves to white rule and the institution of slavery itself failed, of all slave uprisings and threats of uprisings, this one was most unsettling to those concerned about the is-

land's public safety and security, for several reasons: because of the large number of slaves that knew about the plan; because of promises of support from Haiti and some whites; because of the concentration of free blacks and *bozales* (African slaves) in Ponce; because of the huge military force that moved on the municipality once the conspiracy was discovered; and finally because of the large number of slaves eventually punished and executed.

28. Letter from Domingo Roche to Joaquín Mayoral, Ponce, October 1, 1856, BVA. In this letter, the overseer Roche says that even though the plantain crop has been smaller this year because of a lack of water, he has been able to send most of his plantains to haciendas in Ponce.

29. Account Book, Buena Vista, 1847–55, index, BVA. From May 1850 to May 1851, Oppenheimer purchased fifty-four loads, of which only three contained two thousand plantains, while the rest contained twenty-four hundred.

30. Letter from Domingo Roche to Joaquín Mayoral, Ponce, October 1, 1856, BVA.

31. "Memoria topográfica de Ponce," Department of Public Works, June 30, 1846, prepared by José F. Ortiz, GAPR.

32. Scarano, *Sugar and Slavery*, p. 107.

33. Register, January 17, 1846, BVA.

34. Promissory note, "Leonardo Morel, Escribano Real y Público," June 2, 1837, BVA. Although he did not pay interest, Vives had to waive his rights under Law no. 9, par. 1.5, prohibiting embargoes. The loan was paid off in its entirety within two years, on May 20, 1839.

35. Claudio Pesquera, customs administrator, Ponce, January 25, 1837, BVA. Carlos, the son of Salvador de Vives and Isabel Díaz, had been born in Venezuela in 1811.

36. Beatriz del Cueto, "Hacienda Buena Vista: Narrativo de la casa principal de vivienda," San Juan, 1987, CTPR.

37. Letter from Carlos Vives to the City Council [Ayuntamiento] of Ponce, April 8, 1847, BVA.

38. Letter from Governor Arístegui to Carlos Vives, June 12, 1847, BVA.

39. Mumford, *Technics and Civilization*, pp. 113–14. See also Strandh, *A History of the Machine*, p. 96; Braudel, *Civilization and Capitalism*, 1:353–58; and Reynolds, *Stronger Than a Hundred Men*, pp. 17–18.

40. Mumford, *Technics and Civilization*, p. 114.

41. Gimpel, *The Medieval Machine*, pp. 12–13.

42. Herman Kellenbenz, "La industria en la Europa moderna (1500–1750)," in Fontana, ed., *La industrialización europea*, p. 20.

43. Reynolds, *Stronger Than a Hundred Men*, pp. 266–67.

44. Although iron wheels had been built since the Middle Ages, it was not until the nineteenth century, when metal became cheap, that such wheels became common. Ibid., p. 286.

45. Sued Badillo, *Guayama*, p. 35.

46. Gil-Bermejo, *Panorama histórico*, p. 120.

47. Jhoan Melgarejo, "Memoria y descripción de la isla de Puerto Rico mandada a hacer por S. A. el Rey Don Felipe II en al año de 1582, y sometida por el ilustre capitán Jhoan Melgarejo, Gobernador y Justicia Mayor en esta ciudad e isla," in Fernández Méndez, ed., *Crónicas de Puerto Rico*, p. 118.

48. Gil-Bermejo, *Panorama histórico*, p. 120. In 1702, the old San Luis de Canóvanas sugar mill was one of the few in operation moved by hydraulic force.

49. Darío de Ormachea, "Memoria acerca de la agricultura, el comercio y las rentas internas de la isla de Puerto Rico, 1847," in Fernández Méndez, ed., *Crónicas de Puerto Rico*, p. 434.

50. "Cuaderno de riqueza agrícola, año de 1848," PMA.

51. Scarano, *Sugar and Slavery*, p. 215 nn. 27, 31. Scarano calculates the "average estimated production of the five water-powered plantations existing [in Ponce] in 1845" to be "a mere 111 tons."

52. Today when the water reaches the machine shed, the operator has three options: direct the water onto the waterwheel; let the water run on into a canal that leads to another, wider canal in the farmyard; or turn it directly into a tailrace channel that takes the water back into the creek. This last option was chosen most after 1854, when only the second cornmeal mill, run by the turbine, was used.

53. Vallejo, *Tratado sobre el movimiento y las aplicaciones de las aguas*, pp. 146–56.

54. BVA. The order, placed in September 1847, specifies the following parts:

1. One (1) pair 46-inch mill wheels (toothed)
2. One (1) mill-wheel propulsion axle
3. One (1) tightening screw
4. One (1) sheet and six (6) bars [of iron]
5. 50 floor tiles
6. 25 feet metal screen
7. Tentering bearing for runner stone

Total cost, including transportation, import tax, and currency conversion, was $431.57.

55. Ramón Tarrats (and, later, the Tarrats estate) was the owner of a 250-*cuerda* sugar-cane hacienda with a water-powered cane-grinding mill in Barrio Magüeyes. It seems to have had a turbine similar to that at Buena Vista. Agricultural Census, November 1863, PMA.

56. United States Patent Office, "James Whitelaw and James Stirrat, Improvement of Water Wheels . . . , No. 3,153, July 3, 1843." The inventor was James Whitelaw, and the manufacturer, James Stirrat. Stirrat had a thread factory and a bleaching factory, in which he apparently installed the first Whitelaw, or Scotch, turbine in Scotland.

57. Ibid., p. 3 of patent. See Knight, *American Mechanical Dictionary*, p. 231; Safford and Hamilton, *The American Mixed Flow Turbine and Its Setting*, U.S.A. paper no. 1502, American Society of Civil Engineers, May 3, 1922, pp. 1330–39. See also Johnson and O'Reilly, "The Barker's Turbine at Hacienda Buena Vista," p. 58.

58. The first turbine, or "reaction wheel," was attributed to Dr. Barker. Called a "Barker's Mill," it was apparently first mentioned in print in Desaguliers's *Experimental Philosophy* of 1743. Johnson and O'Reilly describe the Barker's Mill in the following way: "It worked on the principle of pure reaction, the wheel moving as the liquid under pressure escaped. . . . Barker's Mill consisted essentially of an upright column or tube with two hollow arms at the lower end, like an inverted T. The end of each arm was perforated tangentially so that a jet could issue forth and drive the entire T, in a manner comparable to the common lawn sprinkler of today" ("The Barker's Turbine at Hacienda Buena Vista," pp. 55–56).

59. Letter from William Kemble to Carlos Vives, New York, August 8, 1853, BVA.

60. Bishop, *A History of American Manufacturers*, pp. 486–88; Depew, *1795–1895: One Hundred Years of American Commerce*, 2:337.

61. Ely, *Cuando reinaba su majestad el azúcar*, pp. 518–24.

62. Letter from Robert Parrott to Robert Bennet, Cold Spring, N.Y., December 5, 1853, BVA.

63. Ibid., and another from James Finlay, Cold Spring, N.Y., December 3, 1853, BVA. See also U.S. Patent Office, "James Whitelaw and James Stirrat of Paisley, England. Assignors to James Finlay, of New York, N.Y. Patent No. 3,153," dated July 3, 1843.

64. Finlay to Bennet, December 3, 1853.

65. Johnson and O'Reilly, "The Barker's Turbine at Hacienda Buena Vista," p. 58. A good description of the improvement introduced by Doble in 1893 appears in Strandh, *A History of the Machine*, p. 107.

66. Bill of lading (September 27, 1853, New York) for items shipped by Maitland and Phelps Co. on the *Velocity* to Sr. Carlos Vives, BVA.

67. Bill of lading (New York, December 6, 1853) for items shipped by Maitland and Phelps Co. on the *Alexander Mitchell* to Carlos Vives, BVA.

68. Letter from William Kemble to Carlos Vives, New York, August 8, 1853, BVA.

69. Contract between Ramón Rosaly and Carlos Vives, April 19, 1854; witness, Miguel Font. Second contract between Vives and Florentino Betines and Agustín Belmi, Ponce, July 16, 1854. Both in BVA.

70. Robert Bennet to Carlos Vives; examples are bills dated July 16, 1859, October 1860, October 22, 1863, October 5, 1864, and October 22, 1864, Ponce, BVA.

71. Betz Penot to Carlos Vives, Paris, July 12, 1862, BVA. It is possible that this was a mill that separated the corn's starchy matter from the oils that permeated it. This explanation appears in a newspaper clipping that Carlos Vives kept in his diary. The purpose of the separation was to kill a microscopic fungus that grows in the crease in the kernel. Unfortunately, the clipping does not indicate the source.

72. Moreno Fraginals, *El ingenio*, 1:250.

73. Box 193, Patents, in Documents, Department of Public Works, GAPR. Patents on inventions were recognized in Ponce for the U.S. inventors Davidson, Gallagher, and Brea, who invented a machine for moving the sugarcane squeezings, or *guarapo*, from one boiler to another by means of steam; for Francisco Salich for a weeding machine; for the English inventor Darton for a machine for making wine and beer; for Ricardo Steward for a steam-powered process for manufacturing sugar and a machine for applying carbonic acid to the cane juice; and for Otto Hoffman for an apparatus for pumping water or *guarapo*.

74. Scarano, *Sugar and Slavery*, p. 98.

75. Legajo 318, expediente 6, December 1, 1853, PMA.

76. Annual report, 1869, BVA. According to this report, "the gear-teeth are trimmed, addressing the smaller end of the channel, by striking with the hammer always straight, and the blade likewise, striking hard in the center and more softly toward the edge. . . . The channels should be straight, from smaller end to larger, and to a depth sufficient to let pass a kernel of ordinary corn."

77. Invoice, Robert Bennet to Carlos Vives, July 16, 1859, BVA.

78. Joaquín Mayoral to Carlos Vives, March 4, 1856, BVA.

79. Note from Domingo Roche to Joaquín Mayoral, January 10, 1856, BVA. Roche's salary was fifteen pesos per month.

80. Letter from Joaquín Mayoral to Carlos Vives, April 20, 1856, BVA.

CHAPTER THREE

1. Braudel, *Civilization and Capitalism*, pp. 104–63.

2. Like, for example, the Aztecs, the Maya, and civilizations in North America. See *RAIC*, no. 8 (February 1879): 112–13.

3. López Tuero, *Maíz y tabaco*, p. 1.

4. Gil-Bermejo, *Panorama histórico*, p. 78.

5. Tapia y Rivera, ed., *Biblioteca histórica de Puerto Rico*, p. 534.

6. Agricultural census, 1864, PMA.

7. "Censo y riqueza: Liquidación de los productos de Yauco," 1846, caja 15, FGE.

8. López Tuero, *Maíz y tabaco*, p. 3. The main varieties of corn in the nineteenth century were yellow, white, red, and spotted.

9. Letter from Domingo Roche to Carlos Vives, April 20, 1856, BVA.

10. Receipt, 1858, BVA. This document breaks down by month the forty-eight *cuerdas* planted in corn on Buena Vista.

11. In addition, as noted in Chapter 2, in mid-1854 another corn mill had been installed at Buena Vista.

12. All prices appearing here were obtained from the receipts for payment of corn purchased at Buena Vista. Mill log, 1850–68, BVA.

13. Last will and testament of Carlos Vives, May 1, 1872, notarized by Luis Becerra, notary public, BVA.

14. Account book, 1870, BVA. In February 1870, Buena Vista bought lots at between eleven and twelve *reales*.

15. Common knowledge had it that in four months the corn got old and weevily. A weevil is a small insect that lays its eggs inside the kernel. As the larva develops, it slowly eats its way out, and by the time the hole in the kernel appears, the corn has lost its value. See López Tuero, *Maíz y tabaco*, p. 27.

16. Letter from Antonio Navarro to Salvador Vives, Ponce, August 10, 1872, BVA.

17. Letter from Manuel Domenech to Carlos Vives, Isabela, April 16, 1871, BVA.

18. Letter from Rosaly y Ferrán to Carlos Vives, Guayanilla, November 19, 1858, BVA.

19. Letter from Joaquín Mayoral to Carlos Vives, Ponce, February 6, 1856, BVA.

20. If they bought corn and could not produce cornmeal because the market could not absorb it, the old kernels turned weevily; at that point they would be mixed with fresh kernels. Letter from Antonio Navarro to Salvador Vives, Ponce, July 20, 1872, BVA.

21. Letter from Joaquín Mayoral to Carlos Vives, Ponce, April 16, 1857, BVA.

22. Single sheet reading "Maíz 1871," BVA. Navarro was the brother of Carlos Vives's wife, Guillerma.

23. Carlos Vives to the Ayuntamiento of Ponce, October 18, 1869, BVA. Later, the reasons for the drop-off in sales of cornmeal will be explained.

24. Single sheet, 1860, BVA. The administrator had calculated that one hundred ears of inferior corn were equivalent to thirty-three pounds, whereas one hundred ears of good corn weighed thirty-nine.

25. Salvador Vives, note, January 18, 1872, BVA. "I discounted the corn 16% for being poor quality." Two other examples: Diego López to Salvador Vives, Guayanilla, February 5, 1873, and a letter from Salvador Vives to H. Serra on May 3, 1874, both in BVA. Three sacks were sent back to Serra.

26. Diego López to Salvador Vives, Guayanilla, February 5, 1873, BVA.

27. Carlos López to Salvador Vives, Guayanilla, February 5, 1873, BVA.

28. "Algunas Advertencias a los Mayordomos" (Some instructions to overseers), 1864, BVA.

29. It "got wet" because most of the corn, as has been noted, was bought on the coast, and a good deal of time transpired from the time it was harvested to the time it was ground.

30. "Algunas Advertencias a los Mayordomos."

31. A geared winch attached to a mechanism called a tentering bearing allowed the mill operator to raise and lower the *corredera*, or runner stone, so that the cornmeal could be ground coarser or finer as desired. For a full description of this technology as implemented at Buena Vista, see Nistal Moret et al., "Hacienda Buena Vista," HAER, no. PR-4, pp. 7ff. and especially 10–11.

32. "Algunas Advertencias a los Mayordomos."

33. Single sheet of paper, BVA. One of the measures taken to keep out weevils was

boiling a kettle of coal tar inside the warehouse; the insects would be driven off by the vapor.

34. Arana Soto, *La sanidad en Puerto Rico*, p. 60.

35. *Revista de Agricultura e Industria* 1, no. 3 (February 1879). Corn contains gluten and mucilage, which contains nitrogen, an element essential to the formation of skin cells, muscles, nerves, and the brain.

36. Díaz Soler, in *Historia de la esclavitud negra en Puerto Rico*, p. 161, reports an interview in October 1945 with the former female slaves belonging to Lasalle; they informed the interviewer that under slavery their lunch consisted of root vegetables and a *sorullo* (a cylindrical mass of cornmeal that would be baked or fried) "as big as my arm," as one of them described it. The evening meal consisted of cornmeal and beans.

37. Fernández Juncos, *Costumbres y tradiciones*, p. 20. *El Buscapié* (named for a sort of firecracker that rocketed around at ground level, "looking for feet to pop under") was a fiery, gadfly sort of newspaper that existed in Puerto Rico around the end of the nineteenth century. Fernández Juncos was its publisher and editor; in it, he espoused many "liberal" causes, including community support of the working class through the establishment of a savings and credit bank that would make credit, theretofore unavailable to the working poor, more accessible. See Baralt, *Tradition into the Future: The First Century of the Banco Popular de Puerto Rico, 1893–1993*, trans. Andrew Hurley (San Juan: BPPR, 1993), pp. 20–21.

38. Brau, *Las clases jornaleras*, p. 48.

39. *Boletín Histórico*, 7:112. The report on the exposition also notes that the meals from the Ferrer and Gilbee mill in Ponce received a silver medal. (Manioc flour comes from the manioc or taro, a root vegetable. It is used to make bread. It had been much cultivated on the island during the centuries of Spanish colonization but had fallen off in importance. In the nineteenth century, there was little demand for the manioc flour produced by Buena Vista; a barrel sold at eight pesos, three pesos more than a barrel of cornmeal.)

40. Legajo 66: Exposition, Carlos Vives to J. Carrera, June 19, 1866, PMA. Although Carlos Vives agreed to send his cornmeal, he noted that within two months it would have weevils.

41. Letter from Joaquín Mayoral to Carlos Vives, March 4, 1856, BVA.

42. Letter from Joaquín Mayoral to Carlos Vives, March 28, 1856, BVA.

43. "Padrón [register] de Capitales y Productos de Ponce," 1872–73, PMA.

44. Leví Marrero, *Cuba*, 12:158.

45. In his book *Antropología socioeconómica del Caribe*, p. 107, Angel de Barrios says that this flour was "Santander flour" not because it was produced in Santander but because Santander was the port of embarkation; it should have been called "Spanish," or "Castilian," flour. This product stood up well to transport and the heat and humidity of the tropics.

46. Nadal, *El fracaso de la revolución industrial en España*, p. 68.

47. Leví Marrero, *Cuba*, 12:159.

48. Cruz Monclova, *Historia de Puerto Rico*, 1:246; Leví Marrero, *Cuba*, 12:159.

49. "Aranceles Generales para el cobro de derechos de introducción y exportación en todas las aduanas de los puertos habilitados de la isla de Puerto Rico" (General tariffs for the collection of import and export duties in the established ports of the island of Puerto Rico), August 3, 1850, in *Despachos de los cónsules norteamericanos en Puerto Rico*, 1:1187, CHR.

50. *RAIC*, no. 6 (November 9, 1868): 185.

51. "Informe de don Pedro Irizarri, alcalde ordinario de San Juan sobre las instrucciones que debían darse a don Ramón Power, diputado por Puerto Rico ante las cortes

españolas para promover el adelanto de Puerto Rico" (Instructions to Power as deputy to Spanish Cortes), in Fernández Méndez, ed., *Crónicas de Puerto Rico*, p. 359.

52. Cruz Monclova, *Historia de Puerto Rico*, vol. 2, pt. 2, p. 901.

53. Hostos, *Historia de San Juan*, p. 294.

54. Cruz Monclova, *Historia de Puerto Rico*, 1:24.

55. Caro, *Ramón Power y Giralt*, pp. 181–86.

56. Ibid. Between March and April 1805, for example, several shipments of U.S. flour arrived in San Juan. The governor fixed the price for the flour at sixteen pesos per hundredweight, while it sold for twenty-five pesos on the open market in San Juan (Morales Carrión, *Albores históricos*, p. 115).

57. Morales Carrión, *Albores históricos*, p. 128. In 1814, Fernando VII canceled all privileges conceded by the Spanish Cortes.

58. Cruz Monclova, *Historia de Puerto Rico*, 1:93, 194, 284, respectively.

59. Flinter, *An Account*, pp. 134–35.

60. Consular dispatch, G. Latimer to Clayton, San Juan, Puerto Rico, October 1, 1849. The increase was from 1 to 1.25 pesos per barrel of foreign cornmeal, five pesos per barrel of flour. *Despachos de los cónsules norteamericanos en Puerto Rico*, doc. 27.1, 1:225, CHR.

61. Legajo 8, expediente 3, July 13, 1848, PMA.

62. *Gaceta Oficial de Puerto Rico*, November 5, 1867.

63. Legajo 119, "Actas de la Junta de Agricultura, Industria y Comercio de Ponce," October 11, 1869, no. 22, PMA.

64. Cruz Monclova, *Historia de Puerto Rico*, 1:440.

65. Jiménez, *El Grito de Lares*, pp. 82–117.

66. Legajo 119, "Actas de la Junta," sheet 8, PMA.

67. Domingo Roche, March 4, 1856, BVA.

68. Joaquín Mayoral to Carlos Vives, Ponce, February 21, 1856, BVA.

69. Joaquín Mayoral to Carlos Vives, Ponce, January 9, 1856, BVA.

70. "Don Eugenio de Torres, Procurador de esta Real Audiencia y apoderado de don Carlos Vives ante el concurso de los acreedores de Ramón Tarrats," Ponce, December 24, 1867, BVA.

71. Last will and testament of Carlos Vives, sworn before Francisco Parra, October 29, 1862, BVA.

72. Cruz Monclova, *Historia de Puerto Rico*, vol. 2, pt. 1, p. 781; Ramos Mattei, *La hacienda azucarera*.

73. Account Book, 1874–75, BVA.

74. Statistical Summary of Buena Vista, 1850–70, BVA.

75. Ibid.

76. Last will and testament of Carlos Vives, sworn before Francisco Parra, Ponce, September 29, 1861, BVA.

77. "Inventario y tasación de los bienes que dejó don Carlos Vives que han practicado los que suscriben jurando no hacer ni un solo fraude" (Inventory and appraisal of goods and property left by Don Carlos Vives, carried out by the undersigned, who swear that no fraud has occurred), Ponce, 1870, BVA.

78. Curet, *De la esclavitud a la abolición*, p. 9.

79. BVA. The rental houses were at the following addresses: nos. 17, 19, 21, and 22 Antocha Street, with another on Marina and another on De León, all in Ponce. From 1872 to 1889, the two-story house with four rooms rented independently, storeroom, and one-story house brought in $11,435.85.

80. Curet, *De la esclavitud a la abolición*, p. 9.

81. Murrieta and Co. to Carlos Vives, London, January 16, 1869, BVA. This house also

did considerable business in Spain, with the port of Aguilar and the electric company. In Argentina its interests included the water authority of Buenos Aires. In 1891, the house was reorganized, becoming Murrieta and Co. Ltd. This occurred after the crisis in the Argentine Republic in 1890 that caused so much harm to Murrieta and other English banking concerns. *RAIC*, no. 7 (May 19, 1891): 138.

82. Six-month report on collection of dividends, 1869, from Murrieta and Co., p. 32, BVA.

83. Six-month reports on collection of dividends, 1869, 1888, BVA. They had similar investments in the Argentinian Funding Loan and bonds in Costa Rica.

84. Probate of Vives estate, Ramón Rodríguez, notary, May 10, 1884, BVA.

85. José Rodolfo Rodríguez, *Cuaderno de Teneduría*, 1863, manuscript transcription of original, BVA. A letter of exchange is a commercial document by means of which amounts of money may be received or paid out at different locations by persons who need an amount of money in a country different from that in which they currently reside. They "purchase" this document by depositing with its issuer, or having on account with the issuer, at least the amount of money indicated in the document.

86. Letter from Palmieri to Salvador Vives, Paris, September 1, 1877, BVA.

CHAPTER FOUR

1. Cifre de Loubriel, *La formación del pueblo puertorriqueño*, p. 314. The family owned six slaves in Venezuela; the other four remained there.

2. Ramos and Acosta, *Cabo Rojo*, p. 76.

3. Curet, *De la esclavitud a la abolición*, p. 11.

4. Here and throughout, the word "creole" will refer to an island-born slave, to differentiate such a slave from one brought from Africa or born somewhere else and brought to Puerto Rico.

5. Leonardo Morel, "Protocolos notariales," Ponce, February 23, 1838, sheet 149, GAPR.

6. Ramón Jiménez, "Protocolos notariales," Ponce, July 24, 1843, sheet 453, GAPR.

7. Curet, *De la esclavitud a la abolición*, p. 11.

8. Letter from Salvador de Vives to Governor Rafael de Arístegui, Ponce, February 15, 1845, BVA.

9. Flinter, *A View of the Present Condition of the Slave Population*, p. 47.

10. Slave Census, 1870, BVA.

11. At Buena Vista these workers were called *labradores*, which is equivalent to fieldworkers or field hands. In 1858, according to the hacienda census, all the slaves with the exception of the cook, a mulatto woman named Clotilde, were called fieldworkers. Slave Census, 1858, BVA.

12. "Instrucciones al mayordomo," in Account book, 1870, BVA. The machetes mentioned were long, narrow blades used for scything grass, cutting down bunches of plantains, and harvesting other fruit.

13. "Algunas advertencias a los mayordomos," 1870, BVA.

14. Ibid.

15. Notes, 1845, BVA. It was calculated that each slave prepared more than one hundred shingles.

16. By chapter 6, article 1, of the "Reglamento sobre la educación, trato y ocupaciones que deben dar a sus esclavos los dueños y mayordomos en esta isla" (Rules respecting the education, treatment, and occupations which slave owners and overseers should give their slaves), 1826, Miguel de la Torre, governor, reprinted in Coll y Toste, ed., *Boletín histórico*, 10:262–73.

17. "Entrada, 1861–1863," BVA. This production record noted the amount sold, its

price, and the cart driver who transported it. There were also free day laborers who would transport the farm's produce, such as Pablo Roca, Manuel Colón, and others (Letter from J. Berne to Carlos Vives, November 17, 1870, BVA).

18. The slave census for Buena Vista in 1869 gives this information on Felipe and the other slaves. It notes that Felipe was marked with black lines, "like a ladder," on both arms. In September 1872, the hacienda's administrator, Antonio Navarro, wrote Carlos Vives about the conduct of Telesforo, "the bomba-dancer." Slave Census, 1869, BVA.

19. As noted throughout these descriptions, many plots of land had names. See also the map of the lands of Buena Vista at the end of the Introduction, where one can note the names of the fields as, for example, "Pza. del Corcho," "Pza. de Ciclón," and so forth, indicating *pieza*, or "lot," plus a descriptive or historical name. This was no doubt for ease of reference when discussing a particular piece of the property.

20. "Protocolos Notariales de Ponce," Luis Capó, notary public, and Last Will and Testament: Salvador de Vives and Isabel Díaz, Ponce, November 15, 1843, both in GAPR.

21. Deposition, Isabel Díaz before Luis Capó, Ponce, May 11, 1846, and letter from Carlos Vives to Joaquín Mayoral, Ponce, February 22, 1857, both in BVA.

22. "Contract for the slave Julio," June 25, 1870, Carlos Vives and José Alomar, BVA.

23. "Contribución de Comercio e Industria, Barrio Quinto," March 1, 1872, BVA. The Vives family paid the treasury an annual tax of twelve pesetas on this slave's earnings.

24. "Obras Públicas," legajo 59, registro no. 14, José Ortiz de la Renta, March 4, 1843, GAPR.

25. "February 11, 1854: Loaned 4 slaves; October 9, 1857: 18 slaves; June 11, 1858: 18 slaves; November 10, 1859: 16 slaves." Receipts, collection of loans for highway, signed by Ramón Tarrats, treasurer, BVA.

26. Account book, 1870, and bills from Simmons Co., Ponce, March 5, 1865, both in BVA.

27. Batlle Bakery, Ponce, December 4, 1871, BVA.

28. Domingo Roche, "Note," October 1856, BVA.

29. "Reglamento sobre la educación, trato y ocupaciones."

30. Díaz Soler, *Historia de la esclavitud negra en Puerto Rico*, p. 137.

31. None of the three generations of the Vives family discussed here lived permanently in the owner's residence at Buena Vista.

32. Flinter, *A View of the Present Condition of the Slave Population*, pp. 39–40.

33. Report from Salvador de Vives to Governor Rafael de Arístegui, February 15, 1845, BVA.

34. "Algunas advertencias a los mayordomos," 1860, BVA.

35. Ibid., and letter of April 15, 1856, BVA. One example is that of Antonio, who was sent to town for a "purge."

36. Dr. G. Moringlane to Carlos Vives, Ponce, July 7, 1870, BVA. This is the case of Santiago, who was having high fevers but because of bad weather could not safely be sent to town.

37. Bill from Dr. G. Moringlane to Carlos Vives, July 7, 1870, BVA. The doctor performed such operations as cauterization and such treatments as those for venereal infections.

38. Letter from Dr. G. Moringlane to Carlos Vives, Ponce, July 19, 1860, BVA. Ten years later, the doctor and medicine bill was still at approximately forty pesos.

39. BVA. In August, September, and November 1861, March 1862, and July 1864, Dr. Cornet visited the estate or saw Buena Vista slave patients at his office in town.

40. Sección Ultramar, Serie Gobierno, Legajo 5082, expediente 1, NHA.

41. Kiple, "Cholera and Race in the Caribbean," *Journal of Latin American Studies* 17, pt. 1 (May 1985): 157–77; letter from J. Mayoral to Carlos Vives, June 25, 1856, BVA. Carlos

Vives spent almost the entire year of 1856 in the Dutch colony of Curaçao; it is not known why he stayed away for so many months, but it is possible that as with many other families, it was to protect himself from the ravages of cholera. Brau, *Historia de Puerto Rico*, p. 249.

42. Arana Soto, *La sanidad en Puerto Rico*, p. 60.

43. Letter from J. Mayoral to Carlos Vives, Ponce, July 8, 1856, BVA.

44. "Instrucción preservativa dictada para su observación por los dueños de esclavitudes en la época en que reina la enfermedad del cólera morbo" (Prophylactic instructions dictated to be observed by the owners of slave populations in the time when the disease of cholera reigns), Juan Lemery, no. 136, Circular Letter no. 6, December 7, 1855, reported by Francisco Ramos in *Prontuario de disposiciones oficiales* (Puerto Rico: Imprenta de González, 1866).

45. The reference is to an outbreak of cholera in the Caribbean in 1833, from which Puerto Rico was spared. See Hostos, *Historia de San Juan*, p. 456.

46. Letter from J. Mayoral to Carlos Vives, Ponce, July 11, 1856, BVA.

47. Letter from J. Mayoral to Carlos Vives, Ponce, July 30, 1856, BVA.

48. Ibid. Since February 11, 1856, Mayoral had been asking for Buena Vista to be cordoned off at its border with Barrio Guaraguao, thinking that the disease might enter from Utuado, but it was not until July 30 that he ordered the estate actually closed off.

49. Ibid.

50. Curet, *Los amos hablan*, p. 98.

51. Letter from J. Mayoral to Carlos Vives, Ponce, November 26, 1856, BVA. Those haciendas with the highest death rate among slaves were Pratt's (with 46), Oppenheimer's (with 43), Ferrer's (with 39), and the Archebald brothers' (with 36).

52. Neumann Gandía, *Verdadera y auténtica historia*, p. 264.

53. Letter from J. Mayoral to Carlos Vives, Ponce, December 22, 1856, BVA.

54. Ibid.

55. Letter from J. Mayoral to Carlos Vives, Ponce, December 15, 1856, BVA.

56. Letter from J. Mayoral to Carlos Vives, Ponce, December 6, 1856, BVA.

57. Ibid.

58. Fortuño Janeiro, *Album histórico de Ponce*, p. 18; letter from J. Mayoral to Carlos Vives, Ponce, November 26, 1856, BVA.

59. Letter from J. Mayoral to Carlos Vives, Ponce, December 10, 1856, BVA.

60. Ibid. The total deaths from the 1856 cholera epidemic were 25,820, of which 5,469 were slaves. Barrios Román, *Antropología socioeconómica del Caribe*, p. 289.

61. Letter from J. Mayoral to Carlos Vives, Ponce, June 4, 1856, BVA.

62. This statement is based on the investigation ordered by Governor Laureano Sanz on March 1, 1870 ("Dirección de Administración no. 367 Reservado, March 1, 1870," p. 174, Río Piedras, CHR).

63. Letter from J. Mayoral to Carlos Vives, Ponce, June 4, 1856, BVA.

64. Legajo 241, "Asuntos varios: Archivos en que anotan los esclavos prófugos que se entregan a ocurrencias notables" (Miscellaneous: Files in which are recorded the runaway slaves who get ideas in their heads and act on them), no. 931, caja 229, PMA.

65. Curet has calculated that the average price for male slaves in Ponce for this year was 670 pesos (*De la esclavitud a la abolición*, p. 11).

66. Contract of sale of slaves: Carlos Vives to José Alomar, May 13, 1860, BVA. At the time of this purchase, Hacienda Santa Isabel had eight hundred *cuerdas* planted in sugarcane, some of which was uncultivated, with forty slaves, a steam cane press, and a concrete house for the sugar evaporator. The Privilege of the Indies was Law no. 5, titled "Fifth Book of the Code of the Indies"; since 1834 it had protected plantation owners against their lands' being foreclosed on by their creditors for nonpayment of debts.

67. Contract for the purchase of slaves, August 19, 1869, BVA. Carlos Vives bought Ramón, Nicasio, Telesforo, Juana, and Jesús, this last slave on July 1, 1864.

68. Census of Slaves, Buena Vista, Ponce, January 17, 1870, BVA. See also Díaz Soler, *Historia de la esclavitud negra en Puerto Rico*, p. 307.

69. See Chapter 6.

CHAPTER FIVE

1. For a more exact notion of the amount of coffee produced each year on the island, to the amount exported one should add nine pounds per capita for personal consumption (Saldaña, *El café en Puerto Rico*, p. 6).

2. Chamber of Commerce of Puerto Rico, *Balanza Mercantil de Puerto Rico*, 1897, "Studies carried out under its direction, 1899–1904," Appendix 3; E. D. Colón, *Datos sobre la agricultura*, p. 289.

3. Colón, *Datos sobre la agricultura*, p. 141. In 1897 agricultural land use was categorized as follows:

Product	Total *Cuerdas*
Sugarcane	61,498.23
Coffee	122,399.76
Tobacco	4,264.07
Frutos menores	93,511.08
Other crops	16,277.23
Pasture (uncultivated)	1,127,537.55

4. López Tuero, "El café, cultivo perfeccionado." There are several varieties of coffee, among them the Bengalese, the Mozambique, the Zanzibar, and the Mauritania coffees, all recognized as having slightly different characteristics, as of course Puerto Rican coffee was discovered to have as well. Coffee contains legumin, caffeine, oils, glucose, dextrine (the gummy or soluble matter present in starch globules), caffetannic acid, potassium caffetannate, a soluble volatile oil, and other substances including minerals and water. "El Café," *Boletín Mercantil de Puerto Rico*, December 5, 1877.

5. *Revista Agrícola e Industrial* 11, no. 13 (July 1879): 195.

6. López Tuero, *Café y piña en América*, p. 13.

7. Brau, *Historia de Puerto Rico*, pp. 176–77.

8. Abbad, *Historia geográfica, civil y natural de la Isla de San Juan Bautista de Puerto Rico*, p. 142. Abbad makes the same observation about other crops on the island, attributing the preference for crops that did not take much work to what he called the "indolence" of the Puerto Ricans.

9. Ledrú, *Relación del viaje a la Isla de Puerto Rico*, pp. 76–77.

10. Report of Pedro Irizarri, mayor of San Juan, "Sobre las instrucciones que debían darse a don Ramón Power, diputado por Puerto Rico antes las cortes españolas para promover el adelanto económico de la isla," in Fernández Méndez, ed., *Crónicas de Puerto Rico*, p. 357.

11. Flinter, *An Account*, p. 186. Because of low prices, Flinter notes, many coffee plantations were simply abandoned by their owners, as occurred also in the English and French colonies.

12. Legajo 117, "Agricultura, industria y comercio de Ponce," 1864, PMA.

13. Legajo 35, caja 34A, expedientes 7, 8, and 9, September 1867, PMA.

14. Reid and Taber, *Los terremotos de Puerto Rico*, p. 71, and Neumann Gandía, *Verdadera y auténtica historia*, p. 266.

15. López Tuero, "El Café," pp. 225–32.

16. Picó, "Deshumanización del trabajo, cosificación de la naturaleza: Los comienzos del café en el Utuado del siglo XIX," in Scarano, ed., *Inmigración*, p. 187.

17. "Fondo de obras públicas," legajo 61, caja 317, expediente: "Relativo al traslado del barrio Río Prieto a Yauco," Asuntos municipales, October 10, 1873, GAPR.

18. *Harper's Weekly*, February 11, 1899, p. 147.

19. Among the most common forms of such agreements were sharecropping, lease of land, and day labor. For an excellent discussion of this subject, see Picó, "Deshumanización del trabajo, cosificación de la naturaleza," pp. 201–7, and Bergad, *Coffee and the Growth of Agrarian Capitalism*, pp. 116–31.

20. *RAIC* 3 (January 10, 1887): 36; letter from L. Villamil and Co. to the governor, July 20, 1901, and another from José T. Silva to the president of the United States, February 2, 1902, both in Fortaleza 2135, GAPR. Second-grade coffee was almost always sent to Cuba.

21. Berenger Cela, "La inmigración francesa en la jurisdicción de Santiago," p. 269.

22. Ibid., and see also Balmaseda, *Tesoro del agricultor cubano*, 1:127, and Ely, *Cuando reinaba su majestad el azúcar*. Ely adds three further factors that influenced the decline of coffee in Cuba: heavy tariffs imposed on Cuban coffee by the United States, soil exhaustion, and the steady increase of coffee production in other parts of the world (p. 144).

23. Silva to the president of the United States.

24. Stein, *Vassouras*, p. 216.

25. *RAIC* 5 (December 1889): 298, and Manuel Ortiz Rubio, "Historia del comercio del café en Guatemala," *Revista de Anales de Academia de Guatemala* 55 (January 1981): 223.

26. José de Diego, "Cuestiones obreras," Chamber of Delegates, January 28, 1893, in *Obras completas*, p. 205.

27. The French market was the largest consumer of Puerto Rican *café superior*.

28. Vendrell, *Diario*, CTPR.

29. Ibid.; Neumann Gandía, *Verdadera y auténtica historia*, p. 81.

30. Twenty-six years earlier, the Corsican merchant Angel Agostini, also owner of a coffee plantation in the municipality of Yauco, had invented a machine for polishing coffee beans. If a blue dye were added to the batch, the coffee became even more lustrous, and this gave the impression on the European market (an impression not always well founded) that the coffee was "fresh." It was this process of husking, polishing, and blueing that gave the large "Yauco"-brand bean (as well as other island brands) its fame around the world and brought it the highest prices on the market. But this coffee that was so highly prized in Europe was rejected by American importers, who bought coffee without giving much attention to its appearance and quality (Scott Truxton, "Report of the Puerto Rican Coffee Industry," November 23, 1904, Fondo de Fortaleza, GAPR).

31. Legajo 4, caja 3, expediente 30, "Expediente instruido con el objeto que paguen contribuciones los que tienen tahonas establecidas de acuerdo con el Ayuntamiento de Ponce," March 21, 1888, PMA.

32. *RAIC* 7 (September 25, 1891): 291; Infiesta, *La feria exposición de Puerto Rico*, p. 242.

33. *RAIC* 20 (January 10, 1887): 36. There was also "*caracolillo*," a bean that resulted "when one of the two grains [inside the cherry] aborts; and then the one remaining takes over and instead of growing flat on one side, becomes more or less convex, though it always has a groove in one of its sides" (Nistal Moret et al., "Hacienda Buena Vista," HAER, no. PR-4, p. 18, quoting and translating from G. Cormaillac, *El café, la vainilla, el cacao y el té* [Barcelona: Sabater, 1903], pp. 21–26). This large single bean is called a "peaberry" in English, and it was especially prized (for its flavor, color, and rarity) in Italy.

34. López Tuero, *Café y piña en América*, p. 33. We should recall that before it can be consumed, the coffee must still be roasted, ground, brewed, and filtered.

35. On September 23, 1870, in a letter to the Ayuntamiento of Ponce (BVA), Carlos

Vives adduces the terrible state of his land in requesting a reduction in his taxes. "The surface extent formed by my agricultural lands is notorious for being arid, rugged, and extremely steep, all qualities that militate against cultivation, and where nothing is plowed and nothing is planted."

36. The bean from coastal plantings is smaller because it matures faster than the bean grown at a higher elevation. Hacienda Boca-Burenes, in Ponce's Barrio Tibes, which lies some two thousand feet above sea level, produced 1,000 cwt. of coffee each year, all of large beans, excellent quality, and therefore high price (*Revista Cafetalera* [1913]: 14).

37. BVA. Carlos Vives and Guillerma Navarro had three sons: Salvador, Carlos, and Guillermo. While Salvador remained in Puerto Rico looking after the estate, Carlos and Guillermo went to Europe to study medicine.

38. Letter from Joaquín Mayoral to Carlos Vives, Ponce, December 6, 1856, BVA. The 1865 inventory states that the pulping machine is in very bad condition.

39. *Riqueza Agrícola*, 1861, BVA.

40. Letters from Carlos Vives to the Board of Roads and Canals, May 15, 1849, and May 17, 1862, BVA. In this second letter, Carlos Vives states that he will not stand in the way of the opening of the new road so long as it is built on the "upper" side of the estate, rather than passing through the main plaza where the machine sheds were, as had been originally proposed.

41. Notes, 1850, BVA.

42. Account book, 1890–93, BVA. These calculations appear on a loose sheet of paper inside the book.

43. The "Informe para Subsidio Agrícola (1893) de Ponce, preparado por Salvador Vives" (Report for agricultural subsidy [1893]), BVA, states that 110 *cuerdas* were planted in coffee, but in summarizing the land planted in *frutos menores*, which were the fruit and vegetable crops that had always been grown on the estate, it states that the amount of land "cannot be determined because the *frutos menores* are among the coffee."

44. Buitrago Ortiz, *Haciendas cafetaleras*, p. 121. The author points out that the parts for the coffee-processing machinery on the estates in Yauco and Adjuntas that were the property of Domingo Mariani (the largest coffee plantations in the region) were made by the Querejeta Sobrinos foundry.

45. Some plantations would dry the coffee before depulping it, so that the outer covering, pulp, and parchment might protect the bean as long as possible. See *RAIC* 7, no. 85 (September 25, 1891): 293.

46. These drums would be from eight to ten inches in diameter and two to three feet in length.

47. Loose sheet of paper with the description of the way these blades worked, BVA. The lower blade divided the cylinder into two perfectly equal halves and so close to the rivets on the drum that they were only a half or third of a line [of rivets] away. The cherry would emerge between the rivets and the blades without the beans' being able to escape. On the upper blade, between the drum and the rivets there should be a distance sufficient that when the blade descended with some pressure, the bean would slip out of the pulp. On the lower blade, the same distance, or a little more, so that once the bean was separated from the pulp it could easily escape without being damaged. The distances were adjusted in accordance with the size of the cherries.

48. *RAIC* 8, no. 102 (June 10, 1892). This operation could also be done in wooden mortars, but there was a risk that the bean would be split or cut (*RAIC* 7, no. 85 [September 25, 1891]: 293).

49. Díaz Hernández, *Castañer*, p. 69.

50. The beans could be washed in a machine, but at Buena Vista the washing was always done manually.

51. *RAIC* 8, no. 102 (June 10, 1892): 179. Guillermo Quintanilla, director of the Agricultural Station at Mayagüez in 1892, summarized the drawbacks of sun drying as follows: "Great cost of construction of sufficient terrace surface, since a great deal of space is needed to dry a hundredweight; and the terrace must have a concrete floor, which is liable to constant deterioration, so that money must frequently be spent on repairs. Delay in drying, which slows other operations on the farm and does not permit sale of product on a specific date after harvesting. Large daily exposure to the possibility of bad weather, and certain losses each year due to unforeseen rain-squalls; these contingencies increasing, along with the consequent losses, in direct proportion to the time the drying takes, and consequently, to the size of the harvest. Greater expense, completely pointless, in the continuous stirring of the coffee and in having to put it out and take it in each day. Notorious inequality of harvests, since the sun, which is the drying agent used, is in constant change as to its effects, there being in no harvest of coffee two lots that are dried under the same conditions."

52. Eugenio Rodríguez, "Solicitud para establecer máquina de brillar café," Yauco, April 4, 1883, Fondo de Obras Públicas, GAPR.

53. "Review of the 1882 Exposition," p. 239. The great virtue of Bauzá de Mirabo's invention was that in a few hours it dried coffee to the degree usually obtained in five days of sun-drying, which represented a tremendous economy of time and labor.

54. *RAIC* 2 (December 10, 1886): 188. Other machines were advertised here as well, including the "Smout thresher," probably a husking apparatus, said also to polish coffee.

55. Infiesta, *La feria exposición de Puerto Rico*, p. 232.

56. *Revista Mercantil*, November 19, 1893. This issue of the magazine carried the following information on Robert Graham's foundry: "In the blacksmith establishment and foundry belonging to the undersigned, all types of machines are constructed for the processing of coffee: a) husking machines for removing the husk from and polishing the coffee (in iron or wood); b) machines for depulping, washing, separating, winnowing, sun-drying, and hot-air drying (an extraordinarily useful apparatus in times of rain), gears and transmissions of all kinds; c) water wheels and winches, small carts suitable for the altitude, belts, as well as the patented Smout Guardiola pulping machine and horizontal washers."

57. Atiles García, *Kaleidoscopio*, p. 184. Graham's hardware store was the old Mateo Rabainne establishment, where from 1850 to 1866 many parts had been manufactured for Buena Vista machinery.

58. Removal of the parchment covering could have been done by hand, in a kind of mortar, but there is no evidence that such a process was ever performed at Buena Vista.

59. Pino and Co. to Salvador Vives, Ponce, February 18, 1886, BVA.

60. Annual Report, Sociedad de Agricultura de Ponce, March 18, 1883, Juan Serrallés, president. This society, founded in 1875, encouraged the development and perfecting of sugar-processing machinery, the immigration of laborers, and, in general, anything that might benefit the industry. See Cruz Monclova, *Historia de Puerto Rico*, 2:439.

61. Comas y Miracle to Salvador Vives, Barcelona, June 23, 1874, and Juan Amell y Milá to Salvador Vives, Barcelona, October 20, 1874, BVA.

62. Murrieta to Salvador Vives, London, January 30, 1880, BVA. In 1888 the *RAIC* noted that England bought very little coffee from Puerto Rico, though its prices were good when it did. A hundredweight of good-quality coffee would bring seventy-two to seventy-eight shillings (*RAIC* 4 [October 10, 1888]: 130).

63. "The price paid for colonial fruit in London by Thomas Kilby Co., 1870–1880," BVA. See also Ciro Flamirón Cardoso, "La formación de la hacienda cafetalera costarricense en el siglo XIX," in Florescano, *Haciendas, Latifundios y Plantaciones en América Latina*, p. 653.

CHAPTER SIX

1. *Gaceta Extraordinaria* (flyer), Juan Martínez Plowes, March 30, 1873.

2. Díaz Soler, *Historia de la esclavitud negra en Puerto Rico*, p. 346.

3. Ibid.

4. *Gaceta Extraordinaria.*

5. It is important to stress that the contracts were with Buena Vista because Carlos Vives had died on September 29, 1872, and the management of the estate fell to Antonio Navarro, his brother-in-law.

6. *Peones alquilados* is the specific term used in the account books.

7. Account book, 1873, BVA.

8. Letter from Antonio Navarro to Carlos Vives, Ponce, August 24, 1862, BVA.

9. Notebook: "Café, 1887," BVA. The harvest generally lasted for four months.

10. Before August of each year, most of the coffee pickers do not appear in the account books that are still available to us today.

11. See Chapter 5, where the rise in the price of coffee is discussed.

12. A coffee picker on a commercial estate was expected to pick about fifty pounds of coffee beans per day.

13. Account book, 1890–94, BVA. For example, on November 21, 1891, Cale brought in eight coffee pickers.

14. Díaz Hernández, *Castañer*, p. 33. Díaz Hernández says that in the period 1873–80 the overseer of Hacienda Castañer in Lares was paid 240 pesos per year.

15. The 1862 inventory of Buena Vista indicates that the overseer was provided with five plates, three cups and saucers, two glasses, one table, two tablecloths, one washbowl, two large pots, four smaller pots, two coffeepots with tops, and one sugar bowl.

16. Guillermo Vives to Salvador Vives, Ponce, October 27, 1898, BVA. In this letter, Dr. Guillermo Vives characterizes Ciprián Valdés, the estate's new overseer, as a man who keeps his eye on the machinery, knows how to plant coffee, and makes good sales of plantains and avocados in town.

17. Letters from Antonio Navarro to Salvador Vives, Ponce, July 20, 1872, and September 10, 1872, BVA.

18. Account book, December 1892, May 8, 1893, BVA.

19. Account book, May 1876, BVA.

20. Field-plot book, June 1878, pp. 1–3, BVA.

21. Salvador Vives to His Excellency the Civil Governor Ramón Gómez Pulido, April 1872, BVA. According to Edward Roehs's catalog titled *La historia monetaria de Puerto Rico*, there is evidence that tokens, or "*riles*," as they were called, were used on the plantations belonging to Manuel Cortada, Sauri y Subirá, Serrallés, Collazo, Juan Pons, and R. Toro and Co., along with others in Ponce. We also know that the coffee plantations Hacienda Baleares (in Lares), owned by the Mallorcan Juan Castañer, and Hacienda Santa Clara (in Adjuntas), owned by the Corsican Domingo Mariani, along with many others, used *riles*. The Museum of Anthropology, History, and Art at the University of Puerto Rico has a magnificent collection of *riles* and other tokens from nineteenth-century sugar and coffee plantations.

22. The word *ril* (plural *riles*) is a slight garbling or contraction of the word *real*; see the interesting essay by Víctor Torres in *Qué Pasa en Puerto Rico*, March 1983, pp. 8–9.

23. Picó, *Amargo café*, p. 145.

24. The account books have no information on the existence of a general store on the estate, as on some plantations, although they do clearly reflect advances on earnings paid in foodstuffs, which presumably would have been distributed from the estate's warehouse.

25. Account book, 1878–79: "Notas del campo," BVA. It is here that information on Corcino's and other workers' advances was noted.

CHAPTER SEVEN

1. Rivero Méndez, *Crónica de la Guerra Hispano-Americana*, p. 224. For a description of the guerrilla skirmish that took place in Yauco, see Delgado Pasapera, *Puerto Rico: Sus luchas emancipadoras*, pp. 530–39.

2. Letter from Guillermo Vives to Salvador Vives, Ponce, September 13, 1898, BVA.

3. Letter from Guillermo Vives to Salvador Vives, Ponce, May 16, 1898, BVA.

4. G. Vives to S. Vives, September 13, 1898. See also Rivero Méndez, *Crónica de la Guerra Hispano-Americana*, p. 224.

5. The conditions of surrender were the following: the garrison would be allowed to withdraw; the Ponce municipal government would continue in its functions; the fire department and municipal police would maintain order until the disembarkation of the American troops at the Ponce waterfront; and the captain of the port, the only Spanish official present in the harbor at the time, would not be taken prisoner (Rivero Méndez, *Crónica de la Guerra Hispano-Americana*, pp. 228–29). See also Cervera Bariera, *La defensa militar*, 6:7.

6. G. Vives to S. Vives, September 13, 1898, and Rosario Natal, *Crisis de la Guerra Hispanoamericana*, p. 231. Rosario says that according to several correspondents, Ponce surrendered four times.

7. G. Vives to S. Vives, September 13, 1898.

8. Rivero Méndez, *Crónica de la Guerra Hispano-Americana*, p. 229; Rosario Natal, *Crisis de la Guerra Hispanoamericana*, p. 229; White, *Our New Possessions*, p. 331.

9. G. Vives to S. Vives, September 13, 1898.

10. Ibid. The reference is to the corruption and arbitrariness of the administration of Governor Laureano Sanz (1868–70 and 1874–75). See Cruz Monclova, *Historia de Puerto Rico*, 2:21–26.

11. G. Vives to S. Vives, September 13, 1898.

12. Picó, *1898: La guerra después de la guerra*, pp. 99 and 123. In Barrio Guaraguao, north of Buena Vista, these gangs burned the account books of Guillermo Arbona's general store.

13. G. Vives to S. Vives, September 13, 1898, and letter from Guillermo Vives to Salvador Vives, Ponce, October 27, 1898, BVA. See also Carroll, *Report on the Island of Porto Rico*, pp. 604, 605, and Picó, *Historia general*, p. 225.

14. Cruz Monclova, *Historia del año de 1887*, pp. 260–62; Quiñones, *Un poco de historia*, pp. 227–32.

15. Quiñones, *Un poco de historia*, p. 229.

16. Cruz Monclova, *Historia del año 1887*, p. 209.

17. Ibid., p. 240.

18. Browne and Dole, *The New America and the Far East*, pp. 1386, 1396.

19. Letter from Guillermo Vives to Salvador Vives, Ponce, October 27, 1898, BVA.

20. Chamber of Commerce of Puerto Rico, "Trabajos realizados por su directiva en los años de 1899 a 1904," Appendix 3, last page; annual reports of the governors of Puerto Rico from 1900 to 1904; and reports from the United States Customs Service office in Puerto Rico.

21. *Boletín Mercantil de Puerto Rico*, September 1899, p. 2.

22. Saldaña, *El café en Puerto Rico*, p. 17.

23. Alejandro Albizu to Breekman Winthrop, August 19, 1904, and *Register of Puerto*

Rico for 1910, p. 154, both in Fortaleza 106, GAPR. Exports of coffee fell to only 8,720,000 pounds.

24. *Boletín Mercantil de Puerto Rico*, September 1899, p. 2.

25. Albizu to Winthrop. Fortuño Janeiro, *Album histórico de Ponce*, reports that production of coffee for export reached only 73,929 cwt. this year.

26. Fortuño Janeiro, *Album histórico de Ponce*, p. 70.

27. Vendrell, *Diario*, CTPR.

28. Ibid.

29. *Revista Cafetalera*, 1913, p. 11; Neumann Gandía, *Verdadera y auténtica historia*, p. 213.

30. Account book, September 23, 1900, BVA.

31. *El Imparcial*, December 29, 1899, xiii. *Revista Tierra*, September 10, 1906, Jaime Annexy. Coffee had been at 24.00 silver pesos, which equaled $14.40 in U.S. currency (Annexy, *Revista Tierra*).

32. Alejandro Albizu to Breekman Winthrop, August 17, 1904, Fortaleza 106, GAPR. At one bank alone, the Territorial y Agrícola de Puerto Rico, defaults on loans to coffee producers totaled $107,168.69. November 23, 1899, Fortaleza 6603, GAPR.

33. "Report of the Committee on Agriculture and Manufacture to Mr. Hartzell, President of the Executive Committee," October 12, 1903, Fortaleza, GAPR. The president's order stipulated that one silver peso would be exchanged for $0.60, one-half peso for $0.30, a *peseta* for 12 ½¢, a *real* for 8¢ (Carroll, *Report on the Island of Porto Rico*, p. 496).

34. "Protección del café," draft of report to Congress, November 1908, p. 12.

35. Holloway, *The Brazilian Coffee Valorization of 1906*, p. 27.

36. "La solución del problema agrícola de Puerto Rico," *Revista Tierra*, July 30, 1906; "Protección del café," p. 13.

37. Carroll, *Report on the Island of Porto Rico*, p. 27; "Protección del café," p. 13. The cost of production was $10.00 per hundredweight in Puerto Rico, while the price of coffee ranged from $11.00 to $15.00 per hundredweight.

38. Federico Degetau, August 15, 1901, and another dated October 9, 1901, Fortaleza 2135, GAPR. On July 20, *Revista Tierra* reported the discovery of forty sacks of Brazilian coffee brought onto the island as beans, sent by James Murphy of New York (*Puerto Rico Herald*, August 24, 1901).

39. "Correspondencia de Puerto Rico," *Puerto Rico Herald*, June 27, 1899.

40. Federico Degetau, August 15, 1901, Fortaleza 2135, GAPR.

41. After about five bad months, the Cuban market did bounce back somewhat, due to paragraph 5 of the 1902 Reciprocity Treaty between the United States and Cuba, which gave products grown on American soil a 20 percent reduction in import taxes. Van Leenhoff to Governor William Hunt, August 25, 1903, Fortaleza, GAPR.

42. José T. Silva to President Theodore Roosevelt, February 2, 1902, Fortaleza 2135, GAPR.

43. *El Comercio*, January 20, 1899, p. 4; *El porvenir de nuestro café*, December 31, 1916; message of Garrard Harris, p. 6; and Department of the Interior, Water Supply, and Irrigation, paper no. 32, 1899, p. 39.

44. Francis Leggett to William Corwine, November 24, 1899, Fortaleza 6643, GAPR.

45. *El Heraldo Español*, November 24, 1902, p. 5.

46. "Protección del café," p. 16. Of the $74 million in coffee imports to the United States, $18 million were Brazilian.

47. *Boletín Mercantil de Puerto Rico*, February 21, 1896, p. 2.

48. Van Leenhoff to Brig. Gen. George W. Davies, August 25, 1902, and another from

William B. Harris to George Colton, December 3, 1909, Fortaleza, GAPR. This fact was reported to Governor Colton by the largest roasting concern on the island, the William B. Harris Co.

49. *Puerto Rico Herald*, July 4, 1903.

50. Scott Truxton to Breekman Winthrop, July 11, 1906, Fortaleza, GAPR.

51. Luchetti, *El empréstito para el café*.

52. *Boletín Mercantil de Puerto Rico*, February 21, 1896, p. 2. In Ponce, coffee *cuerdas* fell from 6,774 to 5,743.

53. Fernández García, *El libro azul de Puerto Rico*, pp. 580–84.

54. Others diversified by selling lumber and charcoal and by making and selling beehives.

55. Henricksen, *Propagación y venta de chinas*, p. 3.

56. BVA. For example, 12,650 oranges were picked at Buena Vista in 1870.

57. Letter from Hammond and Co. to Vives brothers, New York, October 24, 1900, BVA.

58. Letter from Hammond and Co. to Salvador Vives, New York, October 24, 1904, and another from Sgobel and Day to Salvador Vives, New York, November 9, 1906, BVA. This last document reads: "The fruit was beautiful. Clearly you took great care in the selection and packing of same."

59. Dr. Guillermo Vives, former head of the Ophthalmological Institute of Madrid, was famed for his work both in Puerto Rico and abroad.

60. BVA. According to the family financial statements, in 1884 shares in the Tramline earned twelve hundred dollars.

61. By-laws of the Crédito y Ahorro Ponceño, June 12, 1894, BVA.

62. Loose sheet of paper, May 25, 1875, Salvador Vives, BVA.

63. Neumann Gandía, *Verdadera y auténtica historia*, p. 81.

64. Curet, *De la esclavitud a la abolición*; Ramos Mattei, ed., *Azúcar y esclavitud*, p. 69. For example, Guillermo Cabrera's hacienda, to which Buena Vista sold hundreds of sacks of cornmeal a year, was gradually broken up and sold in small pieces of land. According to tax exemption requests by plantation owners in 1876, the following problems plagued the industry: drop in prices, abolition of slavery, drought, hurricanes, lack of credit, and Spanish and U.S. tariff discrimination. *Boletín Histórico de Puerto Rico*, pp. 373–80.

65. Depew, *1795–1895: One Hundred Years of American Commerce*, p. 267.

66. RAIC 80 (July 10, 1891): 208. This agreement was signed in return for giving sugar, honey, coffee, and leather from the Spanish Antilles free entry into the United States.

67. Cruz Monclova, *Historia de Puerto Rico*, 3:27. The agreement was disastrous for island customs collections, because some one-half million pesos were lost each year.

68. Ibid., 2:271.

69. Ibid., 2:782; Carroll, *Report on the Island of Porto Rico*, p. 417. The cracker factories were Besosa Hermanos, Albizu y Arias, Bigas Hermanos, and García y Colón.

70. Carroll, *Report on the Island of Porto Rico*, p. 129.

71. Cornmeal, July 1904 to October 1905, BVA.

72. Letter from Francisco Gatell to Salvador Vives, San Juan, October 24, 1904, BVA. Gatell says that after some difficulty he did sell the consignment.

73. Letter from Baquero y Gándara to Salvador Vives, San Juan, September 14, 1904, BVA.

74. Letters from Baquero y Gándara to Salvador Vives, San Juan, September 13 and October 1, 1904, BVA.

75. Invoice, Baquero y Gándara to Salvador Vives, San Juan, September 14, 1904, BVA. Shipping charges for 7,402 kg (about 15,000 lbs.) were $4.50.

76. Account book, November 27 to December 3, 1904, BVA. For most people, the work-week was four days long until the coffee harvest began, and then it was six.

77. Account book, 1904–5, BVA. For example, during the week of November 27–December 3, 1904, fifty-four hired workers were employed.

78. Account book, December 18, 1904, BVA.

79. Account book, October 16–22, 1904, BVA.

80. Account book, October 30, 1904, BVA.

81. Account book, October 4, 1904, BVA. Although workers were generally paid by the day, there were cases, such as that of José Bautista, in which the worker would be paid by the amount picked.

CHAPTER EIGHT

1. Neumann Gandía, *Verdadera y auténtica historia*, p. 71. Later, Salvador de Vives's son, Carlos, was a Ponce city councilman (*regidor*); he also belonged to the police commission and the meat commission (*El Ponceño*, April 16, 1853).

2. Francisco del Valle Atiles, "El campesino puertorriqueño," in Fernández Méndez, ed., *Crónicas de Puerto Rico*, p. 511.

3. It should come as no surprise that it was a Scotch turbine, since Scotch machinery, especially that manufactured by Mirrlees, Tait and Watson, was common on the island. See Ferreras Pagán, *Biografía de las riquezas de Puerto Rico*.

MANUSCRIPT SOURCES

New York, New York
New York Public Library
  Patents Division

Puerto Rico
Conservation Trust of Puerto Rico
  Buena Vista Archives
    Cueto, Beatriz del. "Hacienda Buena Vista: Narrativo de la casa principal de
      vivienda." San Juan, 1987.
    Vendrell, F. A. Diary: "Algunos consejos para mis hijos resultado de mi experien-
      cia en la vida, lo que les pido lean muchas veces, hasta aprendérselos de mem-
      oria y sobre todo, que lo practiquen en la vida, para ayudarlos a ser felices."
      New York, February 1913. Copy.
General Archive of Puerto Rico
  Colección de documentos Pietri-Mariani
  Colección Jungham
  Fondo de Fortaleza
  Fondo de Gobernadores Españoles
  Fondo de Obras Públicas
  Fondo Municipal de Guayama
  Fondo Municipal de Yauco
  Protocolos Notariales de Ponce
Ponce Municipal Archives
  Asuntos Varios
  Circulares
  Juicios Verbales
  Libro de Actas del Ayuntamiento
  Padrones de Riqueza Agrícola, Industrial, Comercial, Esclava, etc.
  Pasaportes
  Planilla de Riqueza
  Prestaciones al Camino
  Reparto de Subsidio

PRINTED SOURCES

Abad, José Ramón. *Puerto Rico en la feria exposición de Ponce en 1882*. Ponce: Tipografía
  El Comercio, 1885.
Abbad y Lasierra, Iñigo. *Historia geográfica, civil y natural de la Isla de San Juan
  Bautista de Puerto Rico*. 1788. Reprint, Río Piedras: University of Puerto Rico Press,
  1970.
Alegría, Ricardo. *Los dibujos de Puerto Rico del naturalista francés Augusto Plée*. San
  Juan: Instituto de Cultura Puertorriqueña, 1975.
Alonso, Manuel. *El jíbaro*. 1882. Reprint, Río Piedras: Editorial Edil, 1974.

ELEVATION A-A
ELEVACION A-A

North-south elevation of the Buena Vista plaza. From left to right, the coffee mill with its hydraulic turbine, the overseer's house, the stables, the coach house, and the main house. (HAER, drawn by Reinhard A. Valle and Richard A. Howard, 1977)

Arana Soto, Salvador. *La sanidad en Puerto Rico hasta 1898*. San Juan: Academia Puertorriqueña de la Historia, 1978.

Arango, Mariano. *Café e industria (1850–1930)*. Bogotá: Centro de investigaciones económicas de la Universidad de Antioquía, Carlos Valencia, editores, 1977.

Armstrong, Douglas V. *The Old Village and the Great House: An Archaeological and Historical Examination of Drax Hall Plantation, St. Ann's Bay, Jamaica*. Urbana: University of Illinois Press, 1990.

Armstrong, William. *Manuscrito sobre algunos pueblos de la isla*. Ponce, 1910.

Atiles García, Guillermo. *Kaleidoscopio*. Ponce: Imprenta de M. López, 1905.

Balmaseda, Francisco Javier. *Tesoro del agricultor cubano*. Vol. 1. Havana: Biblioteca de la propaganda literaria, 1885.

Bandinell, James. *Some Accounts of the Trade of Slaves from Africa*. London: Longman, 1842.

Baralt, Guillermo A. *Esclavos rebeldes (1795–1848)*. Río Piedras: Ediciones Huracán, 1981.

———. *Tradition into the Future: The First Century of the Banco Popular de Puerto Rico, 1893–1993*. Translated by Andrew Hurley. San Juan: BPPR, 1993.

———. *Yauco o las minas de oro cafetaleras*. San Juan: Model Offset, 1984.

Barrios Román, Angel de. *Antropología socioeconómica del Caribe*. Santo Domingo: Editorial Cultural Dominicana, 1974.

Berenger Cela, Jorge. "La inmigración francesa en la jurisdicción de Santiago." *Revista Santiago* (Santiago, Cuba), no. 26–27, June 1977.

Bergad, Laird W. *Coffee and the Growth of Agrarian Capitalism in Nineteenth-Century Puerto Rico*. Princeton: Princeton University Press, 1983.

Bishop, J. Leander. *A History of American Manufacturers, 1608–1860*. 3 vols. Philadelphia: E. Young, 1868.

Bovey, Henry T. *A Treatise on Hydraulics*. 2d ed. New York: John Wiley and Sons, 1908.

Brau, Salvador. *Disquisiciones sociológicas*. Río Piedras: University of Puerto Rico Press, 1956.

———. *La fundación de Ponce*. Puerto Rico: Tipografía La Democracia, 1909.

———. *Historia de Puerto Rico*. 1904. Reprint, Río Piedras: Editorial Edil, 1974.

Braudel, Fernand. *Civilization and Capitalism: Fifteenth–Eighteenth Century*. Vol. 1, *The Structures of Everyday Life*. Translated by Miriam Kochan, revised by Siân Reynolds. Vol. 2, *The Wheels of Commerce*. Translated by Siân Reynolds. Vol. 3, *The Perspective of the World*. Translated by Siân Reynolds. New York: Harper and Row, 1981–84.

Browne, Waldo G., and N. Haskell Dole. *The New American and the Far East*. Boston: Marshall Jones Company, 1907.

Buitrago Ortiz, Carlos. *Haciendas cafetaleras y clases terratenientes en Puerto Rico decimonónico*. Río Piedras: University of Puerto Rico Press, 1982.

COFFEE MILL
MOLINO PARA CAFE

COFFEE STORAGE AND DRYING SHED
ALMACEN DE CAFE — COBERTIZO DE
LAS CORREDERAS

CARPENTERS HOUSE
CASA DEL MAYORDOMO

STABLES
ESTABLOS

CARRIAGE HOUSE
COCHERA

HOUSE
CASA DE LA HACIENDA

CORN MILL
MOLINO PARA MAIZ

ELEVATION B–B
ELEVACION B–B

PIT
POSO

East-west elevation of the Buena Vista plaza. From left to right, the cornmeal mill, the newer coffee mill, the shed with its drying drawers and storage, the overseer's house, the stables, the coach house, and the main house. (HAER, drawn by Reinhard A. Valle and Richard A. Howard, 1977)

———. *Los orígenes de la sociedad precapitalista en Puerto Rico decimonónico.* Río Piedras: Ediciones Huracán, 1976.

Cantero, J. G. *Los ingenios de Cuba: 1838.* Edited by Leví Marrero. Barcelona: Pareja, 1984.

Caro, Aida. *Antología de lecturas de historia de Puerto Rico.* 2d ed. Río Piedras: University of Puerto Rico Press, 1977.

———. *Ramón Power y Giralt, diputado puertorriqueño a las cortes generales y extraordinarias de España, 1810–1812.* Barcelona: Pareja, 1969.

Camuñas Madera, Ricardo. *Epidemias, plagas y marginación: La lucha contra la adversidad en Puerto Rico en los siglos XVIII y XIX.* N.p.: Editorial de la Universidad de América, Comisión puertorriqueña para la celebración del quinto centenario del descubrimiento de América y Puerto Rico, 1992.

Carro Figueroa, Vivian. "La formación de la gran propiedad cafetalera: La Hacienda Pietri, 1858–1898." *Anales de Investigación Histórica* 2 (1975): 1–105.

Carroll, Henry K. *Report on the Island of Porto Rico.* Washington, D.C.: Government Printing Office, 1899.

Centro de Investigaciones Históricas, University of Puerto Rico. *Despachos de los cónsules norteamericanos en Puerto Rico, 1818–1868.* Vol. 1. Río Piedras: Centro de Investigaciones Históricas, University of Puerto Rico, 1982.

———. *El proceso abolicionista en Puerto Rico: Documentos para su estudio.* Vol. 1, *La institución de esclavitud y su crisis, 1823–1873.* San Juan: Instituto de Cultura Puertorriqueña, 1974.

Cervera Bariera, Julio. *La defensa militar de Puerto Rico.* In Coll y Toste, ed. (*q.v.*), *Boletín histórico,* vol. 6.

Charles, Gerard Pierre. *La economía haitiana y su vía de desarrollo.* Translated by María Teresa Moll. Mexico City: Cuadernos Americanos, 1965.

Church, Irving, ed. *Hydraulic Motors.* New York: John Wiley and Sons, 1905.

Cifre de Loubriel, Estela. *La formación del pueblo puertorriqueño: La contribución de los catalanes, baleáricos y valencianos.* San Juan: Instituto de Cultura Puertorriqueña, 1975.

———. *La inmigración a Puerto Rico durante el siglo XIX.* San Juan: Instituto de Cultura Puertorriqueña, 1964.

Coello, Francisco. *Atlas de España y sus posesiones de ultramar.* Madrid, 1851.

Cole, Arthur. *Wholesale Commodity Prices in the United States, 1700–1861.* 2 vols. 1938.

Reprint, Cambridge: Harvard University and International Scientific Committee on Price History, 1969.

Coll y Toste, Cayetano, ed. *Boletín histórico de Puerto Rico.* 14 vols. San Juan: Tipografía Cantero Fernández, 1914–27.

———. *Reseña del estado social, económico e industrial de la isla de Puerto Rico al tomar posesión de ella los Estados Unidos.* San Juan: Imprenta de La Correspondencia, 1899.

Colón, E. D. *Datos sobre la agricultura en Puerto Rico antes de 1898.* San Juan: Tipografía Cantero Fernández, 1930.

Colón, Isidro. *Nociones de geografía universal.* Ponce: Tipografía Manuel López, 1888.

Córdova, Pedro Tomás de. *Memorias geográficas, históricas, económicas y estadísticas de la isla de Puerto Rico.* 6 vols. 1831–33. Reprint, San Juan: Instituto de Cultura Puertorriqueña, 1968.

Craton, Michael, and James Walvin. *A Jamaican Plantation: The History of Worthy Park.* London: W. H. Allen, 1970.

Cruz Monclova, Lidio. *Historia de Puerto Rico (Siglo XIX).* 3 vols. Río Piedras: University of Puerto Rico Press, 1970.

———. *Historia del año de 1887.* Río Piedras: University of Puerto Rico Press, 1970.

Curet, José. *Los amos hablan.* Río Piedras: Editorial Cultural, 1986.

———. *De la esclavitud a la abolición: Transiciones económicas en las haciendas azucareras de Ponce, 1845–1873.* CEREP: Cuaderno 7 (1979).

Daugherty, Robert L. *Hydraulics.* 3d ed. New York: McGraw Hill, 1925.

Delgado Pasapera, Germán. *Puerto Rico: Sus luchas emancipadoras.* Río Piedras: Editorial Cultural, 1984.

Depew, Chauncey M. *1795–1895: One Hundred Years of American Commerce.* New York: L. O. Haynes, 1895.

Díaz Hernández, Luis. *Castañer: Una hacienda cafetalera en Puerto Rico (1868–1930).* Ponce: Imprenta Universitaria, 1982.

Díaz Soler, Luis. *Historia de la esclavitud negra en Puerto Rico.* Río Piedras: University of Puerto Rico Press, 1970.

Diego, José de. *Obras completas.* San Juan: Instituto de Cultura Puertorriqueña, 1977.

Ely, Roland T. *Cuando reinaba su majestad el azúcar.* Buenos Aires: Editorial Sudamericana, 1963.

Ewbank, Thomas. *A Descriptive and Historical Account of Hydraulic and Other Machines for Raising Water, Ancient and Modern: With Observations on Various Subjects Connected with the Mechanical Arts: Including the Progressive Development of the Steam Engine. In Five Books, illustrated by nearly three hundred engravings.* 3d ed. New York: Breely and MacElrath, 1849.

Fernández García, E., ed. *El libro azul de Puerto Rico.* San Juan: El Libro Azul Publishing, 1923.

Fernández Juncos, Manuel. *Costumbres y tradiciones.* San Juan: Biblioteca de El Buscapié, 1883.

Fernández Méndez, Eugenio. *Historia cultural de Puerto Rico.* Vol. 2. San Juan: Ediciones Cemí, 1970.

———, ed. *Crónicas de Puerto Rico.* Río Piedras: University of Puerto Rico Press, 1969.

Ferreras Pagán, J. *Biografía de las riquezas de Puerto Rico.* San Juan: Tipografía Luis Ferrera, 1902.

Fielding, H., and Stephen Taber. *Los terremotos de Puerto Rico.* San Juan: Negociado de Materiales y Transporte, 1919.

Flinter, George D[awson]. *An Account of the Present State of the Island of Puerto Rico.* London: Longman, Rees, Orme, Brown, Green, and Longman, 1834.

————. *A View of the Present Condition of the Slave Population of the Island of Puerto Rico*. Philadelphia: Adam Waldie, 1832.

Florescano, Enrique. *Precios del maíz y crisis agrícola en México (1708–1810)*. Nueva Serie 4. Mexico City: Centro de Estudios Históricos, Colegio de México, 1969.

————, ed. *Haciendas, latifundios y plantaciones en América Latina*. Rome: Siglo Veintiuno, 1975.

Fontana, Joseph, ed. *La industrialización europea*. Barcelona: Editorial Crítica, 1980.

Fortuño Janeiro, Luis. *Album histórico de Ponce (1692–1934)*. Ponce, 1934.

Gandía, Ramón. *Estado actual de Ponce*. Ponce: Tipografía La Democracia, 1899.

García Rodríguez, Gervasio L., and A. G. Quintero Rivera. *Desafío y solidaridad: Breve historia del movimiento obrero puertorriqueño*. Río Piedras: Ediciones Huracán, 1982.

Gérard, Pierre C. *La economía haitiana y su vía de desarrollo*. Translated by María Teresa Toral. Mexico City: Cuadernos Americanos, 1965.

Gil-Bermejo, Juana. *Panorama histórico de la agricultura en Puerto Rico*. Seville: Instituto de Cultura Puertorriqueña, 1970.

Gimpel, Jean. *The Medieval Machine: The Industrial Revolution of the Middle Ages*. New York: Holt, Rinehart and Winston, 1974.

Gómez Acevedo, Labor. *Organización y reglamentación del trabajo en el Puerto Rico del siglo XIX: Propietarios y jornaleros*. San Juan: Instituto de Cultura Puertorriqueña, 1970.

Grossourdy, Renato de. *El médico botánico criollo*. 3 vols. Paris: Librería de Francisco Brachet, 1864.

Handler, Jerome S., and F. N. Longe. *Plantation Slavery in Barbados: An Archaeological and Historical Investigation*. Cambridge: Harvard University Press, 1978.

Heck, J. G. *The Iconographic Encyclopaedia of Science, Literature, and Art*. Translated by Spencer F. Baird. New York: R. Garrigue, 1851.

Henricksen, H. C. *Propagación y venta de chinas (naranjas) en Puerto Rico*. Washington, D.C.: Government Printing Office, 1904.

Hernández, Pedro H. "Los inmigrantes italianos de Puerto Rico durante el siglo XIX." *Anales de Investigación Histórica* 3, no. 2 (July–December 1976).

Hill, Robert T. *Cuba and Porto Rico with the Other Islands of the West Indies*. New York: Century Company, 1898.

Holloway, Thomas H. *The Brazilian Coffee Valorization of 1906*. Madison: University of Wisconsin Logmark Edition, 1971.

————. *Immigrants on the Land: Coffee and Society in São Paulo, 1886–1934*. Chapel Hill: University of North Carolina Press, 1980.

Hostos, Adolfo de. *Historia de San Juan, ciudad murada*. San Juan: Instituto de Cultura Puertorriqueña, 1966.

Hostos, Eugenio María de. *Obras completas*. Edición conmemorativa del Gobierno de Puerto Rico. Havana: Imprenta Cultural, 1938–39.

Infiesta, Alejandro. *La feria exposición de Puerto Rico, 1493–1893*. San Juan: Imprenta del Boletín Mercantil, 1895.

Jiménez, Olga. *El Grito de Lares*. Río Piedras: Ediciones Huracán, 1985.

Johnson, Robert L., and Patricia O'Reilly. "The Barker's Turbine at Hacienda Buena Vista." *Journal of the Society for Industrial Archeology* 4, no. 1 (1978).

Kiple, Kenneth F. "Cholera and Race in the Caribbean." *Journal of Latin American Studies* 17, pt. 1 (May 1985): 157–77.

Knight, Edward H. *American Mechanical Dictionary*. New York: J. R. Ford, 1874.

Labat, Jean-Baptiste. *Viajes a las Islas de la América*. Translated from the French by Francisco de Oraña. Havana, 1979.

Landels, John G. *Engineering in the Ancient World*. Berkeley: University of California Press, 1978.

Latimer, Eugenio. *José Ramón Figueroa y la fundación de Villalba*. Puerto Rico: Jay-ce Printing, 1985.

Layfield, John. "A large Relation of Port Ricco Voyage; written as is reported, by that learned man and reverend Divine Doctor Eglambie, his Lordships [the Earl of Cumberland's] Chaplaine and Attendant in that Expedition; very much abbreviated." In Samuel Purchas, *Hakluytus Posthumus, or Purchas His Pilgrims: Contayning a History of the World in Sea Voyages and Lande Travells by Englishmen and Others*. 20 vols. Glasgow: James MacLehose and Sons, 1906; reprint, New York: Macmillan, vol. 16.

Ledrú, André Pierre. *Relación del viaje a la Isla de Puerto Rico en el año de orden de su gobierno y bajo la dirección del Capitán N. Baudin*. Translated by Julio L. de Vizcarrondo. Puerto Rico: Imprenta Militar de J. González, 1863; reprint, San Juan: Ediciones Borinquen/Editorial Coquí, 1971.

Lee, Albert E. *An Island Grows: Memoirs of Albert E. Lee, Puerto Rico, 1873–1942*. New York: MacCrellish and Quigley, 1963. ("Published as a public service, on the occasion of its eighty-sixth anniversary, by Albert E. Lee and Son, Inc., San Juan, Puerto Rico.")

Letrone, M. *Curso completo de geografía universal*. Paris, 1855.

Library of Useful Knowledge: Natural Philosophy. London: Baldwin and Craddock, 1829.

Little, Elbert L., Jr., Frank H. Wadsworth, and José Marrero. *Arboles comunes de Puerto Rico y las Islas Vírgenes*. Drawings by Frances W. Horne. Río Piedras: University of Puerto Rico Press, in association with the U.S. Forestry Service, 1977.

López Tuero, Fernando. *Café y piña en América*. San Juan: Imprenta y Librería de Acosta, 1891.

———. "El café." *RAIC* 7, no. 81 (July 25, 1891): 225–32.

———. "El café, cultivo perfeccionado." *RAIC* 7, no. 79 (June 25, 1891): 193–97.

———. *Caña de azúcar*. San Juan: Tipografía del Boletín Mercantil, 1877.

———. *Isla de Puerto Rico: Estudios de economía rural*. San Juan: Tipografía del Boletín Mercantil, 1893.

———. *Isla de Puerto Rico: La reforma agrícola*. San Juan: Tipografía del Boletín Mercantil, 1891.

———. *Maíz y tabaco*. San Juan: Imprenta y Librería de Acosta, 1891.

Luchetti, Mateo. *El empréstito para el café*. San Juan: Tipografía del Boletín Mercantil.

Macauley, David. *Mill*. Boston: Houghton Mifflin, 1983.

Manual del Cafetero Colombiano. Havana: Instituto del Libro, 1969.

Marazzi, Rosa. *Impacto de la inmigración a Puerto Rico*. Río Piedras: Centro de Investigaciones Sociales, University of Puerto Rico, 1975.

Martínez Vergne, Teresita. *Capitalism in Colonial Puerto Rico: Central San Vicente in the Nineteenth Century*. Gainesville: University Presses of Florida, 1992.

Masini, Juan. *Historia ilustrada de Yauco*. Yauco: Yauco Printing, 1925.

Mayol Alcóver, Esperanza. *Islas*. Palma de Mallorca: Imprenta Alcóver, 1976.

Mintz, Sidney W. *Caribbean Transformations*. Baltimore: Johns Hopkins University Press, 1974.

Morales Carrión, Arturo. *Albores históricos del capitalismo en Puerto Rico*. Río Piedras: University of Puerto Rico Press, 1972.

———. *Auge y decadencia de la trata negrera en Puerto Rico (1820–1860)*. San Juan: Centro de Estudios Avanzados de Puerto Rico y el Caribe, 1978.

———. *Puerto Rico and the Non-Hispanic Caribbean: A Study in the Decline of Spanish Exclusivism*. Río Piedras: University of Puerto Rico Press, 1952.

Morell Campos, Ramón. *Guía local de comercio*. Ponce: Imprenta El Telégrafo, 1895.

Moreno Fraginals, Manuel. *El ingenio.* Havana: Editorial de Ciencias Sociales, 1978.

Mumford, Lewis. *Technics and Civilization.* New York: Harcourt, Brace, 1934.

Nadal, Jordi. *El fracaso de la revolución industrial en España, 1814–1913.* Barcelona: Editorial Ariel, 1984.

Neumann Gandía, Eduardo. *Verdadera y auténtica historia de la ciudad de Ponce desde sus primitivos tiempos hasta la época contemporánea.* San Juan: Imprenta Burillo, 1913.

Nistal Moret, Benjamín, supervising historian; Héctor Sánchez Sánchez and Javier Meléndez, student historians. Drawings by Charles F. D. Roberts, supervising architect; Richard A. Valle, architect; Robert Praga and Richard A. Howard, student architects. Record of visit to and study of "Hacienda Buena Vista [Hacienda Vives] [Buena Vista Plantation]." *Historic American Engineering Record,* no. PR-4, 1984.

Olivares, José de. *Our Islands and Their People.* St. Louis: Thompson Publishing, 1899.

O'Neill, Luis Pumarada. *La industria cafetalera de Puerto Rico, 1736–1969.* San Juan: Oficina de Preservación Histórica, 1990.

O'Reilly, Alejandro. *Memoria sobre la isla de Puerto Rico.* Collected in Fernández Méndez, ed., *Crónicas de Puerto Rico,* pp. 239–67.

Ortiz Fernández, Fernando. *Contrapunteo cubano del tabaco y el azúcar.* Havana: Consejo Nacional de Cultura, 1913.

Peñaranda, Carlos. *Cartas puertorriqueñas, 1878–1880.* Madrid: Sucesores de Rivadeneyra, 1885.

Pérez de la Riva, Francisco. *El café: Historia de su cultivo y explotación en Cuba.* Havana: Jesús Montero, 1944.

Pérez Vega, Ivette. *El cielo y la tierra en sus manos.* Río Piedras: Ediciones Huracán, 1985.

———. "Las sociedades mercantiles de Ponce." *Anales de Investigación Histórica* 6, no. 2.

Perfiles de Ponce. San Juan: Puerto Rican Office of Historical Preservation, 1986.

Picó, Fernando. *Amargo café: Los pequeños y medianos caficultores de Utuado en la segunda mitad del siglo XIX.* Río Piedras: Ediciones Huracán, 1981.

———. *1898: La guerra después de la guerra.* Río Piedras: Ediciones Huracán, 1987.

———. *Historia general de Puerto Rico.* Río Piedras: Ediciones Huracán, 1986.

———. *Libertad y servidumbre en el Puerto Rico del siglo XIX (Los jornaleros utuadeños en vísperas del auge del café).* Río Piedras: Ediciones Huracán, 1979.

———. *Registro general de jornaleros, Utuado, Puerto Rico (1849–1850).* Río Piedras: Ediciones Huracán, 1976.

Pictorial Guide to Business: Directory of Puerto Rico. New York: Pictorial Guide Publishing, 1899.

Porrata Doria, Luis. *Estado actual de Ponce: 1899.* Ponce: Tipografía La Democracia, 1899.

Purchas, Samuel. See Layfield, John.

Quiñones, José Marcial. *Un poco de historia colonial.* San Juan: Academia Puertorriqueña de la Historia and Instituto de Cultura Puertorriqueña, 1978.

Ramos, Antonio, and Ursula Acosta. *Cabo Rojo: Notas para su historia.* San Juan: Office of Historical Preservation, 1985.

Ramos Mattei, Andrés. *La hacienda azucarera: Su crecimiento y crisis en Puerto Rico (siglo XIX).* San Juan: Centro de Estudios de la Realidad Puertorriqueña, 1981.

———, ed. *Azúcar y esclavitud.* San Juan: Come-Set Type, 1980.

Register of Puerto Rico, 1910. San Juan: Bureau of Supplies, Printing, and Transportation, 1911.

Reynolds, Terry. *Stronger Than a Hundred Men: A History of the Vertical Water Wheel.* Baltimore: Johns Hopkins University Press, 1987.

Riant, A. *Le café, le chocolat, le thé.* Paris: Librairie Hachette, 1875.

Rigau-Pérez, José G. "The Introduction of Smallpox Vaccine in 1803 and the Adoption of Immunization as a Government Function in Puerto Rico." *Hispanic American Historical Review* 69 (August 1989): 393–423.

Rivero Méndez, Angel. *Crónica de la Guerra Hispano-Americana.* Madrid: Sucesores de Rivadeneyra, 1922.

Roberts, R. C. *Soil Survey of Puerto Rico.* Washington, D.C.: U.S. Department of Agriculture, 1942.

Rosa Martínez, Luis de la. *Lexicón histórico-documental de Puerto Rico (1812–1899).* San Juan: Centro de Estudios Avanzados de Puerto Rico y el Caribe, 1986.

———. *La periferia del Grito de Lares.* San Juan, 1984.

Rosario Natal, Carmelo. *Puerto Rico y la crisis de la Guerra Hispanoamericana.* Hato Rey: Ramallo Brothers, 1975.

Safford, Arthur T., and Edward P. Hamilton. *The American Mixed Flow Turbine and Its Setting.* U.S.A. paper no. 1502. American Society of Civil Engineers, May 3, 1922.

Saldaña, Jorge E. *El café en Puerto Rico: Historia del café en la isla desde su introducción hasta nuestros días y medidas para su rehabilitación.* San Juan: Tipografía Real Hermanos, 1935.

Salivia, Luis A. *Historia de los temporales de Puerto Rico y las Antillas (1492–1970).* San Juan: Editorial Edil, 1972.

Scarano, Francisco A. *Sugar and Slavery in Puerto Rico: The Plantation Economy of Ponce, 1800–1850.* Madison: University of Wisconsin Press, 1984.

———, ed. *Inmigración y clases sociales en el Puerto Rico del siglo XIX.* Río Piedras: Ediciones Huracán, 1981.

Sheridan, Richard B. *Doctors and Slaves: A Medical and Demographic History of Slavery in the British West Indies.* Cambridge: Cambridge University Press, 1985.

Singer, Charles, E. J. Holmyard, and A. R. Hall, eds. *A History of Technology.* 8 vols. New York: Oxford University Press, 1958.

Smith, Robert S. *A History of Dan River Mills (1882–1950).* Durham: Duke University Press, 1960.

Steele, J. Dorman. *Popular Physics.* 1888. Reprint, New York: American Book Co., 1896.

Stein, Stanley. *Vassouras: A Brazilian Coffee Country, 1850–1890.* New York: Atheneum, 1976.

Strandh, Sigvard. *A History of the Machine.* New York: A. and W. Publishing, 1979.

Sued Badillo, Jalil. *Guayama: Notas para su historia.* San Juan: Office of Historical Preservation, 1983.

Tapia y Rivera, Alejandro, ed. *Biblioteca histórica de Puerto Rico.* San Juan: Imprenta de Márquez, 1854.

Vaía, Dailió. *Plantation Tokens of Puerto Rico.* New York: Vantage Press, 1987.

Valle, José G. del. *Memoria, presentada a la Junta Calificadora.* San Juan: Imprenta de José J. Acosta, 1892.

Valle Atiles, Francisco del. "El campesino puertorriqueño." *Revista Puertorriqueña* 2 (1888–89).

Vallejo, José M. *Tratado sobre el movimiento y las aplicaciones de las aguas.* 2 vols. Madrid: Imprenta de Don Miguel Burgos, 1833.

Vendrell, F. A. *Diario titulado algunos consejos para mis hijos resultado de mi experiencia en la vida, lo que les pido lean muchas veces, hasta aprendérselos de memoria y sobre todo, que lo practiquen en la vida, para ayudarlos a ser felices.* CTPR. Copy.

Views of Puerto Rico. San Juan: Hardie Brothers, 1899.

Villareal de Berriz, Pedro. *Máquinas hidráulicas de molinos y herrerías y Gobierno de los árboles y montes de Vizcaya.* San Sebastián: Sociedad Guipuzcoana de Ediciones y

Publicaciones de la Real Sociedad Vascongada de los Amigos del País y Casa de
Ahorros Municipal de San Sebastián, 1973.

White, Trumbull. *Our New Possessions.* Philadelphia: Elliot Publishing, 1898.

Zeno Gandía, Manuel. *La charca.* 1894. Reprint, Mexico City: Editorial Orión, 1965.

NEWSPAPERS

Boletín Mercantil de Puerto Rico
El Comercio
Gaceta Oficial de Puerto Rico
El Heraldo Español
El Imparcial: Diario Político
El Ponceño
Puerto Rico Herald
El Vapor

MAGAZINES AND JOURNALS

El Agricultor Puertorriqueño
Coffee Trade Journal
Grocery World and General Merchant
Harper's Weekly
Journal of Latin American Studies
Journal of the Society for Industrial Archeology
Op.Cit.
P.R. Progress
P.R. Review
Revista Agrícola Industrial
Revista de Agricultura, Industria y Comercio
Revista Cafetalera
Revista de Historia
Revista Mercantil
Revista Tierra
Self Help
La Tronera